·eptio
ex;
re
) s
Ula.
te the core of
and was en-

Ulam's ability to explain events by tracing the continuities in the Russian mentality makes this work a special achievement in Soviet studies and intellectual history.

Born in Lwow, Poland, in 1922, Adam B. Ulam came to the United States in 1939. He received his Ph.D. from Harvard University in 1947 when he joined the Harvard faculty. He is Professor of Government and Director of the Russian Research Center.

His articles have appeared in numerous journals, among them *Commentary* and *Foreign Policy*. He is the author of nine previous books, the latest of which is *Stalin: The Man and His Era*.

Ideologies and Illusions

Ideologies and Illusions

Revolutionary Thought
from Herzen to Solzhenitsyn

Adam B. Ulam

HARVARD UNIVERSITY PRESS
Cambridge, Massachusetts, and London, England   1976

Library of Congress Cataloging in Publication Data

Ulam, Adam Bruno, 1922-
  Ideologies and illusions.

  Includes bibliographical references and index.
  1. Russia—Intellectual life. 2. Russia—Politics and government.
3. Communism—Russia. 4. Russia—Foreign relations. I. Title.
DK32.7.U4   320.5'3'0947   75-25808
ISBN 0-674-44310-1

ACKNOWLEDGMENTS

.I would like to express my thanks for permission to reprint material of mine from the following publications: *The Bolsheviks*, Macmillan Publishing Co., © 1965; "Socialism and Utopia," *Daedalus*, Journal of the American Academy of Arts and Sciences, Spring 1965; "Lenin: His Legacy," *Foreign Affairs*, April 1970, © Council on Foreign Affairs; "Communist Doctrine and Soviet Diplomacy" and "Lenin's Last Phase," *Survey*, Summer 1970 and Winter-Spring 1975; *Stalin: The Man and His Era*, The Viking Press, © 1973, reprinted by permission; "The Uses of Revolution," from *Revolutionary Russia*, ed. Richard Pipes, Harvard University Press, © 1968; "Titoism," from *Marxism in the Modern World*, ed. Milorad M. Drachkovitch, Stanford University Press, © 1965; *Expansion and Coexistence*, Frederick A. Praeger, Inc., © 1968, excerpted and reprinted by permission; "The Moscow Congress: Prudence and Semantics," *The Reporter* 34, no. 9, May 5, 1966; "Moscow Plays the Balance," *Foreign Policy* 8, Fall 1972, © National Affairs, Inc.; "The Soviet Union and the Rules of the International Game," in *The Soviet Impact on World Politics*, ed. Kurt L. London, Hawthorn Books, 1974; "The Convolutions of Terror," *Lugano Review*, Spring 1975.

I am also grateful to the personnel of the Russian Research Center, and especially to Mary Towle and Christine Balm for their help.

v

CONTENTS

Ideologies and Illusions

INTRODUCTION

Some years ago—actually only fifteen or so but it seems like ages—many social scientists and other wise men concluded that the era of ideologies was over. The world, whether in Russia or the United States, was increasingly ruled by technocrats. Old faiths and enthusiams had given way to computers and new scientific techniques guaranteed to solve our social problems and to effect the material and spiritual progress of mankind. There was, to be sure, an unpleasant possibility that the triumphant progress of science might result in the world blowup. But barring such a fortuitous development (and in a way this too would have solved our problems), one could look confidently ahead to the future. Schemes of social welfare, income redistribution, and consumerism were rendering hollow the idealogical panaceas and battle cries of old. As he was getting behind the wheel of his car to go on a paid vacation, the worker could not be expected to devote much thought to whether he was being robbed of the surplus value he had created or to feel humiliated and indignant at having been engaged in production for profit rather than use. One could not deny that there were pockets of poverty and areas of discrimination in even the most advanced countries of the West, but all that was needed to remove them was wise legislation. As for other areas of the world, one did not speak of poverty but of underdevelopment, with the obvious implication that this was only a temporary condition, in the process of being cured through the infusion of Western capital and development. Although the world was in the throes of a revolution, it was a reassuring revolution of "rising expectation." The Communist world presented a somewhat less reassuring picture. But

1

after all, Stalinism had been jettisoned, peaceful coexistence had been proclaimed the goal of Soviet policy, and though Khrushchev's rhetoric often clashed with this proclaimed goal, he spoke beguilingly of "goulash Communism," a close approximation of our "consumerism." One could then be cautiously hopeful that a convergence of the two worlds would not bring about a collision. Communist China seemed to present disturbing exception to this otherwise universal phenomenon of ideological fervor subsiding before material progress and technocratic rationality. But one suspected that the preachments of Marxian militancy and of a socialism of self-denial which emanated from Peking were only a temporary aberration, reflecting Mao's and his fellow sexagenarians' nostalgia for the heroic days of the Long March and the Yenan caves as well as their fury at their revisionist and coexistentialist Russian comrades. The next and younger generation of Chinese leaders was bound to be more in tune with the spirit of the era and therefore to abandon the talk about international and internal holocausts. For the moment, the Chinese Communists' rhetorical militancy was not without desirable by-products, one of which was to weaken the missionary fervor of their Soviet counterparts. When Khrushchev allowed that two generations might pass before America partook of the blessings of Communism, he was undoubtedly giving vent to a secret wish that it would be *his* grandchildren rather than himself who had to deal with Communist China.

No intelligent observer in 1960 could share the nineteenth century liberal's serene confidence in progress: crisis was still the normal state of international politics. But one could be cautiously optimistic that, if a nuclear war was avoided, the logic of economic interdependence and growing well-being would first moderate and then suppress the most explosive ideological conflicts and divisions, whether in a given society or the world at large. Ideologies would not disappear, of course, but one could hope that their clashes would more and more be settled in the voting booth and at diplomatic conferences, rather than in street fighting and on battlefields.

All of a sudden the middle and late sixties erupted with ideological turbulence. Historians will long debate, no doubt inconclusively, what caused this explosion, which in the midst of the greatest period of prosperity known to the West spawned a series of minirevolutions, a plethora of liberation movements, and a rebirth of militant ideologies grafted upon those movements. A number of American cities experienced race riots. Those who had complacently assumed that what was euphemistically called student activism happened only in backward or oppressive societies rubbed their eyes in disbelief as one after another of the most prestigious academic institutions in many Western countries became theaters of student revolt. For many years the democratic process had, through reform, been defusing the revolutionary potential inherent in such movements as the one for civil rights in the United States or for Irish reunification in the United Kingdom; the emancipation of women appeared to have been carried to its logical and satisfactory conclusion. Now suddenly they all emerged in revolutionary garb, the most extreme factions eschewing reform and preaching, if not actually practicing, violence. Causes and movements that had harmlessly dotted the political landscape, expressing the political eccentricities of tiny minorities, acquired overnight a new vitality and strident militancy. Thus, Scottish nationalism and Trotskyism were reborn as movements of intellectual significance.

This bewildering kaleidoscope of causes and cults was baptized by those who do such classifications as the new left. A huge oversimplification and, as I shall show, a wrong adjective. Yet the "left" part of the appellation was undoubtedly apt, for each protest movement, whether directed against sufferings of Catholic Irishmen in the North or against wrongs visited upon women, has had a substratum of radical ideology, sometimes explicitly socialist, but more often vaguely anarchist. It would not do for a protest or revolt to confine itself to a specific social, ethnic, or racial grievance and to eschew anticapitalist, antiestablishment, or antistate goals; in fact, those "antis" have usually been employed interchangeably in the rhetoric.

It was the radical characteristic of the revolt of the sixties, as well as its seemingly elemental nature, which led many social scientists as well as unlicenced sages to proclaim—some despairingly, others exultantly—that the old order had collapsed. Again the definition of this order—whether as capitalism, Western civilization, or repression of all kinds—varied according to the writer's argument. As André Malraux wrote under the shattering impression of the Paris students' strike and "revolution": "We face not the need for reforms, but one of the most profound crises that civilization has known . . . This general rehearsal of the (temporarily) suspended drama created both among the strikers themselves, and among those who observed them, the feeling of the end of a world . . . Our society still has not adjusted to the machine civilization."[1] The analyst-turned-prophets then projected visions of new, sometimes brave, sometimes dismal, worlds. The reader could take his choice as to the future: it would be characterized by universal participation or by general chaos and anarchy. The world would be ruled by Consciousness Three or by a repressive minority. It was entering upon a new era either of democratic socialism or of the breakdown of all forms of authority and hence civilization.

A few years have passed, and it is now almost impossible to recapture the heady atmosphere of those days. The future shock has turned into a prosaic, if perplexing, economic crisis. Social scientists who were then involved with how the assembly line bred alienation must now concern themselves with how to keep the assembly line going and to minimize unemployment. Most of the students and teachers who formerly decried education as irrelevant and middle class have now turned their attention to the growing problem of the financial viability of institutions of higher learning. Events have given an ironic twist to some of the most inflammatory terms and slogans of the revolutionary rhetoric. It was then said that, though political colonialism had become unfashionable, Western monopoly capitalism was keeping the Third World in neoimperialist subjection. Now neoimperalism would seem to be a peculiarly appropriate description of the policies and practices employed by the oil-producing countries, most of them members in good standing of the Third World.

Although the existentialist revolt thrown up by the sixties has receded, the intellectual malaise of which it was both a contributory cause and a symptom continues. Economically, the present state of affairs in industrialized democracies would still appear by the standards of 1935, or even of 1950, a miracle of progress and well-being. Yet intellectually the most fashionable posture has become to lament over the inability of liberal society, and of what is still perversely called capitalism, to create a viable society, both internally and in the world at large. It is perhaps partly because of the loss of influence of organized religion that a mournful moralism has entered the discussion of social and political problems. The ecological movement, generally sensible in its warnings and recommendations, still has an undertone of a masochistic cult, calling upon industrialized societies to repent of their sinful pursuit of materialism. Fashionable schools of historiography have ascribed the sources of conflict between postwar America and Stalin's Russia to America's imperialist strivings. The quest for virtue in internal as well as international politics and the implicit guilt about one's own society are best reflected in the fascination of Communist China for Western observers and analysts, many of whom have no sympathy for Communism per se. In choosing between two Communist societies, one of which represses political dissent entirely and the other, somewhat less so, a person brought up in the democratic and rationalist tradition would be expected to express a grudging preference for the latter. Yet it is Mao Tse-tung's China that has become the object of admiration for much of the new left, and even of sympathetic interest for some of the conservatives. In the present mood, there is no demand for utopias that exhibit cravings for automobiles, washing machines, and nonconformity; perhaps the more that is known and understood about a society, the less utopian it is bound to appear.

What has brought about this intellectual atmosphere is a subject of great complexity, on which philosophers may be unable to reach a definitive conclusion. Equally difficult is perceiving the ultimate consequences of this bizarre politico-intellectual mood through which the world is passing. Yet light can be shed on the ideas, obsessions, and enthusiasms that beguile us by tracing their development in the course of the Russian revolutionary movement, the end product of which was Soviet Communism. The old pre-Marxian Russian left displayed close parallels to the new left, including its revolutionary élan, its occasional ventures into and apologies for terrorism, and the general incoherence of its social and political programs. The statement, "The greatest evil of our society is the spiritual rule by children," could have been the heartfelt exclamation of a disgruntled American or West European conservative at the beginning of the 1970s. It actually appeared in 1909 in an essay by a former Russian radical who described and deplored the effects on the Russian intelligentsia of more than half a century of revolutionary thought and the consequent erosion of traditional rationalistic and moral values among the young.[2] This erosion and an infatuation with revolution for revolution's sake go far to explain the inability of Russian society to preserve democracy once the shackles of tsarism had burst. In its irrationality, quarrelsomeness, and lust for heroics the Russian liberation movement often perpetuated the traits of adolescence. So it is not entirely surprising that for all the democratic and egalitarian values enshrined in the revolutionary tradition, the actual revolution gave birth to an autocratic system, which after a period of despotism stabilized as an oligarchic bureaucracy. The current heirs of generations of revolutionaries who dreamed and struggled for progress and universal emancipation are sexagenerian bureaucrats, who think of domestic politics in terms of their own job security and the rate of growth of the economy, and who follow the tenets of realpolitik when it comes to international affairs.

The history of the Russian revolutionary movement and of its progeny, Communism, presents an incongruous mixture of two contradictory recipes for social change. It is a confirmation both of Mao's "political power comes out of the mouth of the gun," and John Maynard Keynes's "The ideas of economists and political philosophers, both when they are right and they are wrong, are more powerful than is commonly understood. Indeed the world is ruled by little else."[3] Nothing on the record justifies a belief that the interplay of guns and ideas is productive of greater happiness and freedom; if anything, the opposite is true. But the tradition which has Herzen as a founder and Solzhenitsyn as a current representative offers also a consoling proof that even an ideology buttressed by an impressive array of guns cannot entirely suppress the human striving for rationality and the craving for freedom.

PART ONE   THE BEGINNINGS

1 | BAKUNIN, HERZEN, AND CHERNYSHEVSKY

Russian socialism was born as a twin revolt against the native autocracy and Western liberalism. Two names stand out at its beginning: Michael Bakunin and Alexander Herzen. They best epitomize its tone: a tortured, often self-contradictory search for a third solution, its alternating moods of despair at the actual chances of revolution and of a messianic hope that Russia and the Russians might show the world the road to freedom and social justice. Strictly speaking, neither Bakunin nor Herzen can be counted as socialists. They defy classification, and any description—socialism, anarchism, populism—fails to do justice to the extraordinary variety and complexity of ideas that sprang from the pen of each man, to the succession of moods and political positions they adopted in their lifetimes. But they were reaching for socialism by writing and acting in the conviction that a purely political reform was not enough, and that only a wide social and economic transformation would regenerate Russia. With them, Russian radical thought emerges from the drawing rooms of Saint Petersburg and Moscow, appears on the European stage, and in turn begins to feed and form the revolutionary strivings at home.

The legacy of Michael Bakunin (1814-1876) belongs principally to Western anarchism. In his own country, Bakunin left few disciples. But he was in his lifetime the embodiment of the radical ethos, an example of sheer revolutionary energy that passed into history as a characteristic of the whole movement.

Bakunin was one of those natures that arouse either enthusiasm or reprobation. Any attempt at a "sober" biography is likely to be tinged with hypocrisy. An unfriendly biographer will inevitably imply that his rebellious spirit was a function of his disorderly personality, that no conceivable social system, no conceivable occupation save that of a revolutionary could accommodate and appease him. A friendly writer will have to overlook or minimize his negative sides: his racism, xenophobia, and utter irresponsibility, which made him associate with clearly criminal and demented characters, such as Nechaev. But in Bakunin we see, in exaggerated form, the strengths and weaknesses of the Russian revolutionary movement, which go far to explain its history, at once heroic and pathetic, and its final defeat (for that, in a sense, was the meaning of its absorption by Bolshevism), in which there was more pathos than heroism.

Bakunin was born a nobleman and tried his hand at one of the few professions open to his class: the army. After giving up his commission, he served an apprenticeship in the Moscow philosophical and literary circles and then sought escape to the freer world of the West. In "Europe" (which is how, consciously or unconsciously, the Russian intellectuals referred to the West in contradistinction to Russia) this student of German philosophy soon plunged into the radical and socialist movements that put their imprint on the eighteen forties and fifties. Bakunin became—as he was always to remain—what might be called a visiting revolutionary. There was no insurrection, actual or planned—including the ones in Prague in 1848, Dresden in 1849, Poland in 1863, and the numerous attempted revolts in France and Italy—in which he was not ready to fight, lend his assistance as a drafter of manifestoes or a theorist of revolutionary dictatorship, and the like.

The middle period of his adult life was spent in prison and exile. The Austrian government handed him over to its Russian ally in 1851. There is an anecdote that upon being turned over to the tsarist police, Bakunin, in his way always a Russian patriot, exclaimed how good it was to be on Russian soil, even if in chains (which was, a twentieth century writer might say, a Freudian slip, for the actual transfer of Bakunin, who was a fighter for Polish independence, took place on Polish soil, though within the Russian state). The unsentimental Russian gendarme replied: "It is strictly forbidden to talk."

During Bakunin's incarceration in Russia an incident took place that his biographers have found difficult to explain. Nicholas I had a truly Soviet passion for hearing or reading recantations of his imprisoned enemies. It was suggested to Bakunin that he should try. The result was his *Confession* (it came to light only after the Bolshevik Revolution), which the Tsar read with a great deal of interest and, on the whole, approval. In it Bakunin flattered and eulogized the Tsar and denounced Western liberals and parliamentarians. It will not do either to present the *Confession* as does a Soviet biographer, Steklov, who calls it a clever and justifiably mendacious document designed to enable Bakunin to have his sentence softened, or to hedge on this point, as does Franco Venturi, who sees it as "a photographic negative of Bakunin's personality" and its purpose as "consciously . . . to deceive and enlist the sympathies of his royal gaoler."[1] Bakunin would hardly have been human had he not sought an alleviation of his prison regimen, which he felt was killing him (although the next generation of Russian revolutionaries would have scorned such devices; they sought martyrdom, as we shall see in the case of Nicholas Chernyshevsky). But parts of the *Confession* have a genuine and even passionate ring. Some of the explanation must be that the revolutionary often found it easier—and this was to remain sadly true—to talk and to sympathize with the autocrat than with a Western-style liberal and moderate reformer.

Like his gendarme, Nicholas was rather unsentimental, and Bakunin's *Confession* did not bring him freedom. It was only in the next reign of Alexander II that his imprisonment in the fortress was exchanged for exile to Siberia, where Bakunin could at least move around and enjoy human company. Continued imprisonment for a man of his temperament would have ended, as it did for many others, in insanity. From Siberia he found it relatively easy to escape. In 1861 he was back in London, inquiring about the next revolution.

To a superficial observer, Bakunin was a "typical Russian revolutionary" or, worse yet, a "typical Russian": huge, gluttonous, eternally smoking and drinking tea (or stronger stuff), always sponging money from his friends, and disorderly in his habits. This stereotype is as exaggerated as is the other one of the Russian intellectual: fastidious and cultured to a fault. But stereotypes are sometimes more influential than reality. Lenin—and this was not unconnected with his revulsion at much of the Russian revolutionary tradition—displayed the utmost bourgeois sobriety and orderliness in his personal life, and nobody could have been more unsympathetic to any kind of bohemianism. The same traits in turn became ingrained in the official Soviet man, whose conformity—and not only in politics—would make Bakunin and Herzen turn in their graves.

It is almost superfluous to say that Bakunin never worked out a systematic philosophy of revolution or of socialism. His socialism was mostly of a visceral type: revolt against any kind of oppression and injustice, rejection of any palliatives or halfway measures. At one time he was a follower of a version of Pan-Slavism, the idea of a democratic federation of all the Slav nations. But no major radical philosophy of his time failed for a period to interest him or to hold his allegiance: Marxism, Saint-Simonianism, Proudhonism. It was inevitable, however, that in practical politics he should be a believer in the necessity of revolutionary dictatorships, while in theory he believed in anarchism. The latter made him sensitive to the authoritarian potentialities lurking in the teachings of Karl Marx. Marxism was to him but another way of arriving at the centralized oppressive state, and "he who says state says 'oppression,' and he who says oppression says exploitation." Bakunin would have approved what another anarchist, though Christian and pacifist, Leo Tolstoy, said: he who has not been in jail does not know what the state is. For Bakunin's period, with its illusions, this too was a perceptive statement: "Those previous workers having just become rulers or representatives of the people will cease being workers; they will look at the workers from their heights, they will represent not the people but themselves . . . He who doubts it does not know human nature." To Steklov this is a typical "confusion" of Bakunin, which was dissipated by the clear light of Marxism-Leninism, but the Soviet author who died in Stalin's concentration camp probably had time to reconsider his opinion.[2] To be sure, anarchism is excellent as a critique of other political systems, but hardly so as a positive prescription. Like other anarchists before and after him, Bakunin could only repeat: smash the state, destroy every relationship of domination and inequality. But then what? To that impolite question Bakunin, like other anarchists, could only answer with vague suggestions of purely voluntary cooperation, federalism of communes, and similar notions.

Marx and Marxism became for Bakunin, toward the end of his life, as much an embodiment of evil as the tsarist regime. The quarrel between the two men and their followers broke up the First International. In the West, and especially in the Latin American countries, the historic quarrel marked the real beginning of the hostility between the Marxist and the anarchosyndicalist elements of the workers' movement, a quarrel that flared up into open fighting as recently as during the Spanish Civil War. There was a personal element in Bakunin's hostility toward Marx, with whom at times he had friendly personal relations and whose *Capital* he was supposed to translate (though like most similar endeavors of Bakunin, this one remained unfinished). He could write: "Himself a Jew, he attracts whether in London or in France, but especially in Germany, a whole heap of Yids, more or less intelligent, intriguers, busybodies and speculators, as the Jews are likely to be, commercial and bank agents, writers . . . correspondents . . . who stand one foot in the world of finance and the other in socialism."[3]

Anti-Semitism has been, more often than socialist historians have liked to admit, a strong element in the make-up of radical movements. Marx himself was not entirely free from it. But with Bakunin it was a veritable obsession, grounded in his temperament and his self-delusion. Forgetting his aristocratic background, he fancied himself as a representative of the "masses." "They [the Jews] are always exploiters of other people's labor; they have a basic fear and loathing of the masses, whom whether openly or not they hold in contempt." Anti-Semitism flowed into and reinforced his Germanophobia. There was an element of personal pique in his hatreds: he had an unmistakable feeling of inferiority toward Marx. But mainly both the Jews and the Germans epitomized the qualities that Bakunin loathed, possibly because he felt their lack in himself: assiduity, orderliness, a practical business sense. The sum total of those attributes was the autocratic state or, equally bad, the wretched bourgeois culture of the West.[4] Socialism in the West was being ruined by the "Jews" (among whom Bakunin, at times, included persons he disliked even when not by any possible criteria Jewish), who were pushing it into the authoritarian path of Marxism. As for Russia, even Bakunin could not make a Jew out of Nicholas I, but then the imperial house was German in origin and connections, and so were the higher strata of officialdom. Thus, Russian autocracy was "really" German or, as he phrased it at times, "Germano-Tartar." The Russian people, namely the peasant masses, were democratic by instinct but enslaved and kept backward by an alien oligarchy.

Bakunin's personal phobias ought not to obscure the ideological element behind them. What he was against were essentially the main components of modern society: industrialism, the centralized state, organization, and the like. Here for all his peculiarities he was at one with a powerful tradition of Russian populism, the dominant tradition among the revolutionaries until Marxism became influential, and which even penetrated Marxism and gave it much of its appeal and revolutionary energy. What complemented this rejection of the "West" (and Bakunin simplified the task by his fiat that undesirable elements of the Russian reality were Western-German) was a faith in the "people." The latter, who in Bukanin's time meant the peasants, became the repository of moral virtue, as contrasted with the corruption of the Western bourgeoisie. Unsullied by Judeo-Germanic ideas, uncorrupted by Western materialism, the Russian peasant, thank God, had preserved his simplicity and virtue, his inherent democratic instinct, which would make a fit foundation for the future socialist commonwealth. That this philosophy combined wishful thinking with ignorance of the actual conditions of the Russian peasant's life, that it equated material backwardness with moral virtues, and that finally it concealed xenophobia and injured national pride caused by the dazzling progress of the Western nations can be seen more clearly by us than by a Russian revolutionary in the nineteenth century. Yet today we hear similar voices and arguments from Asia and Africa, and they find sympathetic echoes in the West. But what has escaped many critics of Russian populism who see its view of the peasantry as a combination of revulsion against the West and a sentimental idealization of the common man is its inherently undemocratic condescension. The peasant is regarded as the noble savage. He is an apt instrument, if properly led, to wreak terrible vengeance upon the hated government and the exploiting classes, and to show up the contemptible bourgeoisie of the West with their smug satisfaction in their progress and parliaments.

Bakunin's contribution to Russian populism was mostly through the legend of his own personality and his revolutionary skirmishes. In his last years in Switzerland, he was the object of much interest and some veneration among the young radical intelligentsia who flocked to the West in the 1870s. His writings and teachings were among the influences that stirred students in the same decade to go to the people and to try to educate the Russian peasant for the revolution. But leadership of the radical movement and thought had by the sixties passed into other hands. To the new generation Bakunin still epitomized revolutionary energy and intransigence, but their minds did not follow his exuberant anarchism and his dreams of vast peasant uprisings. In his own country Bakunin left no school. His violent anti-Marxism made him a rather embarrassing ancestor for future generations of socialists. In the long line of revolutionary figures that begins with the Decembrists and ends with Lenin, Bakunin stands somewhat to the side, ready to take on any and all proponents of oppression and coercive institutions, and strangely attractive despite his huge faults.

Unlike Bakunin, the advocate of action and violence (if with a touch of Don Quixote), his contemporary and friend Alexander Herzen (1812-1870) represented the intellectual and moral side of the revolutionary appeal. History has been kinder to Herzen. Though to the Russian "angry men" of the 1860s Herzen was something of a phony, advocating revolution from the safety and luxury of his foreign residence, denouncing materialism while living on the income from one million rubles, and assailing them for their bad manners, later radical thought reclaimed and acknowledged his services. Lenin himself was to enroll Herzen among the great precursors of Bolshevism. Liberals and Marxists were to quarrel over whom the legacy of Herzen should belong to. But apart from the politicians' quarrels, he has an undeniable place in the history of Russian literature. His memoirs, *My Past and Thoughts,* is a masterpiece of its kind, one of the most fetching and moving examples of the autobiographic genre in any language. Even his purely political writings have an elegance and charm that elevate them far above the standard Russian radical pamphleteering with its pretentious "people—yes" tone or its heavy sarcasm about the powers that be.

Herzen has always been a favorite among foreign connoisseurs of the Russian revolutionary tradition. This is not unconnected with his quality, both in life and in writings, of a *grand seigneur.* Like Leo Tolstoy, who also pursued his own brand of unorthodoxy in politics and personal behavior, Herzen could not, even if he wished, erase his characteristics of an aristocrat by birth and intellect. Such traits were not without their negative side. Herzen's sensitivity had at times an appearance of snobbery. Most troublesome of all, there was an element of humbug in his frequent declamations against materialism. Two neighboring passages in *My Past and Thoughts* set this in vivid relief. Herzen has just finished a tirade against the West and a scathing indictment of the prosaic materialistic pursuits of the bourgeoisie. Not long afterward he returns to his private affairs. The tsarist government had recently denied him, a political exile, his patrimony. Herzen ran to his banker, the head of the Paris House of Rothschild. The banker informed the imperial government that it would encounter difficultes in the international finance market unless the money were promplty turned over. As Herzen concludes in an amusing passage, the roles were seemingly reversed: like a "merchant of the second class" the Tsar humbly obeyed the edict of the emperor of bankers, and the money was duly turned over to the political criminal. Nor did the enemy of materialism scorn speculation on the stock exchange and in real estate. He was to feel some remorse (mixed perhaps with rancor at his bad judgment) that, when the Civil War broke out, he had banked on the victory of the "forces of reaction," the Confederate States, and sold his American bonds.

It is peevish to expect socialists to be more consistent in their ideas and private life than is the general run of mankind. And Herzen was generous in helping the revolutionary cause and the exiles. But Herzen's tirades against the West's corrupt materialism were mischievous for another reason. They taught—and Herzen's influence on the Russian intelligentsia was at one time enormous— that political regeneration of his country could be accomplished by an act of will, and that sound economic institutions (in fact, a healthy materialism) are *not* a necessary prerequisite of political freedom. The history of Russian revolutionary thought is the history of an ascending revulsion against the humdrum, unromantic aspect of the everyday life of most ordinary people, a revulsion that finally burns itself out in terrorism and is then replaced by a very different, very materialistic preaching of Marxism. A French socialist whom Herzen admired, Pierre Proudhon, wrote in a moment of disenchantment that the people are a "quiet beast" interested only in eating, sleeping, and love-making. Few revolutionaries would subscribe to this unflattering description of the common man, but what irks them most is the adjective "quiet."

Herzen was born of a noble and rich family. He was of illegitimate birth, but his social standing and education were unaffected by this fact. His father was an eccentric aristocrat somewhat in the style of a French nobleman of the *ancien régime,* who affected to disregard conventions, among them legalized marriage. The first political impulse for young Herzen was provided by the drama of the Decembrists in 1825. Herzen was a child of December 14, wrote Lenin. The heart and mind of the fourteen-year-old boy were stirred by the aristocratic martyrs of freedom. Not long afterward, Herzen and his friend Ogarev swore a solemn oath to sacrifice their lives, like the Decembrists, for the liberty of the Russian people. It was a romantic gesture much in the style of Schiller, who was then being read avidly by the youth, but Herzen and Ogarev, both to grow up as men of talent and wealth without the necessity for politics to fill up a void in their lives, always remained true to their adolescent vow.

Not that, like Bakunin, Herzen was a born rebel or a restless conspirator. In different times and in a different society he might well have become a Whig politician and man of letters. But Nicholas' Russia made it easy for sensitive young men to grow up into revolutionaries. Herzen's first arrest and exile from the capital were earned because he merely knew some young people who were alleged to have sung, in private, revolutionary songs. His second exile in Russia was occasioned by the secret police intercepting a letter in which he alluded to the corruption of the police. In 1847 the young nobleman left his oppressed country to find, he expected, a haven of liberty and civilization in the West.

Herzen's ideas of the West had been fed by Romantic literature, German idealistic philosophy, and Western (mostly French) theoreticians of socialism. Though he reached Europe in his manhood, it was still with a youthful shock that he realized that political life in the West did not all turn around the noble and invigorating ideas of republicanism and socialism, and that people in France and Germany were preoccupied with practical concerns and materialistic cares. The revolutions of 1848, after some turbulence and social experimentation, seemed only to have weakened the upper and strengthened the middle classes, and to have enthroned the middle-class viewpoint as the guiding principle of politics. How different from Romanticism! This jarring impact of reality brought out in Herzen the unconscious Russian nationalist. Europe was decrepit and old. The bourgeoisie had had its day. At the very moment of the beginning of its mastery Herzen, like Karl Marx, was wishfully confident that he was watching the death throes of capitalism. Certainly it was not from a French bourgeois or an English liberal that Russia could expect the inspiration for her freedom.

The usual disgruntlements of a foreigner in France accentuated Herzen's ideological distaste. An aristocratic youth in Russia encountered France either in the person of French tutors and servants, or in the form of eloquent diatribes written against tyranny and exploitation by the French philosophes and socialists. Yet the average Frenchman had nothing servile or tyrannicidal about him. He tended to be self-reliant, caustically practical, and possessed of that eternal French cultural chauvinism which made him criticize good-naturedly the French pronunciation of his Russian friends. It was not uncharacteristic that Herzen should feel much better in Italy. This country was then divided into a number of autocratic principalities. The Italian bourgeoisie was much weaker and poorer, and the Italian peasant, closer in his misery to the Russian one, had none of the infuriating traits of his French counterpart. In London, Herzen was to experience disgust but at the same time a certain awe at the supreme self-confidence of this bastion of the capitalist spirit. He could not but admire English liberties and individualism. In Paris, Italy, or even Switzerland one was never quite safe from the long reach of the tsarist secret service, and the local authorities, were at times unhappy because of the presence of conspiratorial foreigners. To the revolutionaries, the British offered the boon of safety, but also the insult of the utmost lack of interest in their affairs.

Herzen's solution for Russia's ills, once he had found the Western remedies and institutions wanting, took the form of "Russian" populist socialism.[5] How consciously this was a rejection of European constitutionalism is indicated by his famous challenge, "Russia will never be Protestant [moderate and materialistic], Russia will never be *juste-milieu* [a prosaic middle-class regime and society], Russia will never make a revolution with the aim of getting rid of Tsar Nicholas and of replacing him with Tsar-representatives, Tsar-judges, Tsar-policemen."[6] What then?

Behind many an unsound theory there is usually some bad history. And in the case of Russia many historical or philosophical hypotheses that lie at the root of "characteristically Russian" political and economic solutions have been fathered by learned Germans. Herzen's learned German was Baron Haxthausen, whose work on the Russian peasant and agriculture was to have a powerful and fateful influence not only on Herzen's but on much other Russian thought, whether conservative or radical in its tendency. Haxthausen was attracted by one feature of Russian peasant life: the communal organization of the Russian village—in Russian, *obschchina*. The commune both before and after the abolition of serfdom in 1861-1863 was the main type of agricultural organization in most of European Russia. The peasants' land was vested in the commune, not in the individual peasant families. In most communes the assembly of the peasants—in Russian, *mir*—would periodically redistribute plots of land among its members, arbitrate the peasants' disputes, and handle similar matters (subject, of course, to the over-all authority of the landlord prior to the abolition of serfdom, and of government representatives afterward). Haxthausen saw the commune as an institution of great antiquity, the relic of ancient communism, which at one time characterized the agricultural organization of all primitive peoples. Russia was lucky to have preserved this grass-roots type of peasant democracy and socialism. It could preserve her from the evils of competitive capitalism of the West, where the dispossessed peasants and craftsmen were being turned into the slum-dwelling proletariat of the Lyons and Manchesters.

To the Russian conservative, a Slavophile, the theory of Haxthausen provided an important intellectual weapon against the apologists for the Western institutions. Here in Russia, they argued, somewhat in the manner of the Southern defenders of slavery before the Civil War, the seemingly backward institution actually represented both the wisdom of the ages and social justice. The people—the peasants—did not need parliaments; they had a superior form of direct democracy. The commune assured its members economic security, protecting them from the uncertainties and degradations that were the lot of the Western industrial proletariat.

Let it be said once and for all, even as an oversimplification, that in fact the commune was an institution of no great antiquity, that the economic security it provided was at best of a very low level, that despite the periodic redistribution of land it did not prevent economic differentiation among the peasants, and that, most important of all, it hampered social mobility, hurt technical improvement in farming, and thus proved a major obstacle, both before and after the freeing of the serfs, to the industrialization and economic improvement in Russia. We can see this today, and more perceptive thinkers would see it toward the end of the century. But a Russian radical of the eighteen forties and fifties recoiled before the picture of the industrialized world with its unregulated factory life, its sordid manufacturing towns, its teeming and brutalized proletariat; it was easy for him to wish to spare Russia a similar experience. For the Russian socialist even more than for his conservative counterpart, Haxthausen's theories strengthened the already existing idealized vision of the commune and provided a way out of his dilemma: yes, Russia would advance to civilization and, beyond that, to socialism, but without the industrial travail of Europe. This thought was pleasing to the national pride lurking beneath radicalism. Who would have expected that backward, autocratic Russia contained within it an institution and a principle which could show the rest of the world the correct path to democracy and socialism!

Herzen's socialism involved, then, a plan for the federation of free peasant communes. First of all there would have to be a liberation of the serfs; they must be liberated with their land, with little or no compensation for the landlords.[7] Unlike Bakunin, Herzen did not dwell with pleasure on the possibility of vast peasant uprisings like those that had stirred seventeenth century Russia. He looked at times for reform from above, and he appealed to the conscience and intelligence of his own class, the gentry. Despite his aesthetic dislike of the bourgeois West, he was a good European, at least insofar as prizing individualism and rejecting the use of violence before exhausting all the possibilites of persuasion and peaceful alteration.

Herzen's main contribution to the revolutionary tradition lies not wholly in his agrarian socialism; his views of the commune and his idealization of the democratic and inherently communistic Russian peasant are not, after all, much different from Bakunin's or from other contemporary radicals. His contribution lies in his role as teacher and inspirer. It was he who through the example of his personality and his skill as a writer and journalist created the classical ethos of the Russian intelligentsia: the attitude of intellectual opposition to authority, of solicitude for "the people," and of consecration to politics as the duty of every thinking and honest man. Herzen was largely responsible for the creation of Russian-in-exile, that state of mind among political emigrés and escapees which held not merely that they were individuals fleeing from oppression, but that they represented their country's moral dignity and that they bore collective responsibility for Russia's political future. And much of the enlightened opinion at home was in the first instance taught by Herzen to accept the exiles' self-appraisal and to consider them the ambassadors of its hope and aspirations.

In London in 1857 Herzen began publishing a periodical, *Kolokol* (*The Bell*). Even earlier he had made efforts at publication and a dissemination of his ideas at home, but it was only with *The Bell* that he became a power in Russian intellectual and political life. Nicholas I had died in 1855, the Crimean War had ended in Russian defeat, and now the autocracy was relaxing its grip. *The Bell,* officially forbidden, found its way into the most influential circles; even Emperor Alexander II was reputed to read it. *The Bell* for a while fitted the mood of transition after the death of the old despot. The regime was bent upon reform, for the military defeat had shown the cost of the obsolete social and political system, and the new emperor had none of his father's obsessive fear of political change. Superficially, there are some resemblances to the post-Stalin era, although the tsarist government had few of the totalitarian regime's devices to contain the liberalization within safe bounds, and none of its propaganda skill to blame past evils on a "cult of personality." But the tsarist government did have equal determination to let no reform affect the basis of its political power.

The Bell at times approved the Tsar's reforming tendencies and promises and at times chastised their dilatoriness. Its main fire was directed at the remnants of the old bureaucratic abuses and at the personalities within the bureaucracy who attempted to continue Nicholas' system. Herzen's genius as political writer acquired for him an audience at home among both moderates and radicals. This success and acceptance were short-lived, however, for Herzen, unaware, had caught the infection of Western liberalism and become a liberal revolutionary (to join the two in his case is not a paradox). For him, any reform had to be only an installment on future and complete freedom and socialism. By the same token he could not understand or sympathize with the new radical breed who viewed reforms with loathing and sarcasm and who wanted the whole social and political system to be smashed at once before a new and socialist Russia could be reconstructed from the ruins. The conflict was prophetic of the future splits in the revolutionary movement: each successive generation was to view its elders with a mixture of pity and contempt, as men who had grown soft and alien to the revolutionary strivings of the people.

In politics as in his private life Herzen was a true child of Romanticism, subject to intermittent bouts of exultation and depression, ready with an exorbitant tribute or with a scathing indictment. The news that the Tsar contemplated freeing the serfs threw him into transports of gratitude. He hailed the rather commonplace emperor as the savior of Russia and addressed to him through the pages of *The Bell* a series of letters containing unsolicited advice on how to overcome the opposition of the bureaucracy and reactionary nobility. This one-sided "correspondence" took at times a ridiculous turn, as when Herzen undertook to advise the imperial family on the upbringing of the heir to the throne.[8] Once the repressive nature of the regime had reasserted itself, Herzen's adulation turned to the severest censure. Essentially this proneness to address the Tsar (and Herzen was by no means alone among the revolutionaries in doing so) was not unconnected with his populism. Did not the peasant believe the Tsar to be his benevolent father and did he not blame the evils of government on the bureaucracy that deceived the Tsar and kept a barrier between him and his people? So ran the stereotype. In a strange and perverse way even the terrorists who later hunted and killed the emperor were the victims of the same emotion, the same belief in the omnipotence of one person: they punished an unjust father who deceived and refused freedom to his people. This heady atmosphere of the revolutionary's intimate feeling about the ruler was to be entirely absent from the make-up of the Russian Marxists. To Lenin, the emperor was that "idiot Romanov" and a person of absolutely no consequence.

The early sixties marked the end of *The Bell's* great influence in Russia. The actual form of the peasants' emancipation disappointed Herzen. Most of all, tsarism horrified him anew by the bloody suppression of the Polish rebellion of 1863. Herzen was among the relatively few Russian intellectuals who have been genuinely and fervently pro-Polish. For all their close ethnic connection (or maybe because of it), and for all their historical links, relations between the Poles and the Russians have usually been unhappy. In Russian public opinion contemporary with Herzen, the Poles fitted a stereotype not too dissimilar from that attached sometimes to the Jews. The Russian radicals saw in the Polish leaders mainly aristocrats and landowners who exploited their (often Russian) peasants. The conservative Russians regarded the Poles as a nation of revolutionaries, vaunting their superior culture and betraying the Slavic race. Herzen's advocacy of Polish independence at the time when the rebellious Poles were killing Russian soldiers rubbed hard against aroused Russian chauvinism.

Among the more radical souls who would have welcomed any rebellion against tsarism, Herzen was losing influence for another reason. To the "men of the sixties," or the "nihilists" as they were sometimes known, Herzen was clearly behind the times. He was a product of Romanticism, whereas they imagined themselves as being disciples of "scientific" materialism. For their taste, Herzen's socialism was too humanistic, too much grounded in the hope of change by evolution. They were in many cases men of humble birth, whose ideological disagreement was enhanced by their personal pique at Herzen's noble manner and the elegance of his language. Their feeling of social and intellectual inferiority was covered up, as is often the case, by biting sarcasm at the expense of the "men of the forties" with their well-intentioned but obsolete and useless liberal ideas (the word "liberal" was already becoming a term of opprobrium among the radicals). The new men, such as Chernyshevsky, aroused in Herzen a revulsion not so much political as aesthetic. He felt in them, as he probably would have felt in the Bolsheviks, a strange preoccupation with revolution as an end in itself rather than as the means of assuring human freedom. Behind their professed materialism and dedication to science he saw a hostility to traditional culture, to everything that might not be "useful," that is, not in line with their political views and ambitions. Appalled by the new radicals, Herzen used a phrase about them that has always been held against him: the young men, he wrote, retained in their mentality the traits of the "servants' room, the theological seminary, and the barracks." This was a direct reference to their plebeian origin, which accused them of vulgarity and of socially envying the older, more "refined" generation. In another attack, Herzen initiated the technique that has since become a commonplace in revolutionary debates, the full elaboration of which we can see today in the exchange between the Russian and Chinese Communists, that of attacking persons who are left of your own politics as being "really" right-wing and serving the interests of reaction. In an article entitled "Very Dangerous" (somewhat affectedly, the title is in English), Herzen proclaimed that the attacks upon him and his position served the interests of the most reactionary part of the tsarist bureaucracy, and that the young radicals might live to be decorated by the government.

This bitterness reflected Herzen's realization that the minds and hearts of the young generation in Russia were being increasingly won over by his opponents. But it also bespoke a feeling of hopelessness about his own political position. Herzen could not for long remain a moderate or an enemy of any revolutionary striving. He already had the psychological trait that was to become the curse of future liberals and moderate socialists up to the October Revolution: the consciousness of being outdistanced in one's radicalism and of being confronted with a more uncompromising and unscrupulous revolutionary resolve that produced inner doubts and a sense of inferiority. How well was Lenin to understand and to exploit this infirmity of the liberal mind!

Herzen, because of his temperament, had to return to the out-and-out revolutionary fray. Despite his deep resentment about new radicals, and despite his lingering hopes in the emperor, any and every act of official oppression and brutality provoked afresh his revolutionary fervor. To the students who then in Russia were becoming the vanguard of revolutionary disturbances Herzen wrote: "Glory to you, you begin a new era, you have understood that the time of whispers, of hidden allusions, of [the secret reading of] the forbidden books has passed." Where should they go when the brutal authorities close down the universities? "To the people, to the people . . . show them . . . that from among you will come the fighters of the Russian people." And the arrest of Chernyshevsky—his main antagonist among the radicals, the man who epitomized to Herzen the narrow "mentality of the seminary"—evoked from him a generous tribute and imprecations against tsarism.

The last years of Herzen's life were clouded with personal and political tragedy. E. H. Carr gives a vivid picture of the turbulent personal life of the revolutionary and his circle, a life poisoned first by the infidelity and subsequently the tragic death of his wife, then by his tortured liaison with the wife of his great friend Ogarev, a liaison that was not allowed to interrupt the friends' intimacy and political collaboration, but which inevitably contributed to Ogarev's moral and physical decline.[9] The decline of *The Bell* as well as personal considerations made him shift his residence to Geneva. Such places had at least a considerable Russian colony, and no Russian could for long remain content in London with its bleak Victorian atomosphere, the horrors of the English cuisine, and the lack of such amenities as French-style cafés, which are almost indispensable to a revolutionary movement in exile. To Herzen, London was an "ant-heap." He had no contacts with English intellectual or political life, and the circle of his acquaintances was almost exclusively among the exiles and radicals of several nations.

Of the new tendencies in European socialism Herzen was no more enamored than of the new Russian radicalism. "Scientific" socialism and the emphasis on the industrial worker were alien to one who had been brought up on the generous, if fantastic, dreams of Saint-Simon and Fourier. "The worker of all countries will grow into the bourgeois" was Herzen's most perceptive if overoptimistic and, by his lights, unflattering judgment. Russian Marxists have never quite forgiven Herzen this dismissal of the industrial proletariat. How could one identify the heroic working class, with its privations and its revolutionary drive, with the mercenary and philistine spirit of the bourgeoisie? His fellow Londoner, Karl Marx, Herzen could not stand. Marx was what he called a "bilious" type of politician, an intriguer who could not indulge in polemics without heaping abuse and filth upon his opponent. Herzen did not share Bakunin's almost pathological anti-Semitism and Germanophobia (though he was not fond of the Germans). But Marx was for him an embodiment of the German bourgeois spirit: formal, unromantic, and devoid of those elements of humor and compassion that he deemed essential for a real fighter for the people's rights. The news that Marx was to address or even to attend a political gathering or banquet was cause enough for Herzen to send his excuses.

Herzen's faith in revolution as a moral principle was to assume a different and to him an unpleasant form among the people who were both his successors and his opponents in the revolutionary movement. he wrote, in referring to the hotheads of "Young Russia" who were disseminating terroristic manifestoes, that he had long since ceased, whether in war or in politics, to lust for the blood of the enemy. "Whenever anybody's blood is spilled somebody's tears will flow." But the future of the Russian revolutionary movement belonged to the unsqueamish sentiments of Chernyshevsky: "The path of history is not like Nevsky Prospect, it goes at times through dirt, and filth, through swamps and ravines! If you are afaid of being covered with dirt or of soiling your shoes then don't take up politics."[10] This is an unfair criticism of Herzen, who was not afraid of being covered with dirt while carrying on his mission, but who simply did not want revolution to soil its hands in unnecessary blood.

Herzen's posthumous "good luck" in being claimed as a spritual ancestor by all branches of Russian revolutionary thought makes his position all the more pathetic. For he would not have felt at home among the liberals with their admiration of Western parliamentary institutions, and he certainly would have loathed Bolshevism. The Communists have always been good at posthumous rehabilitation. The dead cannot be forced to recant, but their shortcomings can be ascribed to their class origins, or to the times in which they lived. And so in the Pantheon of the Communist saints—predecessors of Lenin—Herzen is forced to share the uncongenial company of Chernyshevsky, of terrorists of the People's Will, and of Plekhanov (who also would have cried in outrage at this honor). Nothing is more certain than that, were he transplanted into the twentieth century, Herzen would be found in Paris or in London (in Bloomsbury) stigmatizing Soviet Russia with the same moral fervor that he expended on Nicholas. One can be equally sure that he would couple the lashing of the native tyranny with scorching protests against the capitalist West, its imperialism and its incomprehension that what is going on in

Russia, brutal and tyrannous though it is, may still contain the seeds of a freer and better society. One might even suspect that he would have welcomed the coming of Communism in China as representing a purer, agrarian brand of the ideology, and that he would at first have been thrilled at the epic of the Cuban revolution. Perhaps in looking at Herzen's enthusiasms and disenchantments, we see not only Russia, and not only the past.

With Nicholas Gavrilovich Chernyshevsky (1828-1889) we stand at the real source of Bolshevism. At the age of eighteen Lenin wrote an admiring letter to the great radical, then in exile in Saratov after a long imprisonment in Siberia. And in the office of the Chairman of the Council of the People's Commissars in the Kremlin, Chernyshevsky's works shared the place of honor with those of Karl Marx. Chernyshevsky helped to mold the form of the revolutionary; Marx provided him with the message. But not only Lenin was inspired by Chernyshevsky. In the memoirs of revolutionaries of various political persuasions, or even in their depositions before the police, one often finds a phrase such as, "I became a revolutionary at the age of——after reading Chernyshevsky." The work most often mentioned is the novel that gave Lenin the title for his basic political treatise, *What Is To Be Done?* When it appeared in the early 1860s, this novel and its message were read by the young radicals, as one of them put it, "practically on our knees." But even ten or twenty years later, when its cryptic political allusions could no longer be deciphered by another generation, schoolboys were still entranced and steered into the revolutionary path by *What Is To Be Done?*

In Chernyshevsky we see the effects of a social environment widely different from that which had brought forth Herzen or Bakunin. He was the son of an Orthodox priest. The rank-and-file clergy was practically a hereditary class. Since they could not aspire to the higher ecclesiastical preferments, the clerics lived under material conditions usually not much superior to those of their congregations, which in nineteenth century Russia meant mostly peasants. At the same time they had to have a modicum of education. This combination of poverty, imposed dogmatism, and education tended to make the clerical households a breeding ground for the radical and revolutionary intelligentsia. Not only Chernyshevsky and his closest collaborator, Dobrolyubov, but many other revolutionaries were to spring up from this clerical environment.[11]

This background and the fact that he himself studied for a time in a theological seminary left a definite imprint on Chernyshevsky. His Soviet biographer relates with some distaste that even as a radical and unbeliever Chernyshevsky still liked to attend church services and would cross himself when passing a church.[12] But more important, his strict upbringing by his clerical father bred in the boy a timidity and awkwardness in society that he never shed. Like that other alumnus of a theological seminary, Stalin, Chernyshevsky retained traces of scholasticism in his thinking and writing.

It is important to dwell somewhat on Chernyshevsky's private life and characteristics, not for the sake of what might be called historical voyeurism, but because his personality contributed much to the tone of the later radical movement, and because both he and his fictional heroes became the models for future revolutionary fighters. Again one is tempted to commit a huge oversimplification: Chernyshevsky, below the veneer of extensive education and erudition that he acquired, was the typical Russian man of the people. One finds in him a mixture of peasant slyness and of naiveté; of overpowering if at times sardonic humility, combined with arrogant self-confidence. What other author would address the reader as he does in the beginning of *What Is To Be Done?* "I don't have the shadow of an artistic talent. I even use the language poorly. But that is not important: read on, kind public, you will read this with benefit. Truth is a great thing; it compensates for the deficiencies of the writer who serves it." From the jail, on the eve of his long exile to Siberia, he wrote to his wife: "Our life belongs to history; hundreds of years will pass, and our names will still be dear to the people; they will think of us with gratitude when our contemporaries are long dead." The same man who warned the reader that he had not a shadow of artistic talent proudly told a police official that his name would live in the history of Russian literature along with those of Pushkin, Gogol, and Lermontov.

Chernyshevsky's endurance of suffering was more than heroic; it turned into an obstinacy that borders on masochism. There was in his nature a blend of resignation and defiance that is bred through more than just political persecution. After ten years in Siberia the government let it be known that if Chernyshevsky petitioned for a pardon, he would be allowed to rejoin his family in Russia. The official who brought the message to the exile was greeted with neither elation nor anger. Chernyshevsky answered with a kind of puzzlement: "Thank you. But, look, for what can I 'plead' for pardon? . . . It appears to me that I was exiled only because my head is differently constructed from that of the head of the Chief of the Police, and how can I ask pardon for that?" And to the bafflement and anguish of the official, he absolutely refused to ask for mercy. When as a middle-aged but already physically ruined man he was allowed to return to European Russia, Chernyshevsky quietly continued his literary occupations. To an idiotic question as to how he had felt in Siberia, he replied patiently—and again there was more than just irony in the answer—that those had been his happiest years!

A cynic will see in all this a conscious effort to build a political legend out of one's own life. But the same qualities of endurance, timidity, and resolution are found in Chernyshevsky's private life. He fell in love with a girl from a higher social sphere who was both lovely and much sought after. Chernyshevsky was overjoyed and incredulous that his beloved reciprocated his feelings. In a paradoxical fashion he set about demonstrating to the girl that he had no right to marry and involve another being with his fate, since he was drawn to politics and, though by nature cowardly, he would have to join a revolutionary movement if one arose in Russia and was thus likely to end up on the gallows or in prison.[13] Before their marriage Chernyshevsky made a statement most unusual for the nineteenth century, that he would leave his wife entirely free in every sense of the word. More than that, he declared to his fiancée: "I am in your power, do what you will." To his friends, who warned him about his future wife's character, he said incredibly: "It is all the same to me if I have someone else's child; I shall tell her: Should you prefer, my dear, to come back to me, don't be embarrassed."[14] It was not only love that motivated him but his social conviction that woman had always been oppressed, and now her emancipation must begin by her temporary dominance over man: "Every decent man in my opinion is bound to put his wife above himself; this temporary domination is necessary for future equality." His wife's subsequent infidelities and frivolity were borne by him with the same unshakable patience and contentment with which he endured exile. He never wrote or treated her except in terms of complete affection and devotion. If her behavior, apart from the disloyalty toward her husband, did not meet Chernyshevsky's conception of how an emancipated and politically conscious woman should act or caused him pain, then he successfully concealed it from strangers.[15] After his exile he returned to his Olga and worked hard at uncongenial work on translations for the money to satisfy her slightest whim. What most jars the Soviet commentators about Olga Chernyshevsky is that, with her husband on his deathbed, she tried unsuccessfully to reconcile him to the faith of his fathers.

Chernyshevsky's most important period of activity encompasses the last of Nicholas' and the first few years of Alexander II's reigns. He had abandoned any thought of a clerical career and found himself in 1846 at Saint Petersburg University. After a stint of teaching in the high school, he became a collaborator on the magazine *The Contemporary,* and before long this priest's son, still in his twenties, was Russia's most influential social and literary critic, the intellectual guide of the new intelligentsia. *The Contemporary* had what in terms of Russia in the late fifties and early sixties was a huge circulation—over six thousand—built up through the collaboration of Russia's leading literary lights. Founded by Pushkin shortly before his death, it was to feature Turgenev and young Tolstoy and many others of this halcyon period of Russian literature.

The radical poet Nekrasov, then editor of *The Contemporary,* recruited Chernyshevsky. The latter with his critiques, essays, and articles changed the direction and the significance of the journal. It became the standard-bearer of radicalism. In that respect its influence rivaled and soon surpassed Herzen's *The Bell,* even though the latter did not have to grapple with censorship.

In his aesthetic views and criticisms Chernyshevsky must be considered an ancestor of Soviet socialist realism, though its full and appalling character cannot be blamed on the critic who believed that the artist should be free to write or paint as he pleases. But even in his doctoral dissertation Chernyshevsky condemns art for art's sake and science for science's sake and declares that both spheres of activity should be judged in terms of their utility for society. In his criticisms, this point of view is carried to further lengths. The useful, common-sense technique of taking into account the social meaning and tendency of a given work of art is allowed by Chernyshevsky to affect his aesthetic judgment and at times to push him into absurdities. His friend and fellow editor, Nekrasov, wrote for "the people"; Pushkin did not; hence Nekrasov is a far greater poet. What makes it worse is that Chernyshevsky hastens to explain that he looks at poetry "not at all exclusively from the political point of view." How sadly premonitory is Chernyshevsky's trumpeting of the social responsibility of the writer, the admonition that he should not write "just" poetry, his reminder to Nekrasov that "every decent man in Russia counts on you," presumably to write the poetry of social protest.

Chernyshevsky's observations on the ideal of beauty are not without interest. Why is "the people's ideal" of feminine beauty connected with the image of a hefty peasant wench with rosy cheeks? Because the common people have to work hard, and hence they value the evidence of health and strength. But take a society beauty. Generations of idleness have weakened the muscles; hence the small delicate limbs. That much-prized pallor in a lady of the upper classes is eloquent testimony to the sluggish circulation of the blood. No wonder that headache is a fashionable ailment of the aristocracy: it testifies that its sufferer does not have to work and her blood consequently accumulates in the brain. In the same passage Chernyshevsky somewhat inconsistently ascribes the delicacy and fragility that are the attributes of the aristocratic ideal of beauty to exhaustion from the sensual excesses to which the idle classes resort out of boredom. It is no wonder that such persons as Tolstoy and Turgenev became uneasy about their fellow contributor to *The Contemporary*.

It is fair to observe that Chernyshevsky was by no means the most extreme among his contemporaries in his "social significance" school of literary criticism. It fell to him to defend Tolstoy's *Childhood and Adolescence* from the charge of ignoring the social problem. A novel intended to reproduce the world of a child, he wrote, can hardly dwell on the basic problems of politics or social philosophy. That this defense had to be made, and of such a writer as Tolstoy, and by Chernyshevsky, is an eloquent testimony to the spirit of the times, or at least to that of the radical intelligentsia.

Chernyshevsky's political and philosophical viewpoint was formed under many influences. In his university days he was drawn to Fourierism, perhaps through a vague connection with the Petrashevsky circle, and the vision of the phalanstery as an ideal form of social organization stayed with him to the end. After the usual apprenticeship in the idealistic German philosophy, he fell under the spell of the materialistic views of Ludwig Feuerbach. This philosopher, unfortunately for his reputation, is now remembered mainly for his celebrated aphorism, "Man is what he eats," and for his logical deductions from this principle, like his recommendation to the working classes that they would never conquer their beef-eating aristocracy as long as they fed on potatoes; they should change their diet to beans. Chernyshevsky was very literal in embracing a body of philosophy, and it is no accident that the hero of *What Is To Be Done?* builds himself up for revolutionary work by eating huge quantities of beef. For many a Russian intellectual, and for none more than Chernyshevsky, the acceptance or approval of a philosophical system was not only a matter of intellectual choice but a passionate act of faith. He grasped greedily Feuerbach's dictum that philosophy should be replaced by the natural sciences. Science, the study of man and nature, should replace the systems of metaphysics and idealistic ethics as an explanation of life and a guide to action. Chernyshevsky was a leader in the intellectual revolution of the 1860s, which made the young intelligentsia turn their backs on the German idealism with which men of Herzen's generation had been enamored and look for answers in materialism and scientism. He expressed this new addiction in words that again could come only from his pen: "I am a scientist. I am one of those scientists whom they call 'thinkers' . . . I have been one since my early youth. It has long been my habit and self-imposed duty to consider everything which comes to my mind from the scientific point of view, and I am unable to think of anything otherwise." Chernyshevsky, having rejected Christianity—and he was not alone in this—never lost the need for faith, for absolute certainty. And like the preceeding, the following words appear comical in their conceit only at first, but are full of pathos in their implications: "My mistakes have been only in trifling details which do not affect the essence of my thought."

Like their predecessors who found in German idealism the "arithmetic of revolution," Chernyshevsky and his followers had no trouble in identifying the message of materialism and utilitarianism with an injunction to revolutionary struggle. The philosophical instrument for this tranformation was the celebrated theory of "wise selfishness." It was derived by Chernyshevsky from the English utilitarians, but Jeremy Bentham and John Stuart Mill would have been surprised to see its ramifications in the hands of their Russian disciple. Man is naturally selfish, said the radicals of the 1860s, with the rapture and vehemence that usually accompanies a new discovery. Neither God nor any higher moral law but only self-interest guides him in his behavior. But what is the most rational form of selfishness? A "decent," "real," or "new" man (all those adjectives are used interchangeably by Chernyshevsky) finds his highest interest, the most satisfying sensual pleasure, in serving the interests of society. Selfishness = service to mankind = revolutionary activity (under the conditions of contemporary Russia). In *What Is To Be Done?* various characters go to great, and to the reader exhausting, lengths to demonstrate that their heroic actions, such as giving up a beloved woman, sleeping on a bed of nails to harden oneself for revolutionary work, or other torments, are not, God forbid, consequences of their altruism or of a love of mankind, but simply of selfishness. Chernyshevsky's elaboration of "wise selfishness" has more serious results. It becomes a rationalization of political terrorism. What if a majority is content or ignorant enough to endure life under political tyranny? Should not a "new man," if his inner needs impel him, risk his life for the good of the people? Alexander Ulyanov, for example, in a speech before the court in 1887 did not even pretend that in attempting to assassinate the Tsar he represented the oppressed masses. No, he avowed, he spoke for a tiny minority. His deed was that of a "wise egoist."

The "new men" were immortalized in Turgenev's *Fathers and Sons.* To their conservative or even liberal contemporaries they became known as "nihilists," raucous enemies of all conformity, culture, and tradition. Chernyshevsky's novel was intended largely as an answer to Turgenev's *Fathers and Sons,* which the young generation felt was a slanderous misrepresentation of their ideas. The subtitle of *What Is To Be Done?* is *Tales About New People.* The most remarkable person, the one intended by Chernyshevsky to be the exemplar of the new man's virtues, is Rakhmetov. It is he who eats huge quantities of raw beef and sleeps on nails, thus acquiring enormous stength and hardiness for revolutionary tasks (Chernyshevsky himself was frail and bookish in appearance). Aside from raw beef, Rakhmetov will not eat food that poor people cannot afford: "in St. Petersburg he ate oranges, but refused them in the provinces. Because in St. Petersburg common people eat them, which is not the case in the provinces." He is brusque and to the point in conversation, scorning the effusive politeness customary in a Russian gentleman. Five minutes of skimming the pages is enough to make him see whether a given book is written in a scientific, materialistic spirit; if not, it is trash and not worth reading: "I read only that which is original, and I read it only insofar as is necessary in order to know this originality." As a "wise egoist," Rakhmetov spends his considerable fortune in helping his fellow men. He is obviously—though this cannot be spelled out because of censorship—a revolutionary.

Russian society of the late fifties and sixties was not, unlike our own, jaded by and resigned to the appearance of successive waves of angry young men. The old type of radical à la Herzen was a man of courtly manners and culture. But the "new man" would laugh in your face if you talked of idealistic philosophy, would gobble down food while discussing social problems, and would sneer at everything unconnected with science or revolution. Worse still, the "new man" was being joined by the "new woman," who had cropped hair, talked back to her parents, and intended to study anatomy in order to become a doctor and work among the people. To the conservatives, all these horrors indicated that the relaxation that had followed Nicholas' death had gone too far, that the youth had to be curbed. When within a few years bad manners turned into political terrorism, they had the melancholy satisfaction of reactionaries of all periods: "We told you so." To the older radicals the extravagant mood of the generation whose standard-bearer was Chernyshevsky was saddening, but they saw in it a delayed effect of the constrictions and crudities of Nicholas' times. But though they deplored the crudity of their successors, and could even, as did Herzen in an unguarded moment, attribute it to the low social origins of its leaders, their greatest apprehension was aroused by the political temper of the new men.

In politics Chernyshevsky was as shrewd and cautious as he was naive and preposterous in the artistic field. He was extremely careful not to be openly identified with any revolutionary organization or appeal. His radical ideology and his devastating comments on the autocracy were put forth under the very nose of censorship. Chernyshevsky smuggled them into *The Contemporary* in articles allegedly dealing with such subjects as the events in Austria or ancient Rome, or the French politics of the year of revolutions, 1848. His allusions were clear not only to the initiated but to the public at large. Chernyshevsky's was indeed the model of this "Aesopian language," of which Lenin and his followers were to make good use in their struggle of wits with the censor.

Russian politics of the late eighteen fifties and early sixties presented a fantastic appearance. The most radical people were never very far from petitioning or eulogizing the Tsar for this or that reform. And the most cautious of the liberals were not far from approving a violent revolution if the Tsar would not listen to the pleas for a redress of popular grievances. Chernyshevsky's political activity touched both spheres. In practical politics he was, like most of the radicals and liberals of his day, a follower of Herzen. It was Herzen who in his youth had inspired him with the idea of dedicating himself to the cause of the people and of risking eventual imprisonment or exile. Chernyshevsky's immediate aims for Russia in the 1850s echoed those proclaimed by *The Bell:* emancipation of the peasants with land (which would keep the commune as a basis for future socialism), an end to censorship, and the calling of a national assembly.

But beneath the level of practical politics Chernyshevsky had a fervent revolutionary temperament that could not and would not be appeased by any reforms or schemes of representation. The announcement that the emperor planned to liberate the serfs evoked even from Chernyshevsky an exclamation of admiration and gratitude. Yet not only the character of the promised reform but also a whole complex of feelings and causes pushed him in the direction of an uncompromising struggle with the regime. Herzen's and the liberal gentry's continuing illusions about the emperor increasingly excited the sarcasm and wrath of the radical collabora- tors of *The Contemporary.* Dobrolyubov and Chernyshevsky stig- matized and denounced the moderates and liberals. In hardly veiled allusions they described how the liberals and the middle class abroad, as in France after 1848, had always "sold out" the people and, having secured their own class interests, made peace with the oppressive regime. To them, well-meaning noblemen and bureau- crats were epitomized by Oblomov, the hero of the famous novel of the same name by Goncharov, a "superfluous man" always dreaming of great deeds but never having enough energy and courage to put them into execution.

The passion of the new generation found classical expression in a famous letter to *The Bell* printed in 1860 and signed "A Russian.[16] The author calls upon Herzen to give up his panegyrics to the emperor and his hopes for a revolution from above. He states the classical position of the true revolutionary, "The worse it is, the better for us." Under Nicholas I everybody came to understand that only force could win human rights for the Russian people. Now under Alexander the liberals are confusing the people's minds with nonsensical pleas for patience and moderation: "therefore one now regrets Nicholas. Under him the [needed] work would be car- ried through to the ultimate end," Russia has always been held in slavery because of its idiotic faith in the good intentions of the Tsar- Autocrat. *The Bell* should not burn incense before the emperor:

"Our situation is tragic and insufferable and nothing can help but the axe." And the author throws out the famous challenge, "Call upon Russia to raise the axe."

The letter marked a new era in the Russian revolutionary movement. Revolution and violence had become the only means of cleansing the national life. There was also a more strident voice of class feeling. The tsarist regime shared the writer's contempt for "liberal landowners, liberal professors, liberal authors." This paradoxical hatred by the intelligentsia for the class to which they really belonged and on which they still counted most to ignite the revolutionary fire forms the strongest psychological bond between Chernyshevsky and Lenin.

The actual engagement in the revolutionary struggle followed the proclamation of the emancipation edict in 1861. The long-prayed-for freeing of the serfs was now a fact, and as in the case of every great reform, initial elation was followed by disillusionment. The edict freed the peasants *with* land, but in many provinces they were given less land than they had cultivated while in bondage. These "cutoffs," which went to the landlords, were to remain an important political symbol and issue well into the twentieth century. Most disappointing of all to the radical, the peasants were put under heavy financial obligations, since they were to pay the government (which had compensated the serf owners) in yearly installments for the alleged value of the land. The commune beloved by both the conservative and the radical was retained as the base of the social and economic organization of the Russian village. The "cutoffs" and especially the fact that the peasant had to pay for "his" land, aroused the special fury of the radical. As he had always suspected, the Tsar "sold out" the peasant: the emancipation was a hoax; its provisions benefited only the landlords. That the peasants in some places rebelled, claiming that the Tsar intended to give them land free but that the nobles were cheating them (the intricate financial and administrative features of the reform could only with difficulty be explained to the illiterate masses), was another indication that there was a vast revolutionary potential in the countryside. The years 1861 and especially 1862 became a period of clandestine revolutionary manifestoes. Small groups of students and intellectuals organized themselves into revolutionary circles. The most notable of these, although it was still difficult to speak of a party, adopted the name of *Zemlya i Volya* (Land and Freedom), but there were others: one proclaimed itself as Young Russia. Most of these groups consisted of a press and a handful of zealots.

Chernyshevsky's attitude toward active struggle was not without ambiguities. He claims to have sent an emissary to London to represent to Herzen, once more an activist, how improper it was for him to sit in the safety of England and stir up young people in Russia to dangerous activities. Chernyshevsky's own prudence was so great that though most of the insurrectionary proclamations have been ascribed to him, there is no definite proof that he was the author of any of them. Yet his influence is traceable in practically all the manifestoes. This mild, bookish man became in 1861, along with his coadjutor and closest friend Dobrolyubov, who died in the same year, the inspirer and leader of the revolutionary movement.

Strong evidence connects Chernyshevsky with a series of three insurrectionary proclamations. They were addressed respectively to the students, the soldiers, and the peasants. The last one, composed in the simple folk language, is supposed to have come directly from his pen. It begins, "To the landlords' serfs [actual emancipation was to take place only in 1863], greetings from their well-wishers." The essence of the alleged emancipation is demonstrated to be a fraud and really a perpetuation of serfdom. Who is responsible? Just some bureaucrats and the nobles? But the Tsar himself is a landlord, so why should he not have the interests of the landlords exclusively in view? When will real freedom come for the peasant? When the people will rule themselves, when the peasant will not have to pay the tax, and when he will not be torn away from his family and village to serve for decades in the army. How is this to be accomplished? By a revolution. Let the peasants take counsel with each other, let them approach their brothers who serve as soldiers and prepare for the great day. But until then, they should not engage in piecemeal, isolated uprisings against the government. Only when the movement becomes nationwide will the revolution succeed.[17]

Characteristically, it is impossible in Chernyshevsky's behavior in 1861-1862 to disentangle several skeins of motivation. Did he seek martyrdom consciously, hoping for an early revolution, or was he simply and unreasonably confident that his caution and reputation would protect him from arrest? Probably a little bit of each. The right-wing elements were in full cry after Chernyshevsky as the spiritual if not the actual father of the revolutionary proclamations. One story has it that the governor general of Saint Petersburg, Prince Suvorov (who had the reputation of a liberal and in some circles was being advanced as the future head of a revolutionary regime—such were the fantastic incongruities of the 1860s) sent an emissary to offer Chernyshevsky a passport and advice to go abroad. But political migration in the 1860s meant something quite different from what it was to become in Lenin's day, when there would be a powerful international socialist movement to shelter and support its Russian comrades and to maintain avenues of easy access to the homeland. Even Herzen with his great wealth and cosmopolitan tastes was now leading an unhappy and restless existence abroad, and his influence within Russia, enormous as it had been, was on the wane precisely because he was losing touch with the new generation. And few of the Russian revolutionaries have been as Russian as Chernyshevsky. He stayed.

In the spring of 1862 a series of large-scale fires plagued the capital. The reactionary press blamed them on the nihilists (the phraseology of the proclamation by Young Russia would not rule out its authors resorting to arson); the radicals rejoined that they were the work of the *agents provocateurs* of the right and claimed that in some provincial towns the nobles were setting buildings on fire to discredit the emancipation of the peasants scheduled for the coming year. Whatever the truth—and in view of the multitude of wooden buildings and the wretched safety conditions in contemporary Russian cities it is not necessary to assume arson—the campaign against the revolutionaries and their known or assumed instigators was intensified. Repressions included the closing down of public reading rooms, several schools, and the Saint Petersburg Chess Club, all of them reputed to be infected with the virus of nihilism and alleged to be gathering places for the radical intelligentsia. *The Contemporary* was suspended for eight months. It was inevitable that Chernyshevsky, long under the surveillance of the Third Section, would be arrested. He spent two years in the Petropavlovsk fortress while his case was being "investigated." Legally no proofs of subversive activity could be brought against him, and this, which would not have inhibited authorities under the previous reign, was something of an embarrassment under Alexander. Finally, with the help of some manufactured evidence, the sentence was pronounced in 1864. Chernyshevsky was condemned to seven years at hard labor, but such formalities seldom prevented the tsarist police from detaining a state criminal for an indefinite period. Only in 1883, broken in health, was he allowed to return to European Russia.

Before being sent into exile, Chernyshevsky was subjected to the "civil execution." This barbarous ceremony took place before the public. The prisoner was exhibited on a scaffold wearing a placard with the inscription "state criminal." His sentence having been read, he was made to kneel and a sword was broken over his head. Then in chains he was driven back to prison. Reactions of the audience have been differently described. Most eyewitness accounts agree that Chernyshevsky was applauded by some members of the intelligentsia present at the ordeal. But one account has it that a group of workers hissed the prisoner. To the masses, Alexander was still the Tsar-Liberator and his enemies representatives of the "gentlemen" who resented his benevolent intentions for the people.

The story of Chernyshevsky's martyrdom goes far to explain the feeling of inferiority that Russian liberals always felt vis-à-vis their more radical compatriots. In the face of so much sacrifice and suffering it appeared unworthy to denounce the recklessness of the revolutionary's views, or even to dwell too much on the aesthetic shortcomings of his literary work. This meek and infuriating man scored a moral triumph not only over the regime he detested but also over the moderates who had deplored the savage implications of his views. He and his followers and successors seemingly forced the regime to persist in its barbarous methods, which sapped the meaning of the major political and social reforms of Alexander's time, and thus barred an evolution toward enlightenment and constitutionalism that promised Russia's salvation. Hence the tragedy of Russian liberalism, and a preview of the fate of this doctrine throughout much of today's world.

In the Petropavlovsk fortress Chernyshevsky wrote his *What Is To Be Done?*, the novel that was to play an important role in the formation of Russian revolutionaries and which reveals so much more than do many political treatises and manifestoes of the psychology of political radicalism in the 1860s. Yet except for pornography, *What Is To Be Done?* has all the major characteristics of a bad novel: utter unrealism of situations and characters, lack of literary grace and style, sententiousness, and ponderous moralizing. The author repeatedly addresses, harangues, and nudges "the perspicacious reader" in a way that is unbearable for the most patient of the lot and which must owe something to Chernyshevsky's early theological training. The amazement of the reader of today at the éclat created by the novel is increased when one remembers that it was published at the time of the greatest flowering of Russian prose. This inept, dull, and puerile work fascinated the younger generation, which compared it with the art of Tolstoy, Turgenev, Dostoevsky, and beyond them, with the works of a score of unusually talented and interesting novelists then at the height of their creative powers. Herzen, who felt some responsibility for Chernyshevsky's arrest, praised its "good points." The oracle of early Marxism in Russia, Plekhanov, denounced the critics of *What Is To Be Done?* as "obscurantists." Some argued, with obviously bad artistic conscience, that it should not be compared with *Anna Karenina* but, say, with Voltaire's novels. Yet the comparison with *Candide* is just as devastating, or rather unthinkable, as with Tolstoy's masterpiece. The fact remains, as Plekhanov wrote, "we all have drawn [from the novel] moral strength and faith in a better future," and, "From the moment when the printing press was introduced in Russia until now [the end of the nineteenth century] no printed work has had such a success as *What Is To Be Done?*"[18]

The novel's leitmotif is the story of a "new woman," Vera Pavlovna, daughter of a depraved and meretricious mother and a father weak and servile toward both his employer and his wife.

Brought up in the degrading lower-middle-class atmosphere, Vera surprisingly develops a social consciousness and independence. Pressed by her mother to marry a worthless upper-class lout, she is saved by that veritable *deus ex machina* of the nineteenth century Russian story, the impecunious university student who earns his sustenance as a private tutor. He, Lopukhov, marries her, thus saving her from her sordid surroundings and marriage to the upper-class swain. Need it be said that Lopukhov is a "new man," a believer in "wise selfishness" and a holder of advanced views on the emancipation-of-women question and marriage? Thus, the union of Lopukhov and Vera is a marriage in the eyes of the law only: they have separate bedrooms, each can entertain friends without the other's permission and knowledge, and their social intercourse takes place in the neutral ground of the drawing room where they assemble to drink tea and to hold interminable discussions about the philosophy of life. To be sure, this marital coexistence at times breaks down into a greater intimacy, but the point is well established: their marriage is one of those nominal unions that in the sixties and seventies many an "advanced" woman contracted to escape parental oppression, and in which the "husband" at least in theory made no demands on his "wife." Inevitably Vera falls in love with Lopukhov's best friend, Kirsanov, also a "new man." And so, in order to leave his wife and his best friend to pursue real marital bliss, Lopukhov heroically blows out his brains. But, oh, does he really? First Vera Pavlovna and then the reader is teased into the realization that Lopukhov simulated a suicide and went abroad. The role of the Greek chorus in the book is performed by our friend Rakhmetov. It is he who explains to the disconsolate "widow" her husband's noble ruse, asks her to repair to her real beloved, and scolds her for forgetting in her private grief her social obligations. End of the story? No. Some years later a mysterious "North American," Beaumont, appears on the scene and marries a patient of Kirsanov, now a famous doctor. The young couple settle down to live next to the Kirsanovs, and "they live in harmony and amicably, in a gentle yet active fashion, in a joyous and reasonable fashion."[19] The perspicacious reader does not need telling who this alleged North American really is.

This bare résumé cannot render the full flavor of the novel. Its secondary characters are perhaps as noteworthy as the main ones. Vera's hateful mother, the only person in the book drawn with some artistry, embodies all the brutal and grasping characteristics of the lower middle class. There is a proverbial courtesan with a golden heart and in the same line, but a lower social level, a virtuous prostitute. The latter is saved by Kirsanov, who persuades her to exchange promiscuous amours for a more stable existence of having five or six steady customers. After this period of probation, he himself condescends to live with her, but since he is slated for Vera Pavlovna, the unfortunate victim of bourgeois society has to be killed off by tuberculosis. But having been regenerated by work in a seamstresses' cooperative, she dies happy, warmly recommending her erstwhile lover to Vera Pavlovna.

Throughout the book runs a strange undercurrent of violence. The "new men" are all reason and sweetness, but they can take care of themselves. "What kind of a man was Lopukhov? This will show," whereupon Chernyshevsky recounts his hero's meeting with an upper-class gentleman who marches straight at him: "Now at that time Lopukhov had made this rule. 'I turn aside first for nobody except women' . . . And he marches straight at the gentleman. The individual, half turning back, said, 'What is the matter with you, pig? Cattle!' and was about to continue in this tone when Lopukhov quickly turning around seized the individual around the waist and threw him into the gutter with great dexterity; then standing over his adversary he said to him, 'Don't move or I will drag you into a muddier place.' Two peasants passing saw and applauded; a clerk passing saw, did not applaud and confined himself to a half smile." This passage tells us more than a whole series of political essays.

What might be called direct political and social propaganda is veiled with Chernyshevsky's usual caution in *What Is To Be Done?* Even so, it is hard to understand how the book was passed by the censor, for it is seeded with socialist hints and revolutionary sentiments. The "new men" are clearly socialists. Vera Pavlovna organizes the seamstresses' cooperatives, where the women live and work together and the profits are shared, clearly a version of

Fourier's phalanstery. But the main vision of the better world of the future appears in Vera Pavlovna's dreams, which are set as interludes in the novel. In one of them she sees a society in which poverty and oppression have been eliminated, where women enjoy full equality, and where government and coercion have disappeared. The whole country is covered by flowering gardens (very few people in this utopia live in the cities). In their midst rise palaces of steel and glass, where in the Fourierist fashion thousands of people eat and amuse themselves together. Science has made the deserts bloom and all work light and joyful: "Everybody lives as he wishes." Evenings are spent in dancing and singing, though if somebody prefers to sit in a library or museum, he is welcome to it. Thus, Chernyshevsky's utopian socialism is obviously a throwback to his youthful infatuation with Fourier. The Soviet commentators cannot repress a sigh that in his novel's vision of the future Chernyshevsky seems to have forsaken his materialist viewpoint for this utopian if socialist idyll. But even so, its influence has seeped through to Bolshevism. What are the Soviet Houses of Culture and Rest but the descendants of his glass palaces where the masses spend their time in innocent, cultured, and mirthful occupations?

The epilogue of *What Is To Be Done?* consists of a scene of revelry led by a mysterious Lady-in-Black, in which our two happy couples participate. To the modern reader this scene is bewildering, but to its contemporaries it was the allegory of a victorious revolution, which according to the chronological hints was to take place in 1866. When in that year Alexander II was fired upon, there was some talk in police circles of bringing Chernyshevsky back for an investigation, but this absurd project was abandoned. To the initiated the whole book was replete with revolutionary allusions, and this fact as much as its romantic motif and the daring theme assured its enormous success.

But the appeal of the book deserves even closer scrutiny. To the adolescent the book was simply a novel of adventure and mystery. This genre was to become enormously popular in Russia, and despite the fact that *What Is To Be Done?* is set not among the Red Indians or in Africa but in Russia of the 1850s, it has certain characteristics of the novel of adventure. Did or did not Lopukhov

. . . ? The interminable suspense in clarifying Beaumont's true identity quickens the adolescent's heartbeat with joyful expectation. The dialogue with the perspicacious reader, its hopeless sentimentality wrapped up in hard-boiled realism, the sad end of the virtuous prostitute, the mysterious political hints, the happy and heroic ending—they all appeal to the overserious yet childish mind in a way that *Anna Karenina* or *The Brothers Karamazov* obviously cannot.

To the older generation the appeal lay elsewhere. For them its primary message was one of political and social liberation, especially of women. When the conservative press assailed *What Is To Be Done?* as a shameless brief for free love, this idiotic accusation enhanced the popularity of the novel. Yet Chernyshevsky was an exponent of a somber and humorless morality, and like the more frightening prophets, he had the virtue of practicing what he preached. He would have been shocked at *Lady Chatterley's Lover,* though his moral, "Dare to be happy," is not different from D. H. Lawrence's. *Lady Chatterley's Lover* has as its main motif the deadening effect of industrialization on life and love, and Chernyshevsky levels the same accusation at contemporary Russia with its oppression, especially of women. But then, Lady Chatterley never organized seamstresses' cooperatives.

The novel's characters, fantastic though they are, did have some prototypes in the circle of Chernyshevsky's radical friends.[20] Both Kirsanov and Lopukhov are hugely exaggerated portrayals of his acquaintances. Even the fantastic Rakhmetov is suggested by one Bakhmetev, a rich eccentric who appeared in London, deposited with Herzen a sum of money for the revolutionary cause, and then vanished without a trace, allegedly on his way to establish a socialistic community in some wilderness. Thus, Chernyshevsky's fantasies fitted in with the spirit of the radical youth. For all his shortcomings he was a genius at propaganda: the social and political system is condemned not only because it is unjust, not only in the name of a higher philosophical and historical principle, but mainly because it prevents happiness and the fulfillment of man's most intimate needs. Such a lesson could hardly be gleaned from Marx's *Capital,* but it is part and parcel of the eternal appeal of Communism to the young.

The perspicacious reader of today, if he has navigated his way through *What Is To Be Done?,* will be jarred by one note that remained unnoticed in the quarrel over the novel's alleged moral vices or virtues: Chernyshevsky's condescension if not contempt toward the ordinary run of mankind. What makes it worse is that the novel's professed tone is one of democracy and equality. Chernyshevsky goes to extraordinary lengths to assert the natural goodness of man. It is all the more striking, therefore, when he artlessly reveals an unusual kind of intellectual snobbery. The "new men" are really quite sure that they stand above the vulgar multitude: "We did not see these men six years ago . . . but it matters little what we think of them now; in a few years, in a very few years we shall appeal to them; we shall say 'Save us,' and whatever they say then will be done by all." When Kirsanov's virtuous prostitute dies, the lover-reformer's feelings are described as follows: "His old love for her had been no more than a youth's desire to love someone, no matter whom. It is needless to say that Nastenka was never a match for him, for they were not equals in intellectual development. As he matured, he could do no more than pity her." For Chernyshevsky, the common man is often merely a well-intentioned slob. Vera Pavlovna's mother is derided among other things for her ignorance of French. This intellectual snobbery is not untinged by a social one: Chernyshevsky denounces the degenerate aristocracy of the capital, but he cannot help describing Rakhmetov's ancient and distinguished genealogy. The author's biases, like many of his characteristics, are both disarming and frightening; they are expressed with a disingenuousness that would almost make one believe he is satirizing his own convictions, but they have their source in the frightful intensity of the revolutionary's hatred of the world of the bourgeoisie and officialdom.

It is almost superfluous to talk of Chernyshevsky's "influence" on Lenin or on the subsequent development of the Russian revolutionary movement. Soviety historians hail him as the Great Predecessor. In their classificatory passion they try to fit him into one of their tiresome categories, as a populist, or perhaps a revolutionary democrat with a touch of utopian socialism. They stress—and not only out of duty—that for all his lack of the final grace of Marxism, no figure looms as great in the history of revolution prior to Lenin. The father of Russian Marxism, Plekhanov, is by comparison a dry *raisonneur*. The revolutionaries of the People's Will who offered their lives in fighting the autocracy are the romantic precursors of the men of 1905 and 1917. But Chernyshevsky represents not only the idea and the resolve of revolution. He also mirrors the mentality of the revolutionary: his cunning and naiveté, his ability to withstand and to inflict suffering, both the crudity and the elation of his vision of a better world.

2 | SOCIALISM AND UTOPIA

Socialism and utopia. These two words were once thought to be closely associated, if indeed not synonymous. With all due respect to Sir Thomas More's copyright, creation of utopias is a nineteenth century phenomenon and so is socialism. To seek salvation on this earth, to achieve human perfectibility in this life, would have been almost inconceivable before the onset of rationalism. The wonders and miseries of the industrial age prompted the search for a haven of peace and contentment where science and technology could reign and bestow their benefactions, but from which their fellow travelers, business and competition, would be sternly excluded. Nothing is more productive of intellectual discontent than material progress. The vistas of infinite improvement when seen through the reality of squalor and human degradation lead to an impassioned protest and a reassertion of the golden age, this time thrust into the future.

The organic connection between socialism and utopia becomes more evident when we contemplate the contemporary scene. Seemingly, socialism is the ideology of our age. Regimes that proclaim themselves to be socialist rule one-third of mankind. Just as in the nineteenth century no Balkan country could become independent without its leaders doffing their picturesque native costumes, donning frock coats, striped trousers, top hats, and liberalism, and talking in the jargon of John Stuart Mill and Gladstone, so today the independence of Zambia or Algeria is instantaneously followed by the local leaders proclaiming their adherence to an "African" or "Arab" brand of socialism. But in reality socialism as an ideology has become sterile and unexciting. Scratch its Chinese or Russian brand, and below the thin veneer of Marxism-Leninism you will find intense nationalism, which for purposes of defense and expansion propagates the old slogans and ideas. In the West, socialism as a philosophy rather than a ritual still lingers on. But even there it has in practice coalesced with one or another version of the welfare state. Various Western philosophers, unwilling to relinquish completely their youthful enthusiasms and resentments, are busily rummaging in young Marx trying to clear him of responsibility for the more deplorable aspects of Leninism and Stalinism. But even that venture proceeds without the zest and faith (the all-important word) of the earlier creators of socialism and utopias.

In fact, it has been the decline of utopian thinking that has seriously damaged the capacity of socialism to stir up emotions of fear or hope. Even in that least utopian of socialisms, in Marxism, it is the vision of the final and frankly utopian phase of social development, of communism, which is responsible for much of its appeal. A society of perfect equality and harmony is the final promise of Marxism, the promise which has enabled it to offset the anarchists' charge that it proposed to displace a multitude of capitalists by one, the state. Yet, how meager has been the residue of this promise. When the then heir of Marx, Nikita Khrushchev, attempted in 1961 to portray the blessings of communism, which the Soviet people are scheduled to enter in 1980, he could think of nothing more imaginative than the production of two hundred million tons of steel and free rides on buses and railways. Those are not the kinds of things that stir men's hearts and imaginations.

At the other end of the socialist spectrum a similar disenchantment, "de-utopianism," has stolen in. Wrote Sir William Beveridge in the document that was the foundation of the British Labour Party's victory in 1945, "The suggestion of this Report is that we should find that common objective in determination to make a Britain free of the giant evils of Want, Disease, Ignorance and Squalor."[1] How unassuming in comparison, and prosaic, are the postulates under which the Labour Party won its modest victory in 1964! To close the gap in the balance of payments, to arrest the brain drain, to deprive the upper classes of their still remaining guilty pleasures and pretensions—those are the tasks that British socialism sets before itself. Sir William's manifesto seemed to promise immortality, something that was overlooked even by the most caustic critics of his report and its adaptation in Labour's program (how else can one interpret the promise to abolish disease?). Harold Wilson and his colleagues promise to restore solvency and industrial efficiency.

How can one explain this simultaneous decline of socialism and utopia? There are a number of ready answers. We *do* live in a precarious utopia. Those wonderful advances of science that have made possible the abolition of so many social evils may also lead to the abolition of civilized life. How can one retain a childlike belief in the power of science to work unconditionally beneficent miracles, or in utopias, or in that unhesitating socialism which so stirred our predecessors?

Or, another explanation: we have grown jaded and disillusioned with promises of infinite improvement, of a basic and vast transformation of the conditions of human existence. Freud has left some melancholy observations on this count, and though most of the psychoanalysts and his lay devotees have adhered to the cause of progress, his warnings hover over this Freudian world of ours. Disillusionment with the dreams of human perfectibility and with the (mostly socialist) utopias of the past has given rise in our times to literary fantasies that can be described as antiutopias. They range from works like Zamiatin's *We,* an early protest against Soviet society, to more generalized versions of the future horrors of mechanization and collectivism, such as *Brave New World* and *1984.* The golden age is once again seen to lie in the past. For all the sufferings and imperfections of the pre-1914 Western civilization, the individual was less trammeled by the state and society. And for all his religious and superstitious fears, the average man was free of fear that the basis of civilized life, if indeed not its physical continuity, could be utterly destroyed. What are all our advances in comfort, in mechanical contrivances, and in social justice against this fear?

The antiutopias present a counsel of despair. In the most masochistic of them, *1984,* even the catharsis of total destruction is excluded in order to make the picture of perfect totalitarianism more

genuine because of his speculation (financial, not political) on the victory of the slave-owning South in the Civil War. One might argue, in fact, that it is only natural for a great humanitarian's exertions on behalf of mankind to leave him less capable of attending to and correcting his personal weaknesses.

It is equally indiscreet and dangerous to push too far the analogy between the emotional basis of socialism and that of such movements as fascism and national socialism. Dislike of the modern city with its hustle and bustle inspired William Morris to write his absurd communist utopia. Not much later, awe and hatred of Vienna, of the anonymity and cosmopolitanism of a great city's life, led an unemployed painter to formulate the first premises of his hideous philosophy. Morris thought that the Parliament buildings could be better employed by storing fertilizer in them. One remembers the frantic rage into which Lenin would erupt at the mere mention of the word parliamentarism. The gentle dreams of a Kropotkin, or a Blatchford, their complaints that modern industrial organization has stripped life of its spontaneity and charm, have found harsh echoes in the Nazis' "blood and soil" and in the corporative state of the fascists, from which the ignoble motivations of profit and class interest were also to be expelled. But such analogies can hardly be used as the basis for accusations against socialism or individual socialist thinkers. They appealed to the same emotions and often exploited the same fears and superstitions, but their conclusions were different.

However, it would be both squeamish and unreasonable not to acknowledge the common fund of radicalism to which both the extreme right and the extreme left have made their appeal in the struggle against modern industrial civilization. For lack of a better word, this common fund might be called anarchism. It is engendered by an agrarian society undergoing the birth pains of industrialization. The classical model is that of Western Europe during the first half of the nineteenth century. There we see masses of formerly rural population being transformed into the city proletariat. To the common man, apparently mysterious forces deprive him of his livelihood on the land or in a craft and compel him to sell his labor to the entrepreneur, the hated capitalist. Though economic historians never tire of pointing out that the workman's miserable standard of living still represented an advance over his previous status, such statistics could hardly be convincing to the victim of progress. His previous mode of existence, or that of his father, appeared to have been "natural"; his present mode, as an appendage of the machine, monstrously wrong. People who today advocate urban renewal sometimes run into traces of the same psychology: a more comfortable dwelling does not seem to compensate for loss of the feeling of neighborhood; the "naturalness" of a broken-down house in the slums is perversely prized over a more comfortable apartment. In a "stable" agrarian society almost everybody could consider himself a proprietor of some kind, even in the humble capacity of tenant. In industrial society, as the *Communist Manifesto* convincingly argued, property for the majority in its meaningful sense, in land or in the tools of one's work, was destroyed.

From a similar perspective, preindustrial life must have appeared harmonious and bereft of the catastrophic fluctuations and crises that characterize a commercial and industrial society. Droughts, famines, and the like are forgotten or minimized when contrasted with the instability which in the industrial order is the rule. A new technological invention, constant advances of science, even the improvements in medicine that lengthen life and decrease infant mortality, all lead to periodic overcrowding of the labor market, to loss of jobs, and to uncertainty about the future. It is thus understandable that in the earliest types of socialist and reactionary thinking the machine is asserted to be the enemy of the poor and technological progress itself is said to be responsible for enslaving the masses. A man as intelligent as William Cobbett still could believe that the preindustrial age was one of prosperity and universal contentment and that the population of England had declined as a consequence of industrialization and mechanization. The Luddites were simply the most primitive and direct among those who held the machine to be a diabolical invention destined to ruin the livelihood of millions and to accumulate all wealth in the hands of a few capitalists.

It was equally easy to idealize the political past. In the preindustrial age the average man was hardly aware of the phenomenon of the state. The system of authority under which he found himself was traditional and thus appeared natural. But even the earliest liberal state becomes a welter of laws and regulations, its very pruning of the archaic and obsolete laws having the appearance of constant legislative revolution. The character of this revolution is only too clearly to bolster the interests of industry and commerce, in brief, of the capitalist. The state, whether it enforces the New Poor Law, calls upon armed force to quell popular uprisings and disturbances, or bestows the franchise on the new commercial classes—including Jews and Dissenters—is thus acting in the interest of the capitalist; it becomes the executive committee of the exploiting class.

The sum of those reactions could not fail to produce a frame of mind that has endured to our own day and which has provided the most fertile soil for radicalism of both left and right. The appeal of anti-industrialism is perennial. Even in the countries most imbued with the industrial ethos, a national disaster or an economic crisis will revive the anti-industrial feeling and clothe it in new, if more sophisticated, theories and forms of social protest. In Britain the defeat of Chartism and the triumph of liberalism in politics and economics appeared forever to blot out the old beliefs and superstitions. Karl Marx, whose system and prophecies had been so largely based on the observable tendencies of the English social development of the first half of the nineteenth century, lived to realize, with despair in his heart, how in the first industrial country in the world earlier political turbulence had given way to acquiescence in capitalism, and earlier socialism to tame trade unionism. Yet the slackening of English industrial dynamism led to a rebirth of socialism. Some of its more eccentric varieties, like guild socialism, hearkened back to the anti-industrialism of the left wing of the Chartist movement, repeated the absurd notions of the harmony and stability of the preindustrial age, and sought to impose a quasi-medievalism upon the age of industry and science. Today, such ideas are hardly allowed to protrude from behind the welfare-oriented and bureaucratically-tempered main current of British socialism. No one calls, as the more lyrical of Labour spokesmen did between the two wars, for the creation of a new Jerusalem in England's green and pleasant land. One reason is that a "new Jerusalem" in the opinion of the vast majority of the electorate includes a car for every household—and how can that be reconciled with greenery? But the statesmen and captains of industry of the period of Britain's greatness, who in the past had enjoyed such a good press, have of recent years been increasingly blamed for their alleged heartlessness and devotion to purely material goals. Marx and other critics of triumphant liberalism, so condescendingly tolerated and ignored in their lifetime, have had their revenge.

What stifled the appeal of anti-industrial anarchism in the nineteenth century was a utopia. To be sure, it was not the usual type of nineteenth century utopia in either its plea or its format, but a utopia nevertheless. It was the vision of a society where wonders would be achieved by those very evils decried by the anti-industrialists: technology and the love of gain. Wars, superstitions, diseases would be conquered by the progress of science and by the prudent attention of every man to his material advancement. Poverty would be eliminated not by philanthropy or public assistance but by the inevitable progress of science and education. There liberal utopians saw as the greatest obstacles to the realization of their dreams the anti-industrialists: those quarrelsome agitators who wanted to perpetuate and exploit popular superstitions, those benevolent prelates, mainly of the Anglican and Catholic persuasion, who justly saw in material progress the frightful threat of secularism, and those disgruntled economists and other intellectuals who in every generation oppose the status quo.

But such was the strength and vigor of the liberal utopia that it even achieved domination of the intellectual world. There are few examples of an ideology being capable at once of dominating the political, economic, and intellectual life of society to the extent that liberalism did in the West during the second half of the nineteenth century. Its victory was nowhere so complete as in England, and even there one can find major dissonances and departures from the canon: for example, the social legislation beginning in the forties, the first steps toward collectivism which Dicey dates from 1870, and the rising popularity of imperialism, a cardinal sin in the eyes of a strict liberal, which dates from about the same time. But all in all, it is difficult to exaggerate the extent of the triumph of the doctrine.

The reasons must be found not only in the prosaic fact that capitalism-liberalism "worked," that is, an increasing number of people felt its benefits. It carried the day largely because it was utopian, because it promised blessings and a universality, which no rational analysis of its premises and the world conditions could really justify. Like every other successful ideology, liberalism scorned an apologetic tone and sociological sophistication. Free enterprise was considered not only socially beneficent but also morally imperative. The future scope of the system was to embrace not only Europe but the whole world. Equally impressive was its lack of historical sense, in which respect it rivaled anti-industrial radicalism: for all the historical sophistication of its theorists, the average devotee blamed all the troubles of the world from its beginning to the end of the eighteenth century on ignorance of the doctrines of Adam Smith, Jeremy Bentham, and David Ricardo.

Liberalism was irrational in its very claims on human rationality. It expected people to give up those quarrels, prejudices, and beliefs that give zest to life in order to engage in a sober "felicific calculus" of the pros and cons of every action. But in its heyday this rationalism was relieved by a religious and missionary zeal. The cause of political reform or of colonial emancipation was argued by the nineteenth century liberal entirely without that sense of guilt and hesitation which characterizes his modern descendant's argument. The pre-eminent position of the West was for him a source not of shame but of pride and of obligation to spread the blessings of industrialism and constitutionalism to Africa and India. He would have scorned the obscurantism of talking about "African personality" and the euphemism of "one-party democracy." Rights and obligations of human beings everywhere were held to be identical; their obvious differences in beliefs and customs were discounted as temporary and subject to erasure by the passage of time.

The source of strength of original liberalism was the same factor that would lead to its eventual downfall: its unabashed materialism. By the end of the nineteenth century a liberal of the original breed could argue that the gospel of self-enrichment had, within a few decades, been productive of greater progress in equality and freedom than that wrought by all the religious and moral preachings since the beginning of our era. How far we, even in this remaining bastion of capitalism, have departed from this passionate and brazen belief in materialism can be indicated by the furor created some years ago by an incautious remark of a Cabinet member: "What is good for General Motors is good for the country." For a mid-nineteenth-century capitalist the proposition that what was good for business (and his business) was good for the general welfare was so obvious that it would not have admitted of argument. Not an industrialist but a political reformer and radical wrote in the 1830s: "As the best men in the working class proceed in their attainment of knowledge, they will cease to enforce their mistaken notions, and this will be called abandoning their caste by those who remain unenlightened; and these men and such other men as have power over multitudes of other men, and have sinister objects to accomplish will misinterpret to the many the actions and opinions of those who have become more enlightened . . . In the meantime many of the incorrigible leaders and large numbers of their followers who are unteachable will be wearied out with continued and rapidly recurring disappointments, will draw off to be replaced by better men; and notwithstanding the times of inactivity and despair which will occasionally occur, the progress of actual improvement in right thinking will go on with increased velocity."[4]

The present generation finds such views almost incomprehensible in their heartlessness. Many a liberal viewed a time "of inactivity and despair" like the great Irish famine of the late forties with perfect composure, akin perhaps to the complacency with which the rulers of the Soviet Union must have considered the frightful toll of the forcible collectivization of 1929-1933. But before we place the nineteenth century liberal and today's Communist (and his apologist) on the same level, we must remember that the former's sins were mostly those of omission; *he* did not believe in man-made cataclysms as the means to a better future. But it is from early liberalism that Marxism has inherited its impassioned faith in industrialization and productivity, and its dislike of humanitarian and aesthetic objections to progress.

These arguments explain much of the character of socialist thought in the nineteenth century.[5] Faced by the domination of liberalism both in politics and in the intellectual sphere, socialism went underground, so to speak. It was reduced to becoming either a conspiracy or a utopian cult. It was fairly late in the century before the socialist argument could achieve intellectual respectability or before a socialist movement, as distinguished from a republican or nationalist one with socialist overtones, could frighten statesmen and the middle class. France, especially in 1848, appears to have been an exception to this generalization, but even there we see recurrences of the Jacobin tradition rather than socialism in its purer form.

The utopian character of much socialist thinking represented then a kind of rearguard action which withdrawing radicalism conducted against the triumphant march of industrialism and liberalism. In some ways those retreating had to adopt the same weapons as their enemies. One such weapon was science. Both Robert Owen and François Fourier refuse to yield to anyone in their preference for a small agrarian community free from the evils of industrial life; but it is exactly science that is to make this idyllic community practical. The noble and somewhat demented dreams of both men reach toward something that becomes explicit in Saint-Simon: science becomes a religion, a way of making miracles. Science is not simply part of the frightening process of modernization; in fact, it shows the way to avoid it. Marx's judgment on Owen and Fourier, though ill-humored, is essentially correct: "They still dream of experimental realisation of their social Utopias, of founding isolated *phalansteres*, of establishing Home Colonies, or setting up a Little Icaria—pocket editions of the New Jerusalem—and to realise all these castles in the air, they are compelled to appeal to the feelings and purses of the bourgeois."[6] Marx is equally perceptive in counting Saint-Simon, for whom otherwise he had considerable respect, among the utopians. The

French thinker's cult of science, his advocacy of the managerial elite, do not bring him much closer to the realities of the modern industrial state than are William Cobbett or Robert Owen. His relationship to modern science and to economic planning is no closer than that of Jules Verne to space travel, or that of H. G. Wells to the exploitation of atomic energy.

But Marx's irritation with the then competing brands of socialism was also based on reasons other than their "unscientific" character. For instance, he saw already in 1848 that one could not be a socialist without being utopian unless one accepted capitalism and the industrial ethos of liberalism. For all his earlier flirtation with Blanquism, Marx by then had to tolerate most of capitalism's self-appraisal. Few of its strongest apologists were indeed capable of reaching his height of lyricism on the subject: "The bourgeoisie during its rule of scarce one hundred years, has created more massive and more colossal productive forces than have all the preceding generations together." In *Capital* the praise of the capitalist is even more specific: "Fanatically bent on making value expand itself, he ruthlessly forces the human race to produce for production's sake: he thus forces the development of the productive forces of society, and creates those very material conditions which alone can form the real basis of a higher form of society, a society in which the full and free development of every individual forms the ruling principle."[7]

This bondage to the ethos of capitalism could not have been easy to endure for a man who had written: "The philosophers have only *interpreted* the world in various ways; the point, however, is to *change* it." In a way, Marx must have envied the utopians the free rein they had given to their fancies and their more straightforward condemnation of the capitalists and the powers that be. His doctrine, as Marx must have realized after Chartism receded in England, was also condemned to a long period of political impotence. He had mistaken the birth pains of capitalism for its death throes. Not until capitalism had had its full run would *his* socialism come into its own. The inner conflict between the revolutionary and the philosopher of history stayed with Marx for the rest of his life. Until the 1870s, revolutionary opportunities still beckoned enticingly all over Europe, but they were not the "right kind": they were bourgeois nationalist movements or, in the parlance of his successors, "wars of liberation." To cope with the problem, Marx advanced the theory of permanent revolution, which his Russian disciples were to develop so successfully in the twentieth century. After the suppression of the Paris Commune when the revolutionary flame died down, Marx and Engels sought desperately for a solution of the impasse. As revolutionaries, they granted to the Russian populists, whose socialism ran against the grain of Marxism, that Russia might skip the phase of capitalism entirely, a horrendous and un-Marxist admission. As philosophers of history, they granted to some countries, notably Great Britain, the option of entering socialism peacefully and through parliamentary means. The situation was as depressing as it was ironic: what there was of the militant revolutionary movement in Europe scorned the whole theoretical ballast of Marxism.

The utopian socialist found himself at the same time in an equally difficult predicament. There was no place in the Europe of railways and factories for the small agrarian communities, havens of repose and isolation from the din of the industrial state. Anti-industrialism found its expression then in straightforward anarchism—rejection of authority and centralization, an appeal not to nostalgia for the past, but more directly to class resentments of the present. Anarchists sought the solution of the social problems not in creation of ideal communities; their aim was to preserve the industrial system but without its concomitants, capitalism and the centralized state. This partial capitulation to industrialism would not make anarchism, or its siamese twin, syndicalism, more capable of competing for political power. Anarchism rejects utopia without accepting the reality of modern politics and economics. But it would serve as an invaluable resource for the rebirth of militant Marxism-Communism. It was mainly as a legatee of anarchism that Communism would triumph in Russia and would achieve its greatest influence among the working class of the West. The genius of Lenin consisted exactly in his ability to separate the *revolutionary* part of his program from the scientific and philosophical element of Marxism. Unhampered by historical laws, the Communist would make his appeal to whatever revolutionary potential he could find in society: to the peasant's need for more land, to the worker's dislike of factory discipline, to each national group's desire to preserve its own peculiarities and rights. The supranational, centralistic, and production-oriented aspects of Marxism are muted as long as Communism struggles for power. Once it achieves power, it outdoes the most rapacious type of early capitalism in its insistence on industrialization as the supreme goal of society.

The weakening of the utopian tradition was thus bound to transform the whole nature of socialism and eventually to lead to its decline as an ideology. For without a utopia, or with utopia pushed far away in time, as in Marxism, socialism had to change its focus of interest. One word that characterizes all utopias is harmony. Even its socialist versions stress that opposition to their beneficent schemes is based on either the ignorance or the selfishness of the defenders of the status quo. They are not the almost helpless victims of historical forces which, quite apart from their malice or self-interest, make them behave in an antisocial way. They can be convinced or converted to the new gospel: their *enlightened* self-interest urges them in this direction.

With Marxism, and especially Communism, the key word is struggle. No ideological legerdemain can abolish class struggle, no single revolutionary eruption can overnight transform society and reform human nature. The extreme of this doctrine was formulated by Stalin when he affirmed that the closer one gets to socialism, the sharper becomes the character of class struggle, even in a society ruled by socialists. For the dream of a perfect society, Communism substitutes the cult of the perfect party. In it the fighter for socialism will find what he cannot realize on this earth until the distant day of Communism: perfect equality and infallible authority, brotherhood and discipline. A lyrically minded French Communist sang of his "beautiful Party." But lest one think that even in the party cell he found a haven of repose and harmony, the devotee is sternly reminded that in this most perfect of human institutions there will inevitably and periodically appear the seeds of corruption: revisionism on the one hand and dogmatism and sectarianism on the other. Thus, Communism triumphantly reintroduces what all the utopias attempted to expel from terrestrial existence: sin.

Nineteenth-century Russia provides an interesting example of the organic tie-up between utopian and socialist thinking. Generations of revolutionaries were brought up on Chernyshevsky's *What Is To Be Done?* undoubtedly the most influential utopian work of all times in terms of its impact on its own society. Even before that, the Petrashevsky circle provided an example of how readily socialist-utopian ideas found fertile soil in Russia.

The reasons are obvious. A Russian *intelligent* lived in an environment almost as fantastic as that of the most extravagant utopia. Serfdom, an utter lack of representative institutions, a judicial system the likes of which have not been seen elsewhere since the end of the Middle Ages, were only some of the features separating Russia from the increasingly parliamentarian and liberal Europe. The great reforms of the 1860s did not remove the blight of autocracy; hence, in retrospect they must be seen as accentuating the discontent of society (as the term was then used in Russia) with the government.

From where could salvation come? The thought of merely imitating Western parliamentarism and liberalism filled the Russian radical with a horror equal to that experienced by the most reactionary believer in absolutism and orthodoxy. Backwardness, or to use a currently fashionable term, underdevelopment, creates its own illusions and compensations. This sense of inferiority toward the West led to a strange amalgam of nationalistic and messianic feelings: just because Russia was backward, so it was her mission to redeem the world from the false gods of materialism and parliamentarism, and to point out a more perfect road to democracy and brotherhood. The Russian radical, helped by a learned German, felt that his utopia, the ideal community, was already at hand: this was the village commune, with its alleged grass roots democracy in the form of its assembly or mir. All that was needed was to clean this perfection of some encrustations which had grown over the ages: absolution, the centralized state, and the like. The peasant was seen as a socialist version of the noble savage: an instinctive democrat and communist. The rotten West, in contrast, could present nothing but plutocratic and smug capitalism, which through industrialism was destroying the natural order of society. Unlike the peasant, the industrial worker was thought to be very unpromising. The worker everywhere, said Herzen, was slated for a horrible fate: to become the bourgeois.

Bad history breeds bad theories, which in turn lead to fatal politics. In the service of this ideal and fiction two generations of Russian radicals combatted both autocracy and liberalism. The catastrophic results of the famous pilgrimage to the people in the mid-seventies did not undermine the populist's faith in the peasant. The apathy or brutality of the villager was simply added to the list of aberrations which the Russian socialist had to remove so that the natural peasant communism and democracy might emerge. The very superstition and backwardness of the peasants were to be used in the struggle against tsarism. A group of young hotheads persuaded peasants of a region in the Ukraine that the Tsar wanted them to rise against the landowners and bureaucrats who were frustrating his benevolent intentions toward the people. A similar rationale was invoked on behalf of terror: only assassination of the leading figures of the regime, or the Tsar himself, could shake the people out of their apathy and force the government to yield to the just demands of the revolutionaries and convoke the Constituent Assembly which would duly promulgate the era of demoracy and socialism for Russia.

The alienation of the Russian intelligentsia was bound to produce some startlingly modern symptoms. In a sense, the radicals realized, though few were honest or clear-sighted enough to admit it, that they were fighting not only autocracy and the bureaucratic state but also, and primarily, the inertia and disinterest in politics of a vast majority of their countrymen. The acquiescence of the mass of peasants in their political condition, and the purely materialistic character of their actual aspirations, including the desire of the more enterprising ones to break out of the commune, inspired the intellectual with a distaste comparable to that of a contemporary philosopher when he sees the modern Englishman or American disregarding the injunction of Marx, whether young or middle-aged, and persisting in his enslavement to television and the automobile while remaining blissfully unaware of his alienation. Hence the frantic search for a handle, an issue, to stir up Proudhon's "quiet beast," the people. The anonymous writer (Chernyshevsky or Dobrolyubov?) who wrote to Herzen's *Bell* that a true radical prays for a period of reaction and ought to prefer Nicholas I to Alexander II, because only through suffering can people be stirred up to overthrow the whole monstrous system, stood between two generations of Russian radicals: one with a generous and utopian faith in the people, the other with a longing for struggle and revolutionary cataclysm. The latter would soon find its embodiment in Leninism.

Much of this lusting for violence was unconscious or, as in the case of many a modern intellectual, caused by society's callous indifference to his theories and sufferings. Few radicals were ready to go so far as the very young Tkachev when he held that a regeneration of Russia required that everybody over twenty-five years of age should be liquidated.[8] But an even more fundamental question for socialist as well as utopian thinking must be: to what extent can it be genuinely democratic? The Russian radical, in the words of Zhelyabov, "wanted to give history a push." Is this impatience entirely consistent with that sympathy for the people at large, with that understanding even of their faults and prejudices, and with that willingness to cure them through education and example which must be at the basis of a genuinely democratic feeling? Certainly Chernyshevsky's "new men," the freshly baked doctors and students, are well aware that they stand above the common herd. This was the author and philosopher for whom Plekhanov, Lenin, and many other Russian socialists never ceased to express their admiration and acknowledge their intellectual debt.

For many a Russian radical, as for Dostoevsky's theorist in *The Possessed,* faith in the natural goodness of the common man, never explicitly renounced, was thus to lead to authoritarianism; and their system "beginning from the premise of unlimited freedom concludes in complete despotism." The story of this evolution is writ large in Bolshevism. Russian Marxism grew from and fed upon the earlier populist tradition, but unlike the latter, it was eventually to see in the peasant not a communistic savage but, in Gorky's words, a "heavy, stupid and semi-Asiatic man of the villages" or, to use a more doctrinal definition, a "petty bourgeois" who had to be destroyed before Russia could enter the promised land of industrialism and socialism.

The history of Russian socialist thought, in both its populist and its Marxian varieties, is then a warning—which does not lose its force because of its commonplace and often repeated character—of the dangers of utopian thinking in politics. In the West, triumphant materialism suppressed, at least for a century, the utopias, the nostalgia for a nonexistent agrarian past, and the *cri de coeur* of the alienated intellectual and aesthete masquerading as social protest. The would-be Lenins of the West saw themselves reduced to leaders of small cults or, worse yet, transformed into parliamentarians and academicians. What happened to many Saint-Simonians is characteristic of the encounter between liberalism, as yet in its full vigor, and socialist utopia: from the devotees of a most extravagant cult, they become bankers, industrialists, and canal builders—in brief, servants and propagators of capitalism.

In Russia the revolt against the utopian tradition in radicalism came later—too late, in fact. In 1909, a group of ex-socialists among the intelligentsia published an avowal of contrition under the title *Vekhi* (Russian for "landmarks" or "signposts"). Had the Western intellectuals paid attention to the conclusions of *Vekhi*, perhaps there would have been no occasion for a much later compilation of essays under the title *The God That Failed*. "The greatest evil of our society is the spiritual rule by children," wrote contrite intellectuals as they deplored the domination of myth and immoderate radicalism in Russian political thinking.[9] And those words still have not lost their relevance. But for the Russian intellectuals it was late in the day. Both the intelligentsia and the institutions they abhorred were to be swept under by the movement that derived its ideology from a work by Lenin—ironically also entitled *What Is To Be Done?*

The Bolshevik triumph was bound to revive the socialist-utopian tradition in the West, where liberalism had been buried by two wars and the depression. For the first time, utopia was located in an actual country where visitors, if so inclined, could see the future at work. In this actual Icaria one encountered many features of the previous utopias: equality and an all-wise, benevolent autocrat, first identified as the party, later as a person. Most of all, one encountered planning and full employment, which between the two world wars became themselves objects of a utopian cult.

The destruction of the utopian image of the Soviet Union has been taking place in more recent times. It is characterized not only by the disenchantment of foreign Communists and sympathizers but also by the increasingly apologetic tone of Russian Communism itself. Communism's strength, just as that of liberalism in its heyday, has been derived from its self-assurance and ruthlessness, its ability to terrorize and shame the opponents of its exposition of Marxism. To a man who said, "but this is immoral," Communism answered, "Philistine." Those who dared to point out that things have changed since Marx erected his lofty structure were often shamed out of their doubts by another epithet, "revisionists." The innocent observation, "but this is not what Marx said and what we promised," earned an equally formidable rebuttal, "dogmatist." Today, however, the high priests have increasingly to argue, explain, and even apologize, sure signs of an ideology past its utopian phase.

The organic connection between utopia and socialism appears severed, at least for the moment. It is in the nature of utopia that it must promise not more of the same but an entirely different and marvelous world, and this vision can no longer be sustained by socialism either of the Communist or the democratic variety.

It might be argued that much of the passion, generosity, and naiveté which went earlier into utopian designs goes nowadays into the thinking and writing about international affairs. Some have constructed the vision of a new world order based on the emergent nations. The current critic of Western civilization and its values (and what is all of utopian thinking and much of socialist thought but a critique of the values and traditons of the West?) is tempted to see the new nations as free from the materialism and power striving of the old. They in turn listen gratefully to the Westerner who has instructed them about the evils of imperialism from which they have suffered and who extols their revolutionary élan. But such visions cannot withstand a scrutiny of the facts. The emerging nations are clamoring for automobiles and washing machines. Upon closer examination their brand of socialism is exhibited as nationalism coated by a thin veneer of foreign slogans and symbols.

Have we reached the end of utopianism in radical thought? From other points of view, such as science, the advances of, say, biology have opened perspectives for the creation of utopias undreamed of by the boldest of science fiction writers. But when it comes to the ordaining of man's social behavior, we have grown more sober and—a horrible word to utopians—realistic. Much of the evolution of radical thought can be symbolized by the titles of books that exhilarated generations of Russian revolutionaries. First there was Herzen's *Who Is Guilty?* Then Chernyshevsky's *What Is To Be Done?* And shortly before his death, Lenin wrote an article entitled "Better Less But Better" (though this was about administration and had no philosophical implications). Perhaps we have reached a moratorium, if not indeed the end, of utopias, and perhaps this is not an altogether bad thing.

3 THE MARXIST PATTERN

When it comes to the Marxist concept of leadership, there was a bit of the cult of personality from the very beginning. Marx was, after all, in the tradition of the great socialist system-makers, who conceived their role not merely as politicians and theorists, but as discoverers of new worlds. Saint-Simon was creating a new religion. Fourier thought of himself as the Newton of moral sciences. And over Marx's grave Engels could say, "As Darwin discovered the law of evolution in organic nature, so Marx discovered the law of evolution in human history." Carried away by emotion, Engels was to claim for his departed master and colleague significant discoveries in mathematics. This was already the seed of presumption that was to make Lenin "condemn" non-Euclidean geometry, Stalin formulate linguistic theories, and Comrade Mao leave his imprint on such varied fields of endeavor as nuclear energy and Ping-pong. There is, after all, an element of both childishness and grandiose conceit in the claim of having discovered something which has eluded countless philosophers and historians, of having laid bare that which the whole course of history and civilization has tended to conceal and suppress. Khrushchev was right insofar as the logic of the doctrine is concerned when in the beginning of his indictment of Stalin he asserted "it is impermissible and foreign to the spirit of Marxism-Leninism to elevate one person, to transform him into a superman possessing supernatural characteristics akin to God. Such a man supposedly knows everything, sees everything, thinks for everyone, can do anything, is infallible in his behavior."[1] But the history of the movement is full of instances of what he finds "impermissible and foreign to the spirit of Marxism-Leninism."

During the last quarter of the nineteenth century, beginning as a matter of fact some years before Marx's death, this demiurgelike concept of the leader became somewhat attenuated. Marx himself tended to speak in unprophetlike tones. "Perhaps" appears increasingly in his judgments and analyses. The spirit of the age became uncongenial to leaders cut in a superhuman mold. Engels, after Marx's death, is reminiscent not so much of a prophet thundering out anathemas and evoking visions of cataclysm as of a kindly retired professor encouraging or reproving his pupils, sighing nostalgically over the enthusiasms and impatience of his youth.

Marxism in the hands of the German Social Democracy became indeed weighed down with academic respectability. Kautsky and Bernstein could only with difficulty be differentiated in their personality traits and their style of work from the Schmollers and Sombarts. On the political side, the picture was almost as depressing. The political leaders, not to speak of the trade-union officials, of the German Social Democracy accepted Marxism as a convenient ideology rather than as a bracing revolutionary imperative. In retrospect it is easy to see that prosperity and legality tended to dampen the revolutionary spirit. And, without a sense of struggle and an exhilarating feeling of danger, there was no place for the leader, the man combining an insight into the future and a sense of mission. There are no Napoleons in peacetime armies. Even a person with as much revolutionary élan as Rosa Luxemburg was essentially a theorist. She was endowed with a degree of intellectual toleration and introspection, again qualities that were to prove destructive to or would disqualify the would-be leaders of Communism.

When we turn to the Russian scene, we find, on the contrary, revolutionary leadership in abundance. Soviet historiography is, for a change, not far wrong or tendentious when it depicts the story of nineteenth-century revolutionary movement as consisting of men seeking for—and failing in their endeavors because they could not find—*the* theory. The pages of the nineteenth-century Russian

history are full of Lenins and Plekhanovs *manqués*, seeking a key
to the understanding of the social reality and to the vast task of
transforming it into a better world. From the Decembrist Pestel,
who got as close as one could at that early time to laying down a
blueprint for a totalitarian state, to Tkachev, who in his ideas on
revolutionary organization and mechanics and his notions on
propaganda was to anticipate Lenin, many of the revolutionaries
longed instinctively for a comprehensive theory of political action,
for an ideology that would show why and how the existing regime
must be brought down. What aroused their despair was the very
intractability of the material they had to work with, the apathy and
ignorance of the peasant masses. This, in turn, spurred revolutionary thought into channels of conspiracy. But conspiracy itself un-
guided by a systematic theory is ineffectual as a guide to revolution, at least under modern political conditions. Thus, what was the
purpose of all the heroics and sacrifices of the People's Will? The
only aim on which its members could agree was convocation of a
universally elected Constituent Assembly. But, as the more perceptive of the members of the People's Will saw, to the great
majority of electors to the assembly such concepts as "democracy," "socialism," and so forth would have been completely
incomprehensible. Thus, the Russian revolutionary of the seventies
and eighties found himself in a predicament somewhat similar to
that of a member of the New Left in the America of the 1960s, and
in both cases the impasse arrived at by the conflict between revolutionary principles and revolutionary temperament was to lead to
wild visions of violence and to cataclysms.

It becomes understandable why Marxism did not exert an earlier
and greater impact on revolutionary thought in Russia. Marxism
teaches patience, the Russian revolutionaries were impatient.
Furthermore, especially in the last quarter of the century, Marxism
had already begun to be bedecked with professional and bourgeois
respectability, which infuriated men brought up to Chernyshevsky's *What Is To Be Done?* and its triumphant exaltation of all
forms of nonconformity. Just as to the modern Western radical the
orthodox Soviet-style Communist Party with its ritual and organization is somewhat "square" and old-fashioned, so to a rebellious

Russian youth of the era, Marx's vision of the industrialized and centralized state was prosaic and repellent. Most of all, the promised land of revolution was to be postponed for what appeared like eons of time, while the idiocy of rural Russia was being transformed into bustling towns and scientifically run farms, and while those corrupt bureaucrats and landlords, so much hated that they almost inspired perverse affection, were being replaced by coldly efficient and calculating industrialists and bankers. This prospect was so repellent that it inspired a *cri de coeur* from Tkachev when admonished by Engels for his impatience: "It is Russia's backwardness which is her great fortune, at least from the revolutionary point of view."[2] Long before Mao Tse-tung, some Russian radicals clearly perceived that true revolutionary spirit cannot cohabit with a highly developed economy.

What then secured the eventual triumph of Marxism in Russia? Mainly the efforts of a small group of devoted and remarkable men. The Bolshevik Revolution, wrote Maxim Gorky in a moment of frankness, was the work of a "numerically tiny group of the intelligentsia leading a few thousand workers who have been indoctrinated by it."[3] Or even more precisely, it was led by a few men who by the force of their personality managed to push Marxism to the fore in the revolutionary movement. When the revolution happened, Marxism was in the wings. As the other contenders for power, the liberals and the Socialist Revolutionaries, dropped out, militant Marxists boldly embarked on their venture. That individual leadership was of crucial importance has been admitted by all the main parties to the drama. The Bolshevik Revolution would not have taken place without Lenin and himself, Trotsky was to write. Had only Gershuni lived, the Socialist Revolutionaries were to sigh, Lenin would not have been able to mesmerize his opponents and followers alike; their own party would not have disintegrated into innumberable factions. If only the Russian liberals, as represented by the Kadets, had possessed a real leader rather than those ineffectual professors and lawyers! If only the early hope of democratic revolution,Kerensky, had not turned out in the end to be a conniving windbag. Even on the right the same questions and regrets have been voiced over the last fifty years: Why was there no Witte or Stolypin among the Tsar's wartime Ministers? And the one general who attempted to stem the tide of the revolution, Kornilov, revealed himself in the words of a colleague as a man "with the heart of a lion and the brains of a sheep."

But even before its supreme triumph and tragedy, the rise and development of Russian Marxism was extraordinarily influenced by the qualities and characteristics of a few men. Among them three stand out—Plekhanov, Lenin, and Martov. It is not too much to say that without any one of them the events of 1917 would have taken a different turn. Of Lenin's contribution it is superfluous to speak. That Russian Marxism arrived at this turning point of history in the condition to play a decisive role was largely the achievement of Plekhanov. That it was not to develop more vigorous antibodies to Bolshevism was largely the fault of Martov Plekhanov's intellectual heritage (as against his actual person, which counted for little in the events of 1917) and Martov's scruples explain the events of 1917 almost as much as Lenin's determination.

The careers of the three men intersected at several points. Much of the history of the Russian Social Democracy between 1898 and 1914 is comprised, in fact, of the collaborations, quarrels, and reconciliations of these three men.

Plekhanov was the master. Indeed, paradoxical though it may sound, his was the most important contribution to the future triumph of Marxism in Russia. Almost singlehandedly between 1883 and 1900 he created Marxian literature in Russian. Equally important, he established a niche in the international socialist movement for Russian Marxism, then consisting literally of just himself and his two faithful coadjutors, Vera Zasulich and Axelrod, and built the foundation for those international contacts and sympathies that were to enable Russian Marxism to survive and thrive in exile. When in the 1890s the Russian revolutionary movement began to revive after its virtual destruction in the preceding decade, it would have been almost inconceivable for young intelligentsia radicals to be tempted to imbibe Marxism and to forsake the much more romantic and activist gospel of renascent populism without this distant and already renowned figure, without his cogent and sarcastic criticism of other radical ideologies, and, not least of all, without the example of his personality. Plekhanov, from a distance, was ideally suited for that hero worship which is the cementing ingredient of revolutionary movements. Not merely a writer and theorist, he was one who as a young man and member of the Land of Freedom group had "walked in the shadow of the gallows," as he would often remind his disciples. He had then had the supreme courage to denounce the terrorist tactics of the People's Will, but this defiance, instead of being, as in the case of the renegade Tikhomirov, a prelude to abandoning the struggle, was for Plekhanov the beginning of a yet more glorious and harrowing revolutionary career. For more than a decade, he had carried the fight against both the tsarist government and the main currents of Russan radical thought, all the while struggling against poverty and a debilitating illness. For a Russian intellectual with his keen sense of inferiority about the "civilized West," it was an impressive achievement for Plekhanov to be recognized as an equal by the leading German luminaries of Marxian thought. When the scandalous heresy of revisionism erupted within the bosom of the Social Democracy, Karl Kautsky, fearful of offending his old comrade, entrusted the Russian with the task of refuting Bernstein's noxious views. To Lenin and Martov, then in Siberian exile, Plekhanov must have appeared almost superhuman. Imagine Karl Kautsky, the ruling deity of Marxian scholarship, asking a Russian for help in a dispute about theory!

But it was in this moment of crisis and triumph that Plekhanov showed himself both very Russian and, in his defense of orthodoxy, very prophetic of the future ferocious intellectual intolerance of the Bolsheviks. Berstein was called not only a dissenter; he was a virtual traitor to the cause. The dogmatic structure of Marxism was for Plekhanov not merely a theoretical framework for a political movement but an all-embracing faith, the canons of which no one had the right to tamper with because of private doubts or the weight of statistical evidence. A socialist party could not degenerate into a debating society; it had to be a fellowship of the faithful. Thus, in a burst of intellectual intolerance Plekhanov really destroyed his own position as *the* leader of Russian Marxism at the moment when it was being transformed from a miniscule sect into a political movement. If all that there is to an ideology is merely the definition of orthodoxy and the suppression of heresy, then the main qualification for leadership becomes not intellectual but organizational ability. There is a deeply ironic quality to the apostolic succession in Russian Marxism: Plekhanov virtually enthroning Lenin as his successor, just as Lenin was to install Stalin as his own, and both men coming to regret bitterly their actions, yet being unable to undo them. Both sought fitting instruments of repression: Plekhanov of theroetical dissent within the fledgling movement, Lenin of political opposition within the ruling Bolshevik Party. Both were to assume that their chosen lieutenant would remain an obedient and deferential pupil, and both were to recoil at discovering that the new man meant not only to snatch the party out of their hands, but to transform it in his own image.

With the Second Congress of the Russian Social Democratic Party in 1903, the Plekhanov phase of Russian Marxism ended. It was he who helped to create Bolshevism by taking Lenin's side and ensuring that on the issue of Lilliputian proportions, as it then appeared, about whether the editorial board of *Iskra* should have three or six members, Lenin's followers should prevail over Martov's. Plekhanov was to remain a figure of great intellectual prestige, whose support was sought by both the Mensheviks and the Bolsheviks in their interminable squabbles, whose word was still law on an intricate problem of Marxian theory, and whose help was called upon when it came to enlisting the services of rich and influential sympathizers. But it was mainly as a monument of the past that he was sought out by Russian visitors to Geneva. With advancing years and economic security, he reverted, as people do, to the manners of his class, the Russian gentry. Formal and reserved in behavior, he would at times scintillate with wit and erudition. A deferential visitor would be dragged through art collections and museums and treated to a lecture by the man who had laid down the canons of Marxian art criticism. But irreverent or disputatious visitors were told to brush up on their Marxism, or their argument would be cut short by a withering glance and those now famous words: "You were not even born when I already . . ."

As in that other veteran revolutionary, Prince Kropotkin, 1914 reawakened in Plekhanov the Russian patriot. His bondage to

Germanic ideas and mannerisms disappeared, and to a shocked fellow-socialist, who inquired "how about our German comrades," he replied that it would be a great pleasure to him to bayonet some of them.[4] October found him a complete stranger to his country and to the movement that he had created. Shortly before his death he barely escaped being lynched by a band of anarchist sailors. This was a vivid demonstration of his own rueful prophecy: the Russian working class would only disgrace itself by a premature seizure of power.

Plekhanov set great store by the question of personal style. His first doubts about Lenin were aroused by the latter's admittedly laborious and awkward prose. Leon Trotsky, with his brashness and flamboyance, he disliked from the first. Such scruples in a revolutionary may appear both comical and pedantic. Yet a Russian Marxist before 1917 was bound to feel that the essence of his creed required, strange as it sounds to our ears, a *civilized revolution*. The disgrace of tsarist Russia lay precisely in the uncivilized character of its social and political relations. An anarchist or a populist could think of revolution as consisting in unleashing a mob's fury. Some members of the People's Will looked not unfavorably at the anti-Semitic pogroms that followed the assassination of Alexander II. They represented a welcome sign of the breakdown of law and order, a necessary prelude to a popular uprising. But to a Marxist such sentiments were impermissible. Yet, the triumph of the Bolsheviks in 1917 was predicated precisely on their abandoning this "civilized" concept of the revolution, of giving in to and abetting the anarchist feelings of the masses, of conquering power under essentially anarchist slogans.

It is not too much to describe the dispute between Martov and Lenin as being about revolutionary manners and morals, rather than about ideology properly speaking. In Lenin, the disciple of Plekhanov clashed with the disciple of Chernyshevsky. After the revolution Lenin was to sigh repeatedly over its various "uncultured" aspects, urge that Russia must learn from "the civilized West," scoff at bohemianism and contrived bad manners. But he also used to repeat that "one does not enter the realm of revolution in white gloves." There was a strange quirk in his character that made him delight in trampling on legal norms and customs, hanker after violence, and elevate terror to a principle of administration

To Martov, in contrast, the most vivid memory of his childhood remained the scene of the Jewish pogrom in 1881 in Odessa, when his own family was in jeopardy. From then on he could never, in the famous revolutionary phrase of the 1860s attributed to Chernyshevsky, call upon Russia to "raise the axe." Though he was a convinced Marxist and, under the Russian circumstances, could never unconditionally repudiate violence, Martov found it repugnant. World War I was for him a tragedy and an absolute evil.[5] For Lenin it was a unique opportunity to breathe the militant spirit once more into Marxism and to embark upon world revolution.

The relationship between the two men who embodied the two opposing currents of Russian Marxism is of great psychological interest. Their friendship turned after 1903 into a bitter personal hostility, yet each man retained a strange attraction for the other. Lenin was to struggle hard against his love for Martov, as Krupskaya wrote in her sentimental way. But more than this "love" was at stake. Martov came to epitomize for Lenin the whole humanistic and hence futile side of the Russian revolutionary tradition: a man who in principle was an uncompromising Marxist, yet in every concrete revolutionary situation was filled with doubts and qualifications. The language used by Lenin about his old friend after the Revolution—"cretin," "Miliukov's lackey," and so forth—gives the impression of Lenin trying to exorcise Martov and Martovism from his own nature, not giving in to the temptations of thinking that the Revolution and the socialist state could be won and preserved in a more humane way. Martov for his part could never overcome a certain juvenile admiration for his old friend's daring and defiance of rules. In the memoirs of his youth, he was to write nostalgically of the young Lenin of the 1890s, still willing to learn rather than to be an oracle, still devoid of that morbid intolerance and suspicion toward people which was to characterize him later on. Pathetically and revealingly Martov could add, "I was *never* to notice any element of personal vanity in Lenin's character."[6]

This last remark contains a clue to the tragedy of Martov's life and to that of Russian Marxism. Countless times before, he had excoriated Lenin for his presumption and intrigues. In 1903 Lenin was out to steal the party journal. In the revolution of 1905-1906 he authorized "expropriations," armed robberies supposedly for the party treasury but in fact joined in by criminal elements. After 1910 Lenin was, in Martov's words, not a political leader but the head of a sort of Mafia bent upon seizing the Russian Social Democracy. In 1917 he abandoned Marxism for adventurism and anarchism. Yet at each point Martov drew back from drawing consequences from his indictments and from pressing to take countermeasures. Had he thrown his already considerable prestige behind such a move, Martov could have been instrumental in expelling Lenin from the party in 1907, when the majority at the London Congress was roused to furious indignation by the revelation of scandals and crimes perpetrated by the Bolsheviks. In July 1917, when the troops were being moved to Petrograd to quell what had been clearly an attempted coup by the Bolsheviks, Martov accused Kerensky of following in the footsteps of Thiers and setting out to massacre the revolutionaries. And in October, while condemning the this time successful Bolshevik seizure of power, Martov still could not bring himself to advocate countersteps. Revolutionary events on the scale of October could not after all be traced, he felt, to the will of oi. man or to the conspiracy of a power-hungry group. They had to be traced to the aspirations, however misguided, of the "masses." A true revolutionary and Marxist could not forcibly oppose the "masses." The Mensheviks, then, had to educate the people or, as Martov phrased it before October, work to "isolate the Bolsheviks morally." After the Revolution even Martov could not maintain that it was the "masses" who had instituted systematic terror, shot or imprisoned veteran political leaders, and finally sent him and other Mensheviks into exile. But in 1922 he still could not discern any element of "personal vanity" in Lenin's make-up!

It would be a gross oversimplification to trace Martov's predicament solely to his personal weakness for Lenin. It was, in part, the product of the intellectual's eternal feeling of inferiority toward the activist. To be sure, Martov was not an armchair philosopher; he had been a revolutionary propagandist and organizer. But in October it was the Bolsheviks who were making the revolution. Most of all, the fears and scruples that disarmed Martov and at the crucial point emasculated the non-Bolshevik left are traceable to its concept of its own ideology. It would have been a repudiation of everything that he and his comrades believed in to assume that in the Russia of 1917, the "freest country in the world," one man or one party could effectively change the course of history, that the Marxian laws governing the development of society could be suspended or rendered invalid through a conspiracy. Hence, the real answer to Communism, comical as it sounds to us, was to fit it into the categories of Marxian historical orthodoxy. Wrote Martov in 1921: "We grant to the Bolsheviks that they represent, in essence, the final stage of the destruction of feudal Russia, but we fight them because they are fulfilling this Jacobinical role badly and because . . . they corrupt the proletariat and render it impotent . . . We view the further development [of Russia] as going on *from* Bolshevism rather than returning to a phase before it."[7]

This judgment is truly pathetic from the perspective of nearly fifty years later, for it influenced the dwindling band of Mensheviks in Paris, Berlin, and finally New York to wait quietly for the forces of history to assert themselves and for the blinders to fall off the eyes of the Russian working class. But interestingly enough a variant of the same opinion was expressed by Lenin during his last illness. Appalled by the already evident bureaucratization of the Soviet regime and by the squabbles among his would-be successors, he expressed deep doubts about his lifework. Not that he could ever repudiate the Great October; but the Revolution was seen by him as a violation of the Marxian canon, allowable and legitimate only if its subsequent course were to endow it with a socialist and humanistic content. The sick man's inner dialogue, the conglomerate of his doubts and hopes, is expressed in a language that at times borders on the incoherent. October had represented a unique chance. The complete hopelessness of the situation had by the same token increased the strength of the workers and peasants tenfold and opened "for us the possibility of laying the foundations of a civilization in a different way from all other Western European countries."[8] It was not wrong to conquer power and then "already on the basis of worker-peasant power and the Soviet system to start catching up with other nations." By "catching up" Lenin clearly meant not only industrialization and modernization; he also meant "culture," the word standing in his lexicon principally for humane treatment of the ruled by the rulers. This kind of culture was notably missing in old Russia, and much as he had authorized and approved terror during the Revolution and the Civil War, Lenin incongruously looked forward to a period when socialism would be combined with, would come to mean in effect, this humane, "feeling" attitude toward people. He himself would not see this promised land, but his followers would.

Plekhanov, Martov, and Lenin epitomize three different temperaments of Russian Marxism, three different styles of leadership. Plekhanov, the father of Russian Marxism, turned from his populist activism to the vocation of intellectual leadership. The leader's function was to diagnose the forces of history, to certify the given historical moment as suitable or inappropriate for a revolutionary breakthrough. It was not his role to improvise, to stir up human emotions, to struggle for the sake of struggle. The long exile, the virtual isolation of his last years and finally his tragic end—dying neglected and scorned by the very movement that he had done so much to build and preserve—were thus a price paid for the excessive premium put upon theory as against life. It is incorrect to speak of Plekhanov's moderation or democratic scruples as being responsible for his political failure. It was, on the contrary, his own brand of extremism: his extreme devotion to doctrine. This devotion made him tolerate, at times support, Lenin and the Bolsheviks before 1914 because, for all their undemocratic temperament and behavior, he saw in them a legitimate offshoot of Marxism. His condemnation of Bolshevism at the moment of its triumph in October again proceeded not so much from his revulsion at the tactics employed or even from his Russian patriotism, but from ideological scruples. How could one have socialism or a socialist revolution if the working class did not constitute the majority of the population?

Another dimension of Plekhanov's tragedy was his lack of that keen appetite for political power which is an almost inevitable component of political success. He was abundantly endowed with pride or, if one prefers, vanity. But he could not endure the strain of continuous polemic, the tedium of constant watchfulness for the opponent's moves and intrigues. Charismatic leadership was not part of Plekhanov's equipment. How could it be? He hewed to the notion of the political leader being the intellectual guide. It had been his revulsion at the romanticized notion of political leadership which had been partly responsible for driving him away from populism. Several months before his death in 1918, in a conversation with Vera Zasulich, he wondered whether and where the two of them, by now completely isolated relics of the earliest era of Russian Marxism, had gone wrong. He could find no answer nor grounds for self-reproach: "Did we fulfill our vow? I think we fulfilled it honestly. Isn't that true, Vera Ivanovna, honestly?"[9]

Whereas Plekhanov viewed politics from a severely intellectual angle, which forbade him to depart from his doctrine even when the realities of the political situation cried for flexibility, for Martov the message of Marxism was essentially moral. He savored in Marxism mostly its quality of dissent, its challenge to all established forms of authority, to force and routine as factors in social relations. The intellectual content of his ideology saved Martov from being an anarchist pure and simple. But when it came to a conflict between orthodoxy and the "people" or the "masses," Martov always found himself in a quandary. In a way, and much more than Plekhanov, he was curiously apolitical. That politics requires a notion of authority, that the business of government consists largely in the pedestrian tasks of collecting taxes, legislating, and administering—these commonplaces never found a wholehearted acceptance in Martov's philosophy. A man of such a make-up could never have entered government without a feeling of guilt, without a feeling that to govern is to betray. And this syndrome was strong enough within the non-Bolshevik left to contribute signally to its defeat in 1917.

Scruples and attitudes of a similar kind were not absent even among the Bolsheviks.[10] It took all of Lenin's determination to strip the party of its remaining democratic "superstitions," to compel and cajole its top ranks into accepting the idea first of one-party rule, then of strict intraparty discipline and the prohibition of factions. Just as he had taken over the most anarchic of revolutions and turned it into the foundation on which would be built the most centralized and despotic state of modern times, so he had to transform a movement, which in its inception was as democratic as it was socialist, into a prototype of a totalitarian party. That Lenin had a dictatorial temperament was discerned by Trotsky as early as 1903. But the evolution of the Bolsheviks into a party strictly controlled from the top proceeded by fits and bounds, by accident as well as by design. It would not have been possible without first the authoritarian character of imperial Russia and then World War I. In the post-October period, every abrogation of democratic rights within the party was justified as temporary and as owing to a special emergency: first the Civil War, then the Kronstadt revolt, then the need of rebuilding the country's economy.

One aspect of Lenin's role, therefore, was that of a great improviser. However close emotionally and even ideologically he may have been to Martov, politically he stood at the opposite pole. An astute observer hit the nail on the head when he wrote that for Lenin an ideological problem never existed in a vacuum. It was always considered in connection with its organizational consequences. Or, to paraphrase, considerations of political power colored every ideological problem. To be fair, this association was, for the most part, unconscious and uncynical. Yet the end result was the atrophy of what had remained of democracy and freedom of expression within the Communist Party. Martov and Lenin, the two men once linked by Marxian orthodoxy as well as by intimate personal bonds, thus traveled in opposite directions. One arrived at a point where dissent became almost the sole measure of his political position; the other at a position where the problem of power almost crowded out every other political consideration. For all of Lenin's hopes, for all his grief at the news that the companion of his early struggles was also ill and dying, he could never have admitted that Martov had been proved right.

Each of the three men had his own brand of intolerance, and this factor contributed in no small measure to the poignant tragedy of their lives. An essentially kind and warmhearted man, Plekhanov could not tolerate intellectual disagreement. He greeted revisionism with the famous aphorism: "Either Bernstein will bury social democracy or socialism will bury him.'' Who knows, maybe the memory of this phrase in a textbook of party history stuck enough in Krushchev's mind to prompt him to his memorable ''we shall bury capitalism.'' This intellectual prickliness of Plekhanov prevented him also from throwing his weight decisively against Lenin on the many occasions before 1914 when such a stance could have definitely isolated the Bolsheviks and changed the whole course of Russian Marxism. Although Plekhanov loathed Lenin's adventurist tactics, he was swayed by the fact that the Bolsheviks recognized his own theoretical authority and stuck to the fundamentalist interpretation of Marxism, whereas the Mensheviks included some who leaned toward the ''parliamentary fallacy'' or even—terrible to say—revisionism. When the Bolsheviks' ''tactics'' were shown to be not merely aberrations but a breach with the whole ideological tradition, and Plekhanov finally thundered against them, it was too late. History could not be reversed by a few quotations from the *Capital.*

In Martov, intolerance extended to the whole problem of governing. No government was wholly justified or could have pure hands. Every act of repression, every hint of the use of physical force, was illegitimate. Thus, this devout Marxist, like Bakunin, could have taken as his motto the aphorism of Leo Tolstoy: ''Nobody who has not been in jail knows what the state is''—a sentiment logical for a Christian anarchist, but not for a believer in centralized political and economic power.[11] This notion of political power as being somehow impure prevented Menshevism of Martov's variety from becoming a positive force during the Revolution. And it fatally weakened the position of his more realistic comrades who tried to shore up the Provisional Government. If Martov, who was the conscience of the party, was against repression, how could Tseretelli or Dan work wholeheartedly for the suppression of the Bolsheviks, for tightening up military discipline, or for setting limits to the anarchy that was engulfing the country? During the Civil War, Martov and his group preserved exemplary loyalty toward the Bolshevik regime which was already persecuting them, banning their newspapers, and dissolving soviets and trade unions dominated by them. Martov was unsparing in his criticism of those Mensheviks who were participating in anti-Bolshevik regimes. In return for this support, at the end of the Civil War Martov's partisans were in effect banned from political life. He himself, the man "whom Ilich never ceased to love," according to the testimony of Krupskaya, had to become once again an exile.

Martov's tragedy epitomizes the drama of what might be called "pure social democracy." Standing between revisionism on the one hand and communism on the other, it emasculated Russian democratic socialism of any political influence it could have had without in turn restraining the growing totalitarian tendencies of Bolshevism. The failure of Menshevism in Russia was to have consequences transcending the boundaries of the country; it was the forerunner of the tragedy of the non-Communist left in the world at large. For all the electoral successes of socialism in Great Britain and in the Scandinavian countries, it was but a pale ghost of the movement that in the first decade of the twentieth century promised to inherit the earth, or at least the West. And in due time, democratic socialism was to stand equally abashed before the phenomenon of the New Left. One could not approve of its methods, of its militantly anarchist spirit, but how could one take one's stand on the side of authority, of the state?

As against the intellectual intolerance of Plekhanov and what might be called the libertarian intolerance of Martov, Lenin displayed a more involved complex. Of his emotional dislike of both parliamentarism and the entire legal and administrative paraphernalia of the bourgeois state, one does not have to speak at length.[12] Until 1914 he chafed under the democratic and parliamentary phraseology of the European social democracy, sighed at the strange spectacle of the meetings of the second International, where revisionists and, worse, members of the British Labour Party and of Poale Zion rubbed shoulders with militant Marxists. World War I was for him a liberating experience: the militant Marxists could now shed the debilitating post-1870 parliamentary and democratic tradition, toss aside the very name "social democracy" like a "soiled child's shirt," and revert to the earlier and revolutionary traditions of the movement. The supreme quality of political leadership, being able to realize when the moment has come, was thus his in 1914, as it was again in 1917.

The post-November leadership of Lenin stamped him as one of

the few great historical figures capable both of carrying out a revolution and of mastering it. He set himself resolutely to reverse the trend toward anarchy that had made the triumph of Bolshevism possible. The deepening tragedy of his last years consisted in his increasing concern that the Soviet state might have been conceived in sin against the precepts of Marxism, and that this fact would weigh heavily and fatally upon its future development. But this worry could not make him turn to the remedies he abhorred: anything smacking of Western constitutionalism or free political life. So in his last illness, confronted by the already all-too-visible phenomena of bureaucratism and a passionate struggle for power among the ruling oligarchy, Lenin still sought to cure the Soviet political system through homeopathic prescriptions: an administrative reform, such as the addition to the Central Party organs of fifty or more "rank and file proletarians," and so forth. It thus fell to this believer in historical necessity, to this thoroughgoing Marxist, to discuss the future of the movement and of the state he had built in terms of personalities: not the majestic forces of history, but the personal characteristics of Trotsky, Bukharin, or Stalin were going to determine the future of Russia and Communism. Stalin's "rudeness," as Lenin put it in his *Testament,* loomed as important for the country's future as the rate of Russia's industrial growth, and who now can say that it was not to prove even more important?

Thus, paradoxically, the movement that by its very creed rejects the notion of charismatic leadership, which extolls the forces of history as against whim or the random striving of individuals, has been most dependent on and most affected by a series of leaders who, whether against their wishes (Lenin) or with their ready concurrence (Stalin), assumed semidivine status and adulation. Even the dissident and democratically inclined branches of Russian Marxism stressed, though not so drastically as the Communists, the role of the teacher-leader, as in the cases of Plekhanov and Martov. To come down to our own days, it is characteristic that various offshoots of militant Marxism have become known by the name of and indeed cannot be separated from their leader: Castroism, Titoism, Maoism. In the case of the last, the cult of the leader has reached proportions that have never been surpassed by a political movement. Even at the height of the adulation of Stalin, his discipleship and ideological descent from Lenin were acknowledged; the names of Marx, Engels, and Plekhanov were allowed to appear in the most slavish works devoted to the "genius leader of the world proletariat." But the cult of Mao is *sui generis:* the more recent outpourings about the Great Helmsman mention no predecessors, admit no teachers. From nuclear physics to table tennis, the thought of Mao is to be the inspiration of the Chinese and, indeed, the whole world. One has to go back to the most extravagant of the Roman emperors to find a parallel to this deification of a political leader.

What, then, is responsible for this exaltation of the role of the leader in Marxism and especially in its Communist offshoot? First of all, the doctrine was important for the political movement, which had need for an ultimate authority in its interpretation of and response to the shifting political and social circumstances. Then, as Marxism became implanted in Russian soil, it entered a society where radical thought looked at politics not merely as one of many departments of life, but as the supreme discipline encompassing those spheres which in the West had long been relegated to religion, aesthetics, or the individual's personal philosophy. In that sense, Russian radical thought of the sixties and seventies of the nineteenth century bore a striking resemblance to the New Left of today. Marxism, in competing with and overcoming populism, had absorbed its universalist pretensions, its view of politics as the way of life. The leader had to become not merely statesman and teacher, but hero and prophet as well. And when the whole premise of the rationality of the political process was challenged by World War I, Lenin was bound to triumph over Plekhanov and Martov.

PART TWO   MEN IN POWER

4 | LENIN'S LAST PHASE

With his stroke on May 26, 1922, Lenin's ailment of some two years' standing was revealed as a cruel and relentless illness, which was to claim his life in nineteen months and, even more cruelly, to strip him completely of the capacity for work in ten months. From the period of his relapse in the middle of December 1922 to what we are told was his last intervention in politics on March 6, 1923, Lenin could work but little and intermittently, the work consisting mostly of reflections and memoranda dictated to his secretaries. To a casual reader, these writings may appear to have a random and disjointed character: a bit about cooperation, reflections on a book about the Russian Revolution, a homily about administration and the need for improvement in Soviet agencies, bitter reactions upon hearing of his collaborators' methods in dealing with the nationality problem. For most people, the crucial document to emerge from Lenin during those days is his so-called *Testament,* containing succinct characterizations of six leading Soviet figures. Indeed, what has attracted the most attention is the interplay of those personalities, as well as the drama of the stricken leader struggling against both disease and the solicitude of his doctors and attendants who wanted to isolate him from the turbulent world of party and state affairs, him who could not conceive of life without political activity. These factors have put in shadow the *Testament's* historico-philosophical reflections and strictures on the art of governing and administration, which appear simply to repeat what Lenin had said before. Are those reflections, then, the mere musings of a sick man realizing that time is growing short and that he must once more, perhaps for the last time, impart counsel and warning to those whom he had led in revolution and war?

Lenin's last writings in fact represent much more than that. Read carefully against the background of current Soviet politics, they impress one with their unity of purpose and main concern. They can be grouped under three headings. First is the strand of historico-philosophical reflections about the October Revolution, the "permissibility" of revolution under the circumstances of Russia of 1917, the future fortunes of the revolution, and its possible spread. Second is a whole series of admonitions about administration, the art of governing, and the need for culture or civilization when it comes to that art. And finally, comes the category that will always attract the student and the general reader to the neglect of the other two: Lenin's reflections on the personalities of his closest collaborators as well as his criticisms of some of their policies, contained both in the "Letter to the Congress" and "About the Nationality Question."

The unifying thread throughout these main themes can be best discerned by noting how frequently in these last writings of Lenin's there occurs the word "culture," and how his concern with culture or its absence colors the writer's references both to historical events and to personalities: "If for building of socialism you need a certain level of culture . . . we need a cultural revolution to become a completely socialist country . . . It would be an unforgivable piece of opportunism, if we on the eve of the entrance of the East [onto the main historical stage] and its awakening were to undermine our authority there through the slightest act of *rudeness* . . . Stalin is too *rude.* " These quotations, derived from such seemingly unconnected pieces as the reflections on Sukhanov, an article on cooperation, a memorandum on the nationality problem, and the "Letter to the Congress," could be multiplied manifold. Culture and its relatives—toleration, politeness, the ability to "attach people to oneself" (a necessary qualification for the Chairman of the Gosplan!)—are constantly cited by Lenin as necessary prerequisites of the art of governing, as both the means and the ends of achieving socialism. As against them, one has to combat rudeness, chauvinistic insensitivity, illiteracy in both the literal and the metaphorical sense of the term, and similar phenomena reflecting a lack of culture. Civilization is thus important not only in personal relations but also from the political, indeed the historical, point of view. It is a high standard of conduct that Lenin would require of rulers. For example, Ordzhonikidze, a Communist boss in the Caucasus, may well have been justified as a private person in hitting a man who insulted him. But Ordzhonikidze was not a private person; he was a virtual ruler of the Caucasus. Hence, Ordzhonikidze had no right to indulge his irritability, and his behavior was gross and inexcusable.[1]

Lenin, to be sure, was not prudish in his language. When an occasion seemed to warrant it, he could use a vigorous expression. Thus, a recent *Lenin's Miscellany* shows him, in a letter to a lady, using in the heat of a polemic a word which, though much favored by the New Left, was usually eschewed by the orthodox Marxists with their late nineteenth-century sense of decorum. Lenin's essential concern for manners, however, reflected a basic tenet of his: socialism was possible only through an advance in culture. That advance, although dependent on the growth of the material base, was also dependent on purely human considerations. Tsarist Russia was condemned not only on account of its political and economic backwardness but also because its system spelled the uncivilized, sometimes inhuman relation of ruler to ruled. The uncivilized behavior of the tsarist bureaucracy was particularly evident in its treatment of the non-Great Russian nationalities. To overthrow the tsarist system and burgeoning capitalism was therefore not enough. When it came to human relations, the new socialist state, even in its initial phase of development, had to demonstrate its superiority over the prerevolutionary world. There could be no question of softness toward the class enemy. But "it is another thing when we ourselves, even when it comes to trifles, fall into imperialist ways toward the oppressed nationalities, thereby completely undermining the genuineness of our principles,"[2] Lenin wrote in reference to Georgia and to the means being employed by Ordzhonikidze in integrating the Caucasian republics. Grossness and bullying ways on the part of officialdom had survived the Revolution, and unless they were soon remedied, not only could one question the whole achievement of the last five years, but the appeal of Communism to the nations of the Orient would be undermined. Suddenly a minor personal squabble in Tiflis had in the sick leader's mind become symptomatic of a major danger that threatened the progress of the Revolution throughout the world. To the majority of his collaborators Lenin's fears must have appeared vastly exaggerated, the product of excessive sensitivity and apprehension fed by illness, and so they were to be described at the Twelfth Party Congress by Abel Enukidze, then a strong partisan and friend of Stalin. But as one ponders the lessons of almost fifty years that have passed since Lenin's warning, one must render homage to the acuteness and foresight of his perceptions.

The problem of how men behave in power, the realization that a devoted and courageous revolutionary could still exhibit characteristics making him unfit for a position of political authority, increased Lenin's already deep interest in the general and vastly important question of government and control in a socialist state. Beyond the personal qualification, the personal culture of those in authority, lay the dilemma of political power. How to deal with it had preoccupied Lenin since the morrow of the Revolution. But now the problem received a new twist: his illness prevented him from that continuous supervision of and intervention in administrative affairs which had delighted Lenin when well. As he could no longer struggle personally against the sheer inertia of the administrative machinery, his mind turned more and more to problems of organic solutions and devices against what he had always viewed as the original sin of the Communist state: bureaucratism. Its root cause he again identified as the lack of culture: in his *Pages from a Diary* the problem of education, of literacy, becomes basic to all others: "We ought to try to deal with that semi-Asiatic lack of culture, from which we still have not been able to emerge, and from which we would not be able to emerge without serious efforts, even though the opportunity for it is here, for nowhere else are the masses so interested in cultural improvement as in our country."[3] Lenin's impatience appears at first excessive. Russia had barely emerged from years of devastating foreign and civil war; her economy was still in ruins; yet the creator of this new world demanded something that usually takes years of patient, strenuous effort and of domestic stability: the vast educational uplift of a whole people. But Lenin's hurry becomes understandable in the context of his other preoccupations and writings of the last phase: just as authoritarian abuses were to be checked before they could harden into administrative routine and threaten the Revolution, so a dramatic effort had to be undertaken to raise the level of culture of the masses; only then could the government that was run in their name become truly theirs.

In the background of all these disquisitions on culture undoubtedly lies the problem tackled by Lenin in his notes "About Our Revolution," which are reflections on Sukhanov's on the tumultuous events of 1917. Sukhanov's invaluable book—long slighted abroad in comparison with Trotsky's *History,* a work of undoubtedly higher literary but lesser historical merit—avoids the pomposity that so often mars Trotsky's style. In it the Russia of the old radical intelligentsia seems to be viewing, half-sardonically, half-sympathetically, its own progeny, the Revolution. But these details and the inherent irony of the situation, on which at another time Lenin's attention would have fastened and which would have provoked his own ironic comments, now have for him only secondary significance. His interest centers around those elements of Sukhanov's book that a casual reader in his pursuit of the unfolding drama would most likely overlook, the scraps and bits of theoretical reflection and what Lenin classifies as Menshevik pedantry. Take this statement of Sukhanov's: "Russia has not reached that level of development of the forces of production which would allow the establishment of socialism."[4] Lenin is properly scornful here. Have not all the Mensheviks, all the heroes of the second International, repeated that piece of wisdom a thousandfold? But Sukhanov and those other gentlemen had seen nothing yet! If they believed that the Russian Revolution was "against the rules," let them but wait: there would be other revolutions, in the Orient, which would be even more "impermissible" by the canons employed and revered by those pedants.

Yet for Lenin, as for every other genuine follower of Marx, such answers, or rather taunts, could not be entirely convincing. There is another, almost pathetic motif in his rationalization of the October Revolution, namely, what else they could have done: "What if the complete hopelessness of the situation having by the same token increased the strength of the workers and peasants tenfold opened for us the possibility of laying the foundations of civilization in a different way from all other Western European states.'' [5] In the phrase "laying the foundation of a civilization" is one more variant of that theme of culture which veritably obsessed the sick man. He is arguing not only against Sukhanov and his ilk but also against his own doubts on the subject, doubts that he had communicated to his memorandum on the nationality problem dictated three weeks before. Have such foundations really been laid, and if so, are they secure? Against the background of the Caucasian affair, of Lenin's bitter disappointment in his colleagues, and of his continuous irritation, even when well, at the countless incidents of bureaucratic red tape and abuse, could one really be sure? In "About Our Revolution" Lenin polemicizes not with Sukhanov but with his own thoughts and doubts. Through his mind must have run the more pregnant warning of Plekhanov about the danger of the Russian working class taking over power prematurely and consequently disgracing itself. Lenin concludes with neither an apology nor a recantation: yes, the Revolution was both permissible and necessary, and history will show it as such.

But if it was not in his nature to admit the possibility of defeat, neither would he gloss over an inherent difficulty or defect. And so, in his last weeks of political activity he devoted a great amount of time to measures that would cure the "unculturedness" of the Soviet system, that would remove those blemishes which threatened its historical role both at home and as an inspiration and leader for oppressed people elsewhere. The most abstruse historico-philosophical problems becomes at the next moment a very concrete one. Here Lenin talks about the laws of history, of what Marx had to say in 1856, about processes that would take decades if not centuries. Yet the very next page, or rather session with his secretaries, finds Lenin urging an exemplary punishment for Ordzonikidze and discussing what administrative and personnel practices would cure the twin evils of bureaucratism and Great Russian chauvinism. Through all these preoccupations runs one thought, the same concern.

Personal considerations added poignancy to this concern. Lenin found the regimen imposed on him by his illness at first irksome and then something worse. He came to believe that the extent of his isolation from political affairs was dictated not by medical but by other considerations: "Vladimir Ilyich became convinced that it is not the doctors who give guidance to the Central Committee but the Central Committee which instructs the doctors."[6] In brief, he was persuaded that there was a determined effort to keep him from affairs of state. The Secretary General of the Central Committee, Stalin, had been selected to serve as liaison with the doctors. Yet Stalin, with whom Lenin had had prior clashes concerning the method of setting up the USSR, was in Lenin's eyes bent upon whitewashing the line adopted by Ordzonikidze. All in all, there is no question that it was Stalin who was the main target of Lenin's irritation. But this fact, for understandable reasons, was allowed to overshadow Lenin's general dissatisfaction with the setup and personnel of the party's highest organs. Stalin's responsibility vis-à-vis Lenin was laid upon him by the Politburo as a whole, although one might have thought that somebody personally closer to the stricken man and his wife would have been a more logical choice for this task, which required the utmost delicacy and understanding. It could not be ignored that the Secretary General was not abundantly endowed with such qualities and that, unlike Zinoviev, say, he had never lived for long in Lenin's entourage. We know that Stalin tried at least once to lay down the invidious charge, but continued as liaison with the medical men at the urging of his Politburo colleagues. We do not know Stalin's side of the whole affair, not having been vouchsafed his reply of apology to Lenin's note of March 5, 1923, nor Lenin's reaction to it.

But it is clear that, though Lenin was especially piqued by Stalin, politically he was disillusioned by the whole personnel of the party high command. His characterizations of his six closest collaborators—Trotsky, Stalin, Zinoviev, Kamenev, Piatakov, and Bukharin—are hardly those of unqualified praise or enthusiasm for any of them. The sum total of all Lenin's reservations is to convey a strong impression that these six people were neither separately nor collectively able to lead the party and state. Lenin concluded that the Politburo of the Central Committee as then constituted was incapable of exercising what today is known as collective leadership, largely because its members (at least Stalin and Trotsky) were incapable of harmonious collaboration with each other, but also because of certain personal characteristics of all six individuals involved.[7] What Lenin had to say about these six was not likely to increase their liking or regard for each other. But more important, the effect on the rank and file of the party members, had the "Letter to the Congress" become known to them at the time that Lenin intended it to become known, would most likely have been devastating: the authority of the Politburo would have been undermined. For those who were not sufficiently *au courant* with Lenin's thinking and his concerns of the moment, the "Letter" might have contained enough in the way of internal inconsistencies to make plausible the argument that it was the product of illness and of the bitterness resulting from it.[8] However, had the delegates to the Twelfth Party Congress been allowed to see all the pertinent documents, it is more likely that they, or at least many of them, would have interpreted the "Letter" as Lenin's vote of no confidence in the party leadership as then constituted. It is unlikely that the triumvirate of Zinoviev-Stalin-Kamenev would have been allowed to have its own way, as it largely did at the Congress, and quite possible that the delegates would have forced the Central Committee to abide by Vladimir Ilyich's wish and to dismiss Stalin as Secretary General. If , however, the relevant documents—the "Letter" and the nationality memorandum—were not to become immediately and widely known, Lenin's aim was bound to be frustrated, for the danger to their collective position would incline the Politburo members temporarily to lay aside their squabbles, fears, and resentments of each other. This is precisely what did happen at the Twelfth Congress, and even Trotsky was to be but a partial exception to the ruling group closing its ranks.

Beyond personalities and his personal and family feelings, Lenin looked to far more fundamental issues and solutions. The "Letter" begins, after all, "I would strongly advise that the Congress should undertake a number of changes in *our political system.*"[9] Not in the personnel, nor in the powers of this or that body, but in the system.

The Civil War had barely ended, the guns of Kronstadt had hardly been silenced, when the party awoke to the realization that it was the sole political power in the Communist state. The intraparty debates touching on the Workers' Opposition and related factions were at least connected with this problem. But to many who had accepted Lenin's characterization of the dissident groups as largely anarchosyndicalist in spirit, the problem remained of how to prevent the party from congealing into an elite organization, how to keep it from the almost inevitable corruption consequent upon its special position. Some Communist leaders went so far as to debate in public the desirability of permitting other socialist parties as a kind of loyal opposition. Such a solution, at least in 1921-1922, would have been intolerable to Lenin. He put his faith in the efficacy of the control organs within both the party and the state. In fact, Lenin comes close to developing a theory of the threefold division of powers in government—one which has nothing to do with the classical one of Montesquieu. In the writings of his last period Lenin envisages the three branches as being policy formulation, administration in the proper sense of the word, and control.

But how, Lenin asks, can you have a single party state and yet an effective system of controls and checks on its rule; how can you have a state administration infused with the party spirit and yet separate and independent of the party? Here Lenin wrestles with the problem which in many ways would remain a fundamental one for Communist-run societies, straining the ingenuity of Stalin, Khrushchev, and more recently Mao. But for Lenin even this complex problem is only part of a still vaster one: how can the party-administration-control problem be fitted into the task of the cultural uplift of the working class, of making the Soviet state truly one of the workers and peasants. He then reduces a complex historical problem to a practical one: what is to be done immediately and concretely to bring this about? We are reminded of Michael Pokrovsky's dictum that for Lenin, every theoretical problem had an immediate organizational or propaganda application. Lenin answers his own question: "I envisage the whole business as follows: a few tens of workers, entering the Central Committee, can better than anybody else, undertake checking and improvement . . . of our apparatus."[10] The Central Committee, then composed of twenty-seven ordinary members, is to be increased to fifty or even one hundred. Such an increase, Lenin writes in the "Letter," would accomplish several aims: better work in the Central Committee, less danger of a major split within its ranks, and improved supervision of the whole network of the Soviet administration.

Here it is: the character of the highest party organs is to be basically changed. No longer will the central organ be composed just of notables, currently forming themselves increasingly into personal factions. There will be a Central Committee, the majority of whose members will be alien to the petty squabbles of the Stalins, Zinovievs and Trotskys, and whose very presence may make the party hierarchs mend their ways. The newcomers are clearly to come from the rank-and-file workers and peasants, since they should not have had a long period in any official position; otherwise they would have acquired undeniable habits and biases. This is a delicate way of warning that the Central Committee should not be expanded merely in numbers, as was to be done at the Twelfth Congress, and then to only forty members. Rather, its whole character is to be changed: the new people are not to be partisans of any of the current bigwigs; they are to be completely independent, completely foreign to the quarrels that currently split and endanger the highest organs as well as the party and the country. Lenin truly recommends "changes in our political system."

With this recommendation and its expected effects, all the divergent elements of Lenin's main concern are brought together: the quarreling party potentates are to be restrained; their power individually and collectively is to be seriously curbed. They will not be able to retreat into the more exclusive precincts of the Politburo, for there also the "simple workers and peasants" are to be present, vigilantly watching and if need be censoring their leaders' behavior. The infusion of these workers is bound to take the curse off the Menshevik lament: it will be the workers' and peasants' government. Although the dying leader, like many in his situation, grew disillusioned with his closest collaborators, he still retained his faith in the common proletarian. Being present while the highest matters of policy were discussed, those unspoiled proletarians would grow more sophisticated and cultured. They would most likely provide material for the next generation of leadership in the party and state. And hopefully they would also be free from the habits and biases acquired by their seniors and would not repeat the errors and transgressions of Stalin, Ordzonikidze, or Trotsky.

At the same time, there is at least a hint that the newcomers should not for awhile take an active part in determining policies. Otherwise Lenin would have had no reason to emphasize that they were to be present at all meetings of the Central Committee and to read all its documents—something that should go without saying. Did Lenin, without formally proposing such a division, envisage the Central Committee as consisting for some time in the future of two categories of members: "professionals" as well as "watchers," the former discussing and enacting policies, the latter keeping them straight? If so, the new members' function reminds one of Bagehot's monarch, whose prerogatives were to be informed, to give advice and warning. Or one might reach for another variant of the same idea: the practice in the Russian Communist Party in the late 1950s and early 1960s of holding some plenums of the Central Committee in the presence of a large number of nonmembers who were officials and experts interested in the subject under discussion. In all cases the germ of the idea, if not the motivation, is the same: to provide checks and controls on the highest political bodies: the Cabinet, the Central Committee, the Politburo.

From his disquisition on the problem of control, Lenin passes to the closely related subject of administration and the struggle against bureaucratism. How much the two problems were enmeshed in Lenin's mind is best proved by comparing his draft of an article on "The Rabkrin" with its final version. The phrases relating to the Central Committee in one version at times are applied to the Central Control Commission in the other. Or take this passage: "Our Central Committee has turned into a highly centralized and authoritative group, but its work does not correspond to its authority. This should be remedied by the measure I have proposed, and members of the Central Control Commission ought to be present in a stated number at every meeting of the Politburo, ought to become a cohesive group which 'without regard for personalities' ought to make sure that nobody, neither

the Secretary General nor any other member of the Central Committee should bar them from making inquiries, checking documents and making absolutely sure that they know everything and
that [political] affairs are being settled correctly.''[11] Here, if you
please, is to be the second line of defense against arbitrary
authority and the oligarchical transformation of the party: not only
the new members of the Central Committee but also the Central
Control Commission are to watch over the Politburo as well as over
the ''old'' members of the Central Committee.[12] That Lenin
wanted members of the Central Control Commission delegated to
meet with the Politburo to act as a ''cohesive group'' has an
eloquence of its own. He felt, and justifiably, that when it came to
its prerogatives, the Politburo (with one partial exception) was
itself quite a cohesive group.

But the problems of control and administration, while closely
connected, are not quite the same. Lenin's criticism of the Rabkrin
has always been related to his personal feelings about its former
head, Stalin. But this element was perhaps overstressed by many
commentators and made them overlook or slight some interesting
sidelights of his remarks. They bear a paradoxical character.
Ostensibly Lenin demands a closer link between the party and state
control institutions. The Rabkrin, he writes, like most other
branches of the state administration, is not properly imbued with
party spirit. But the exemplary institution in this respect, the one to
be emulated by the Rabkrin, is none other than the Commissariat
for Foreign Affairs, the Narkomindel. Such a characterization of
the Narkomindel must have led to considerable bewilderment in
party circles: if there was one state institution that by current standards appeared virtually apolitical, it was the foreign ministry.
Headed by a man eschewing party disputes and high policy matters,
George Chicherin, the Commissariat was already becoming a haven
for ex-Menshevik experts and for Bolshevik dignitaries who,
because of past political sins or indiscretions, were believed better
suited for diplomatic rather than political work. The whole thrust
of the Narkomindel's work was to secure foreign recognition and
credits for Russia, and in pursuit of this task Chicherin would feel
constrained to clash occasionally with both the Comintern and
those party zealots who looked contemptuously at the whole busi

ness of formal diplomacy and international amenities. To set up the Foreign Commissariat as a model for the Rabkrin, for the whole Soviet administration, must have appeared incomprehensible, possibly giving further evidence of Lenin's declining powers.

But the paradox does not appear as great in light of what Lenin meant to convey by saying that the state apparatus, with the exception of the Narkomindel, represented for the most part but a relic of the past. The statement in itself is of course a considerable exaggeration, just as is Lenin's categorical declaration in the draft of his article on the Rabkrin dictated on January 13 that the foreign ministry is superior insofar as, unlike other commissariats, it has been completely transformed in spirit and personnel: Were there more rank-and-file workers and party members in the Narkomindel than in the Rabkrin? Most unlikely. But then Lenin specifies that the Narkomindel is freer than are other agencies from the sins of bureaucratism and that it works directly under the Central Committee of the party. The ministry, in brief, is more efficient, and it works not at the behest of some party bigwig or faction but for the party as a whole.

Thus, in a roundabout way Lenin defines his prerequisites for sound administration: efficiency and noninvolvement in the personal side of politics. The state administration is to be imbued with the party spirit, but it is to be free of party politics. In his "Better Less But Better," Lenin develops the notion of this scientifically trained, nonpartisan civil service. He recommends examinations and special training for an elite corps of three to four hundred civil servants within the Rabkrin. Since it goes somewhat against his grain to urge such a nonpolitical development, in typical fashion he makes the reservation that by learning to administer, he does not mean learning in the schoolroom sense. What he has in mind are obviously what are now called managerial skills. And where are these Soviet officials to learn such skills and collect relevant literature? In the United States and Canada, and only when these two countries prove impractical are the neophytes in public administration to go to Britain. One almost suspects that the Harvard Business School of the Elton Mayo period would have best suited Lenin's requirements.

Lenin's last writings present, then, in kaleidoscopic form,

though not fully developed because of his peculiar circumstances and the peculiarities of their style, a theory of government. If in the Revolution and the Civil War the key word was "struggle," then for the preservation and development of a socialist society it is "culture." Culture precludes arbitrary or intrigue-riven political leadership. Hence, at the highest level of political decision-making Lenin wants to erect a multiple system of control that will keep one man or one faction from having full power or, contrariwise, to prevent constant strife and intrigue in the Central Committee and the Politburo. Within state administration the reforms projected by Lenin look to an elite, scientifically trained public service free from the sins of both old and new Russian officialdom. It is only such a system of government that will expedite a great cultural uplift of the working class, enable it to become the ruling class in the true sense of the word, and then propel society as a whole toward socialism. To Lenin in his last phase all aspects of government appear interconnected: seemingly small details assume great historical importance. One man's manners may take on serious consequence; the reorganization of an agency may become the key to vast political transformations: "for me everything is connected with the tasks which the Rabkrin upon its reorganization will face; our whole labor, policies, tactics, strategy."[13]

Lenin's last writings had little effect on the course of Soviet history. The development of the control organs and their role in the configuration of Soviet politics following Lenin's death moved in a different direction. The one key suggestion made by Lenin in his final reflections was about the Central Committee, and it is sometimes asserted that the Twelfth Congress acted in the spirit of the ailing leader's mandate by increasing the number of the Central Committee members, from twenty seven full members and nineteen candidates, to forty and seventeen respectively. But a cursory look at the names of the newcomers will not discover any of the plain workers or peasants whom Lenin had wanted there to act as a check on the party elite. And on many other of Lenin's proposals and concerns the record of the Twelfth Congress is poor. What can be seen, however, from Lenin's last writings is the breadth of his perspectives during those final months and the relevance of some of his reflections to problems that are as perplexing to Communist systems today as they were in 1923.

5 | LENIN'S LEGACY

Official anniversaries are for the Soviets not merely occasions to celebrate and eulogize a famous man or event. They are also—if not mainly—occasions for that self-congratulation of which the Soviet regime has made such a rite, and against which the most uninhibited patriotic oratory on a similar occasion in the United States would appear a pallid understatement. In fact, the USSR celebrates its thanksgiving several times a year. In speeches and editorials the pretext for the celebration is usually disposed of in the first few sentences and perhaps reverted to again at the very end. In between (and usually at length) the listener or reader is treated to production figures *then* and *now,* to assurances of the invincible might of the Soviet Union and yet of its peaceful intentions, to news of the startling achievements of Soviet science, and so forth.

Should the occasion be a major one and the speaker or writer a leading party figure, this general prospectus of Soviet progress in all branches of endeavor is supplemented by a kind of state-of-the-union survey of the troublesome, yet owing to the correct efforts of the party and government generally hopeful and reassuring, domestic and international situation; of the threats to world Communism from dogmatism and sectarianism on the one hand and of revisionism on the other, both being unmasked and overcome through correct remedies prescribed by the Central Committee; of the diversionist strivings of the Maoist clique, which are increasingly perceived and resisted by the masses of the Chinese people, who are unwilling to abandon their traditional feelings of friendship and gratitude to the Soviet Union; of the dangerous game that Zionism, in alliance with imperialism, is playing in the Middle East, a game which is being patiently exposed and countered by the USSR.

While all these elements were present in the massive celebrations of Lenin's hundredth anniversary in 1970, for a change, statistics, achievements and policy announcements were not allowed to obscure the object of the celebrations. That was Lenin's year, and in its descent from a continuity with his achievement, the Soviet regime saw a source of strength that was as important—and this was not a mere oratorical phrase—as its material achievements since the Revolution.

This in turn reflected not only a natural reverence for the principal mover of the October Revolution, and for the man who until 1922 had guided the Soviet state through its earliest and most perilous years. It also reflected a feeling, no more difficult to comprehend for a contemporary Western mind than for somebody brought up in the classical Marxian tradition, that the Soviet state and society are ruled in the name and spirit of Lenin, that through the tragic vicissitudes of the last fifty years or so it is Lenin's teachings and spirit that have protected and guided the Communist experiment.

This political mystique began immediately with Lenin's death. "Lenin lives, Lenin is more alive than those actually living," sang a Soviet poet. The mere concept of the Lenin Mausoleum would have appeared distasteful to an earlier generation of revolutionaries, including the man whose remains it shelters, who had an unfeigned sense of personal modesty and simplicity. But to the oligarchs who succeeded him, the cult of Lenin was the only unifying force and the main link with political legitimacy. His name was invoked on all sides of the intraparty struggle that raged until the late twenties. What had begun as a political contrivance then became the main ingredient of the official ideology of the civil religion, as it were.

Stalin built his cult upon that of Lenin. Subsequently, under the slogan "Back to Lenin," the party sought to recover from the numbing effects of Stalinism. And today, when so many features of Soviet society and of the official creed have been questioned and occasionally, if clandestinely, assailed, it is a source of strength to the regime that these protests have for the most part been made in the name of rather than against Leninism. The passions and enthusiasms of the Revolution, of the industrialization drive, of the de-Stalinization period—all these are by now extinguished. But every day long lines still form in front of the Lenin Mausoleum to parade silently and reverently before the leader. The mausoleum no longer contains the remains of the man who for much longer than Lenin presided over the destinies of the country, and who, in fact, sacrilegious as it might sound to the contemporary Soviet generation, left a much stronger impact on Soviet institutions. For all the recent and careful rehabilitation of Stalin, it is most unlikely that he will ever be restored to anything like moral and political equality with Lenin. The latter remains master and teacher, and as such he is celebrated.

The unique position of Lenin explains even if it does not fully excuse the Soviet sensitivity when it comes to his biographical data. Already in the relatively easygoing days of the twenties, the publication of materials concerning Lenin's life and activity was becoming selective. Later and predictably, as the situation grew worse, successive editions of Krupskaya's memoirs of her life with her great husband grew more and more panegyrical and politically oriented. A reverent fictionalized account of the Ulyanov family published in the thirties still drew official wrath because of its excessive discussion of Lenin's ancestry and of the non-Russian elements of his ethnic background. Many of the most important documents concerning Lenin's personal and what might be called personal-political life have been released only when it suited the needs of current leaders. Thus, it was Khrushchev's campaign against Stalin that enabled notes of the secretaries attending Lenin during his last illness to see the light of day. Many documents of equal if not greater importance must still be locked in the archives; we know, for example, of the existence of memoirs by those who were at one time close to Lenin, such as Kollontai's, which the Central Committee in its wisdom has not thought fit to clear for publication.

Now, some of the selectivity shown in the release of Leniniana by their Soviet guardians has a direct connection with what they understand to be the essence of Lenin's legacy to their own society and the world at large. One can, up to a point, sympathize with their distaste for the current biographical fashion in the West: its psychoanalytic orientation, its mainly iconoclastic thrust, and its inordinate curiosity for intimate detail. But beyond this natural sensitivity to anything that might furnish ammunition for a sensationalist treatment of the life of the maker of the Revolution and the Sovet state, one detects a more general determination to stress those elements of Leninism which are useful in defending current Soviet reality and to minimize or ignore those which would serve as a basis for its criticism.

Lenin was a great revolutionary and a great restorer, a passionate patriot and a fervent internationalist. This combination of opposites enabled him to carry the Revolution through to its logical conclusion in the virtual dissolution of the Russian state, and then to rescue Russia from the Revolution and lay the foundations of the most centralized state of modern times. It is no wonder that to the outside observer of the first phases of the Bolshevik Revolution, Lenin and his followers appeared as "nihilists" bent upon wrecking the old and utterly incapable of creating a new social order. Even to some of his followers Lenin's pronouncements after his return to Russia in 1917 smacked of anarchism rather than socialism. "He has occupied the place vacated by Bakunin," exclaimed one of his followers upon hearing the April theses. The whole orderly world of theoretical Marixism—its canon of stages of historical development dictating the appropriate political forms—ceased to be of any interest to Lenin as contrasted with the imperative need for revolution.

But Lenin defied not only the Marxian historical laws. The whole rationalist tradition of the doctrine, its democratic accretions, appeared to him a burdensome ballast. His "State and Revolution," written supposedly as a critique of anarcho-syndicalism, comes close in its postulates to anarchism: the state and its whole machinery are not to be reformed, they are to be smashed; the need for professional bureaucracy is decried, social and economic egalitarianism extolled. "As long as there is the state there is no freedom; when there is freedom there will be no state." No need exists for material incentives: all officials and managers should be paid the worker's wages. It is unlikely that today these postulates of Lenin's are often repeated.

Yet within a few months of writing this tract, and with power in his hand, the other Lenin began to emerge. The leader and statesman supplanted the revolutionary. The task of running society became for him between 1918 and 1922 increasingly not a simple matter of revolutionary will and enthusiasm, but one of expertise and discipline. Few could have foretold in 1917 that the man who then adopted an existentialist view of revolution, who pleaded for what in the parlance of the New Left is called participatory democracy and an end to all centralized authority—for what else under the circumstances was meant by the slogan "All Power to the Soviets"?—would within a year decry the workers' takeover of factories, plead for retention of specialists in the army and industry, and extol the necessity of material incentives.

It was natural for the left Communists to exclaim that he had betrayed the Revolution. Outside observers commented gleefully that, confronted with the practical problems of governing, the Bolsheviks had to give up their fine theories and revert to the humdrum ways of the past. When the New Economic Policy was introduced in 1921, Marxist purists enjoyed their one moment of triumph. Lenin had finally admitted what they had been saying all along: Russia was not ready for socialism! All such criticisms contained partial truths, yet they missed a more basic truth: Lenin, even if he often disregarded the letter of Marxism, sought and discovered its original spirit. It was a sound instinct that already had him in 1914 seeking to rename his party "Communist." World War I had undone the effects of a century of liberalism and parliamentarianism; Marxism, if it was to secure power, had to recapture its earliest militant and conspiratorial tradition and to shed those democratic and humanitarian elements that had begun to dominate it after 1870, when it seemed as if the main struggles ahead would be resolved at the ballot box.

With power in the hands of the Bolsheviks, the next urgent task, that of laying down the material prerequisites for a socialist society, could not be entrusted to the whimsical ways of a democracy. Neither the state nor industry could be turned over to the workers. The trade unions had to remain subordinate to the party. Lenin then saw the sense of Marxism—and this provides a thread of continuity between his pre- and post-revolutionary policies—as primarily an ideology of social engineering.

This theme of Lenin's pragmatism, of his "revolutionary common sense," is sounded repeatedly in Russia. And just as the true story of Lenin's personal modesty has been used to lash the personality cults of Stalin and Mao, so this stress on Lenin's practicality, on his impatience with metaphysical and theoretical subtleties, carries an important lesson. Against the allurements of the New Left in the West (so strikingly similar in some of its attitudes to the Russian populist tradition from which Lenin emerged but which he rejected in his youth) and of the voices of dissent in the Soviet Union, the regime is able to invoke the supreme authority. It was to a dissident party member who complained of being persecuted that Lenin wrote in words which could be taken from today's *Pravda* editorial: "A decadent petty bourgeois intellectual when he sees an untoward incident or injustice whimpers, cries, loses his head, his self-control, gossips and puffs himself up to talk nonsense about the 'system' . . . the proletarian . . . seeing something wrong goes about correcting it in a businesslike way." To be sure, even in his "anarchist" phase Lenin never advocated rebellion for rebellion's sake or indulged in gloomy disquisitions on alienation or on modern industrial society and science subverting the sense of human existence.

To him, all political activity and struggle were intended to advance specific goals. Rather than dehumanizing society, industrialization was for Lenin, as it must be for every genuine Marxist, the main vehicle of social and cultural progress. There is no doubt that he would hold much of what passes for radical social thought in the West as obscurantism, having nothing to do with socialism. And one must unhappily grant the Soviets that in the eyes of the father of the Revolution much of current dissent in Russia would appear as the kind of squeamishness and bourgeois hypocrisy he decried in those who protested revolutionary terror and repression of political opposition.

And yet, just as one cannot accept the official image of the monolithic Lenin, one cannot assume his unqualified approval of current Soviet reality. One has to remember not only the revolutionary leader uninhibited about violence and deception and the statesman who after October restored authority and put down anarchy, but also the man who in his last months of political activity grew horrified at some of the aspects of the system he had helped build. It was not only the intrigues of the oligarchs of the Politburo that filled him with apprehension about the future of the socialist experiment but the whole phenomenon of bureaucracy, of the new ruling class becoming entrenched in the Soviet system. One cannot credit Lenin with much genuine democratic feeling: the very concept of socialism as social engineering implied elitism, as did his concept of the party enunciated as early as 1902 in *What Is To Be Done?* But both to himself and to others Lenin always rationalized this elitism with the belief that the party would retain a close contact with, and the "feel" of, the masses, that it would rule on their behalf rather than as a severe schoolmaster. The party was to be a vanguard, not an oligarchy. To us, of course, such hopes appear unrealistic, but to Lenin they constituted a cardinal part of his political philosophy. There remained in his make-up, after all, a small remnant of the social democrat: the old order was to be destroyed, not only because it had been condemned by the forces of history, but also because it was offensive to human dignity. And in today's Soviet society it would be easier to imagine Lenin as approving the repression of dissident individuals or groups than to see him as tolerating the bureaucratic complacency of the ruling group, the lifeless ritual that Soviet official political life has become, and the smug self-congratulation in which the regime is constantly indulging. The strength and vitality of the Soviet state and it peoples offer a startling contrast to the petrified form of Soviet political life. Such is the ambiguous legacy of Lenin to the society he helped create.

This ambiguity is even more pronounced and the achievement more puzzling when it comes to another major dimension of Lenin's activity. He was an international revolutionary for whom the Russian Revolution was to be but a prelude to a much wider one, and the Soviet state but the beginning of the historic process leading to an eventual world federation of socialist states. Here the success of the venture initiated by Lenin has been truly breathtaking. From those few men who gathered in Moscow in 1919 and established the Third International, Communism has grown into the world's most widespread ideological movement. It has conquered China, swept over Eastern Europe, and reached into and become a contender for power in practically every country in the world.

In contrast, the Western capitalist system, which loomed like a colossus against the sole embattled and backward Communist state of the day, has withdrawn from vast areas of the world. Its ideology, liberalism, is no longer a triumphant, self-confident creed as it was before 1914; its remaining practitioners are increasingly beset by doubts and a sense of guilt. Again, history has seemingly vindicated Lenin's insight: his rupture with the letter of Marixism in favor of what he considered to be its spirit. International socialism, to be effective in the twentieth century, could not remain a loose confederation of radical parties, such as the Second International had been; it had to become a centralized, disciplined, and ideologically homogeneous movement. It could not, through a slavish adherence to doctrine, confine its activities to highly advanced industrial societies. The weak and vulnerable links in the international capitalist system are the economically backward and colonial areas. Hence, according to Lenin, Communism had to concentrate its activity there and blend its appeal to class war with a call to national struggles of liberation against imperialist oppressors.

The whole history of world politics since 1945 has attested to the correctness of Lenin's insight and his prescription. Yet how depressing he would find the present situation and prospects of world Communism!

That Communism should have become a servant of Russian nationalism, that after the emergence of other Communist states it still would not be truly international, and that the whole movement and ideology should have turned into an arena for contending nationalisms—all this would have seemed to Lenin monstrous. Yet the personality of its founder as well as the historical circumstances dictated this fate for Communism. In his own mind and his public pronouncements Lenin was a fervent internationalist. Often he had called tsarist Russia "the prison house of nationalities." His very love for his country made him detest that gross bullying boorishness which the prerevolutionary officialdom displayed in its dealings with Poles, Jews, and other national minorities of the empire. How searing was his indictment and how clear his insight not long after the Revolution when he said of the Bolsheviks, who thought of themselves as the vanguard of the world revolution: "Scratch a Russian Communist and you will find a Russian chauvinist." Just as Lenin cannot be blamed for the full extent of the Soviet state's bureaucratic degeneration, so the veritable worship of Russian nationalism instituted by his Georgian successor and only slightly moderated by the present rulers cannot be laid to his account.

But the whole thrust of Lenin's political philosophy as well as of his political activity made it inevitable that nationalism should become the moving force behind Communism. By extolling the monolithic party, by making political dissent impermissible, by demanding submission of all other forms of social activity to politics, he abjured all the restraints and cautions that liberalism sought to place between the state and the individual. In such an absolute state in the twentieth century only nationalism could provide a strong link between the rulers and the ruled. The Revolution was won in the name of an internationalist ideology, but revolutionary Russia could be saved only by an appeal to Russian nationalism, as the Bolsheviks had already recognized during the Civil War when this nationalism was unabashedly invoked against foreign intervention, as it was again in 1920 against the Poles.

It was utopian thinking, then, to expect that those Russians and russified Jews or Georgians, who of necessity assumed the leadership of world Communism, would be able to subordinate or even to distinguish their interest as rulers of a state from their duty as soldiers of the world revolution. And after a generation of socialist construction and ideological indoctrination, this inability of the doctrine to evoke supreme loyalty was explicitly recognized when in the moment of its mortal danger the Soviet regime called on its people to fight the invader "for our country, for Stalin," and not for the Revolution or for Marxism-Leninism. In the official historiography, the war that saved Communism, World War II, remains the Great Fatherland War. Stalin himself claimed on the morrow of this victory that it was the *Russian* people which had saved the *Soviet* state, not only because that people was the most numerous but also because it was the most loyal of the nations of the USSR. There is no better testimony as to what has constituted the real strength and basis for cohesion of the Soviet Union and what has been largely a facade.

How weak, then, the tie of ideology was to prove when it was not buttressed by the national interest! It would have been a bitter disappointment for Lenin to witness how the very spread of Communism had eroded its unity. After all, the sacrifices and privations of the Revolution, as well as of revolutions to come, were justified in his eyes by the imperative need to banish war as well as exploitation. Whatever the number of victims claimed by revolutionary terror, it was insignificant as compared with those claimed by World War I. Yet such calculations and rationalizations hardly carry much conviction in view of the experience of the last twenty-five years, when some of the sharpest antagonisms and the most dangerous conflicts have arisen between Communist states themselves. History has turned around many of the dicta and formulas of Marxism-Leninsim; instead of being applicable to the capitalist world, they can be seen as fitting that of Communism.

There is no better example of the inherent contradictions of a social system than in the Soviet state, where the constant need to raise the material and cultural level of the people clashes with the vested interest of the party oligarchy in preserving unimpaired its monopoly of power. Imperialism was in Lenin's formulation the highest, in other words the last, phase of capitalism, and imperialist rivalries were the main cause of wars. Yet the most significant and potentially dangerous international conflict of today is not between two capitalist powers but between the two great Communist states. And it is only the vast preponderance of Soviet strength and not a common ideological inheritance that secures the unity of European Communism. The argument can even be made that the current rulers of the Soviet Union have betrayed Leninism, that he never would have licensed the persecution of writers and intellectuals, for instance, or the invasion of Czechoslovakia.

But in the most fundamental sense, it is history that has betrayed Lenin. History has vindicated his tactics but has repudiated his hopes. Most important, Communism has not proved a solvent of national animosities and a path to world peace. Militant nationalism, in fact, to paraphrase Lenin's statement about imperialism, appears as the highest phase of Communism. Goethe's exclamation about how grey the dogma and how green the tree of life was one of Lenin's favorite quotations. This saying was as paradoxical as was much of his lifework, for he saw himself as an orthodox Marxist and a defender of the doctrine against revisionism of all kinds. But he was himself a revisionist when it came to discarding much of the theoretical apparatus of Marxism in order to rediscover the essence of the doctrine and to put it to practical use. His great strength was his ability to equip Marxism with the weapons necessary to fight twentieth century battles—weapons it eschewed or abandoned as it grew, along with nineteenth century Europe, more moderate and democratic. Thus, the zeal of a doctrinaire blended in him with the political skills of a practical politician, and this combination was responsible for much of the Bolsheviks' success.

But by the same token Lenin could not endow his successors with his own personality. In due time the doctrine was bound to degenerate into a lifeless ritual, and political pragmatism would harden into cynicism. The state that Lenin helped save from utter anarchy, in many ways a greater achievement than his seizure of the Revolution for Bolshevism, would grow enormously in power and prestige. But this growth reflects primarily the vigor and ability of the Russian people rather than the superior virtues of the new social system. The spread of Communism throughout the world would in turn reflect the power and prestige of the Soviet state rather than the inherent appeal of the doctrine. And once Communism loses its exclusively Russian coloration, it becomes entangled in its own national and imperialistic rivalries.

To his followers, then, Lenin stands not only for the heroic days of the Revolution but also for the hopes of those distant days when Communism, though confined to a single backward and devastated country, still exuded more faith and self-confidence in its ability to mark a new era in the history of mankind than it does at present when it is the ruling ideology in countries with nearly one-third of the world's population. There are frequent calls for unity among the contending factions and for efforts to recoup the fervor and purpose of earlier days, but it is unlikely that they will prove effective.

Lenin was abashed to realize after the Revolution, he tells us, that Marx had had little to say as to how a socialist society is actually to be run. The father of scientific socialism had been primarily an analyst of early capitalism, the discoverer, Marx had believed, of those self-destructive elements in a capitalist economy that eventually must bring about its collapse and clear the path to a higher and better form of social organization. Lenin's achievement was similar insofar as he sought to discover and exploit the weaknesses and vulnerabilities of the liberal and social democratic traditions. Economically, Western civilization proved much stronger than Marx had expected or hoped. But politically and psychologically it has proved much less resilient and tough. The realization of this disparity is the basis for calling Lenin the greatest political organizer and strategist in this century. History has confounded his hopes about Communism, but has not as yet refuted his perceptions as to what is weak and vulnerable in the system Communism seeks to destroy.

6 | LENIN, STALIN, AND TROTSKY

On March 5, 1923, for the first time in more than thirty years Vladimir Ilyich Ulyanov forgot that he was primarily a party member and a politician. He was a man who had been insulted both personally and through rudeness to his wife. Whether he had just learned for the first time the full details of Stalin's pressures on Krupskaya, whom Stalin bullied for discussing politics with the sick Lenin in contravention of the Politburo's order, or whether he sensed his coming complete disability, he abandoned any restraint, any veiling of sentiments in political phraseology. Summoning his secretary at 12 noon, he asked her to take two letters, one for Trotsky and the other for Stalin. He felt very ill.[1]

He wrote to the man whom he had elevated to be the party's chief officer, in whom he had put full trust, and toward whom he had displayed a fatherly solicitude extending to such details as finding a larger apartment for his family and insisting on Stalin's taking a full rest: "Dear Comrade Stalin: You permitted yourself a rude summons of my wife to the telephone and a rude reprimand of her. Despite the fact that she told you that she agreed to forget what was said, nevertheless Zinoviev and Kamenev heard about it from her. I have no intention to forget so easily that which is being done against me and I need not stress here that I consider as directed against me that which is being done against my wife. I ask therefore that you weigh carefully whether you are agreeable to retracting your words and apologizing, or whether you prefer the severance of relations between us."[2]

The letter was not sent the same day. Lenin reread it on March 6, and Krupskaya begged him not to send it. She then asked the secretary not to deliver it. But the latter, on March 7, felt that she could not disobey Lenin's implicit instructions. She waited on Stalin with the letter, informing him that she must have his answer immediately. He dictated an apology, the text of which we do not know. Copies of Lenin's ultimatum went to Zinoviev and Kamenev. Stalin's apology could not be delivered to Lenin on the same day, as his condition took a turn for the worse. When and how he received the apology, the guardians of the party archives have not seen fit to inform us.

This letter was an act of desperation and self-indulgence on the part of the sick man. He must have known that Stalin would apologize and would remain the Politburo's chief watchman over him. Zinoviev and Kamenev had not helped Krupskaya when she first told them of her mistreatment, so why should they help now? The reader might well ask why the dictator, though to be sure a crippled dictator, was so helpless. Why not dispatch a letter to all the Politburo, all the Central Committee members, demanding that Stalin be dismissed, asking that he himself be allowed to live and die as he pleased, and not in incarceration? To repeat, Lenin was caught in his own trap. He had always acted or pretended to act in the name of the party, of the Central Committee, had always said "we," "on behalf of." Any other behavior would have been taken as a sign that he was deranged. If the events surrounding Lenin's illness and death deeply affected Stalin's future behavior, as we must believe that they did, then we can understand the fantastic extent of the "cult of personality" that Stalin erected. Apart from his vanity, he never wanted to find himself in the position of his predecessor. He wanted to be so much above everyone else that, even if debilitated, at his orders a militiaman on duty in the Kremlin would shoot the most powerful of his lieutenants.

The letter to Trotsky was written with the same haste, and it was telephoned to him before being delivered, the answer to be communicated "as soon as possible." In it, Lenin once again was trying to break the iron ring surrounding him. Would Trotsky take upon himself the defense of the Georgian case? "The matter is now being prosecuted by Stalin and Dzerzhinsky, on whose objectivity I cannot rely. Quite the contrary." Lenin enclosed his December memorandum on the nationality question with its devastating criticism of

Stalin and others. If Trotsky would not agree to plead the case of the Georgian dissidents, would he return the materials to Lenin? Trotsky's telephone answer must have been pusillanimous, for now in utmost despair, trying to force the issue into the open, Lenin threw all caution and the party regulations to the wind. He wrote on March 6 to the Georgian dissidents, with copies to Trotsky and Kamenev: "I follow your case with all my heart. I am appalled by the coarseness of Ordzhonikidze and the connivance of Stalin and Dzerzhinsky. I am preparing for you notes and a speech."

Trotsky's behavior in the matter was unheroic. What is more, it displayed fantastic political blundering. Since Trotsky's own version of the story departs from the facts as they can be gleaned from the documents that he himself retained and which are now in his archive, it is well to go into the incident in some detail.[3]

Lenin's letter spoke for itself. Trotsky was to retain the nationality memorandum *if* he was going to defend the Georgians in the Central Committee and presumably elsewhere. Return of the memorandum would signify that he had refused to take up the case. Trotsky did return Lenin's typescript (for some reason only one copy was typed), which meant his refusal, but he also made a copy of it for his own future use, something that Lenin had not authorized him to do if he was not going to take the case. The contents of Lenin's devastating attack were not communicated by him to anybody else. In his memoirs Trotsky claimed lamely that Lenin did not want him to acquaint anybody, even Kamenev, with the contents of the nationality memorandum. This is palpably absurd: how could Lenin want Trotsky to defend the Georgian case before the Central Committee and lend him for that purpose the only copy of his document if the gist of his criticisms was to remain secret? And as we have seen, on the very next day, March 6, hoping to shame Trotsky into action, Lenin sent Trotsky and Kamenev copies of his wire to two Georgians who were not even members of the Central Committee, in which he made abundantly clear his attack on Stalin and that he was preparing notes and a speech on this subject.

Trotsky must have felt some shame at his behavior, for later on in March, when Lenin was already hopelessly paralyzed, he made some feeble moves in the Politburo on the Georgian issue. He proposed a recall of Ordzhonikidze from Transcaucasia and defended, though not very strongly, the Georgian oppositionists. He enclosed a copy of his motions in the Politburo for Lenin's secretary, the very same one who had handed him the explosive memorandum and then had to take it back.[4] But not a word in Trotsky's motions about Stalin and Dzerzhinsky or about an exemplary punishment for Ordzhonikidze. There the matter might have rested, buried with Lenin's nationality memorandum and nobody but Trotsky knowing its full contents, but for the courageous action of the chief secretary of the paralyzed leader, Fotyeva.[5] The party Congress was about to meet, yet not a word had been spoken about Vladimir Ilyich's memorandum, which she knew he wanted to become widely known. On April 16 she wrote to Kamenev as Chairman of the Politburo, giving the full story of the incident.[6] The fat was in the fire. Trotsky was caught on two counts. First, he had kept secret from the Politburo the fact that he had received a communication from Lenin. Second, he had let Vladimir Ilyich down, by not making the fight that Lenin had begged him to make. He had shown himself both devious and fainthearted.

It was now possible for Stalin to assume the pose of injured innocence. He wrote to members of the Central Committee: "I am greatly surprised that those articles of Com. Lenin which, without a doubt, are of a distinct basic significance, and which Com. Trotsky received as early as 5 March of this year—he has considered admissible to keep his own secret for over a month without making their content known to the Political Bureau or to the C.C. plenum, until one day before the opening of the Twelfth Congress of the party."[7]

Trotsky attempted an explanation, which he circulated to the Central Committee the very same day. It speaks for itself. Yes, he did receive a memorandum from Lenin on March 5. "I made a copy of it as a basis of my corrections to Comrade Stalin's theses on nationality (which were accepted by Comrade Stalin) and also of my article in *Pravda.*" Lenin's memorandum had a great importance, but "on the other hand it includes a severe judgment on three members of the Central Committee." Now Trotsky says that he sees no alternative but to acquaint the members of the Central Committee with Lenin's piece (which was going to be distributed among them anyway), but he promises to let it go no further. "If no member of the Central Committee, due to intra-Party considerations, will bring the memorandum in one form or another to the knowledge of the Party or the Party Congress then I for my part will consider it as a silent authorization relieving me from personal responsibility in the matter in connection with the Party Congress." The reaction of the party oligarchs to this explanation, which would not have fooled a schoolboy, can well be imagined. Next day Trotsky addressed another more detailed letter, in which he got even more entangled. He, Trotsky, had no idea as to what Lenin planned to do with his piece on the nationality problem. Trotsky repeats that he had copied it *only* to make some corrections in Comrade Stalin's theses on the national problem. Won't the Central Committee state that he had acted absolutely correctly? As to whether Lenin's memorandum ought to be published: "The problem should be decided according to the political desirability of such a step. I could not take the responsibility alone for such a decision and hence turned [the document] over to the Central Committee."[8]

In his panic Trotsky passed to threats. He wrote to Stalin on April 18 that the latter had assured him that he had acted correctly in the matter and that Stalin would write to the members of the Central Committee in this vein. Why had Stalin not written this letter yet? (Their conversation took place only the day before.) If he did not write it immediately, he, Trotsky, would demand that a special commission investigate the matter and the insinuations made about him: "You better than anyone else can estimate that if I haven't done it up to now it was not because such a step might hurt me."[9] Stalin must have smiled as he complied with this request and wrote to the Committee members that Comrade Trotsky's behavior in connection with Lenin's memorandum was perfectly understandable and correct.

Few are the cases of brilliant and clever men being caught so red-handed and piling up one fatal political error upon another. Trotsky's explanation of his behavior, written when he was already in exile from Stalin's Russia, is pathetic in its half-truths and attempts to gloss over the facts, which are clearly spelled out in the papers he himself kept and which are now in his archive. He tried to shift the blame to Kamenev, invented conversations with Lenin's secretary that obviously could not have taken place, and the like.[10] He ended up by crediting himself with having acted with great magnanimity toward Stalin, whom he could have crushed then and there if he had chosen to do so.

What were in fact the reasons for his behavior? Here one must admit that upon receiving Lenin's letter and the enclosed memorandum on March 5, Trotsky was put in a difficult position. He was bound to reveal the fact that he had received the communication, if not indeed its contents, to the other members of the Politburo. Then, had he pledged to pursue the matter further, he would have had to attack Stalin, Dzerzhinsky, and Ordzhonikidze at the meeting of the Central Committee, where most likely he would have been opposed by all his colleagues from the Politburo and defeated, even though he could have invoked Lenin's authority. This course at least would have had the virtue of forthrightness. By refusing to take up the Georgian case and clandestinely copying Lenin's memorandum for his future use, Trotsky thought he was taking the safest course. Lenin might recover and tend to the business himself. If not, he would produce the bomb against Stalin in his own good time, while in the meantime nobody could accuse Trotsky of breaking the solidarity of the Politburo and intriguing with the sick man. He could not have foreseen that on April 16 Fotyeva would take it upon herself to reveal the whole story to his colleagues.

In addition, there might have been another element of calculation in Trotsky's conduct. Suppose that he had carried the struggle to the Central Committee and managed, against considerable odds, to impugn Stalin's position. Who would have been the beneficiary? In his memoirs written in 1929 Stalin, of course, is made the villain and the enemy. But in 1923, much as he hated Stalin, Trotsky saw Zinoviev as his chief rival for Lenin's mantle. Any discrediting of Stalin, much as it would have pleased Trotsky, would have redounded to the advantage of the Zinoviev-Kamenev faction. They held a majority on the Central Committee, and in all likelihood they would nominate the next Secretary General of the party. In the country and to the world Trotsky was clearly the second man in Russia. But within the party, among both its oligarchy and the membership at large, the situation was quite different. "Comrade

Trotsky has no idea about the local Party organizations, he is a military man," said Anastas Mikoyan, then a young delegate at the Eleventh Party Congress.[11] Trotsky had warm admirers and fervent partisans, but to the oligarchs he was a relative newcomer to Bolshevism, and to the rank and file a specialist on military and economic problems. If he was going to succeed to the leadership, it would not be through the party organization. Hence, it was perhaps safer to leave the leadership in the "neutral" hands of Stalin rather than to add it to the already preponderant mass of assets held by Zinoviev and Kamenev.

Such calculations took place against the now virtual certainty that Lenin would not return to the helm. On March 7 his condition deteriorated still further. On March 9 he suffered yet another major stroke. This time he was completely incapacitated. Full paralysis of the right side was joined with aphasia. He could speak only with difficulty and but a few words. No more dictation. No more conspiracies. Amazingly enough, his indomitable will still persisted. He tried to communicate by signs, would fly into a rage at being misunderstood. At times he would chase out the doctors and nurses, and could be appeased only by his wife or sister. He could no longer resist when in May he was taken from the Kremlin, where he had lain all this time, to Gorki.

In his absence the event took place that he had so fervently hoped to attend, the Twelfth Congress of the Communist Party, the first one since 1903 in which he could not participate (excepting the Sixth Congress in 1917, when he was hiding but with which he was nevertheless in communication). Kamenev, who opened the proceedings, gave reassuring news about Lenin's health. He was getting better, the danger had passed, they could hope for "a full recovery of Vladimir Ilyich."[12] Those with any inkling of medical knowledge or just with common sense could wonder how a man who had been in failing health for some time and who had had three major cerebral strokes within a few months could ever be expected to achieve a "full recovery," or to resume even a small part of his previous duties. Equally honest was Kamenev's other assurance: the Congress was being run according to Vladimir Ilyich's wishes.

The Politburo faced the Congress with the appearance of iron solidarity, but behind the scenes were already the first signs of the future struggle for the succession. During an earlier discussion on who should deliver the central report, usually given by Lenin, there had been a veritable Gaston and Alphonse act with the oligarchs seeking to avoid this invidious and envy-attracting honor. Finally Zinoviev accepted the charge. Within the party and the country at large there was considerable confusion as to what was going on in Lenin's absence, who was going up, who down, the particulars. This confusion was reflected in the traditional greetings to the Congress from factories, youth organizations, and the like. Some of them hailed as "our leaders" Lenin and Zinoviev; some coupled Trotsky with the sick man in their greetings. The more prudent saluted "Lenin, Zinoviev, Kamenev, and Trotsky," or even more wisely omitted any name but Lenin's. In at least one organization the faith in internationalism still burned brightly: they hailed Lenin, then Klara Zetkin, the old war horse of the German Communist Party, and only then the fraternal trio of Kamenev, Zinoviev, and Trotsky. But no one thought of paying a special tribute to the modest, self-effacing man who was the Secretary General of the party.

The outward unity of the top leadership was dictated by imperative reasons. Again there was turbulence both within the rank and file and outside the party ranks. Various workers' groups had sprung up that continued to propagate the slogans of the old Workers' Opposition, which reflected dissatisfaction with the New Economic Policy and the appalling living conditions among the city proletariat. At the Congress there were open complaints against the dictatorship by the Politburo, which, as one delegate put it, had become "an infallible pope."[13] Few could sense the direction in which political events were moving; thus, the individual among the oligarchy who attracted most criticism and obviously aroused most fear was Zinoviev. The perennial malcontent, Osinsky, praised two members of the directing triumvirate, Stalin and Kamenev, but implied that he would like to see Zinoviev with his "general's" manners out of there. Zinoviev (who at the time was credited with much the same guile and skill that has since become associated with Stalin's name) sought to disarm his critic. What was all this talk about power, about him and other members of the Politburo being power-oriented? "Please lay off, Comrade Osinsky," he begged. They all already had more power than they knew what to do with. Their only thought was for the good of the party. "Nobody worries about power."

Stalin's performance was masterful. If he was embarrassed by the knowledge that many in the hall had read Lenin's strictures about him, he did not betray it. He warded off criticisms with a joke or irrelevancy. Somebody had complained about the lack of freedom of speech at this Congress. How could he have said that, wondered Stalin, for this Congress had been better prepared by the Central Committee than any previous one? Osinsky was warned not to try to stir up any trouble among the ruling group. Stalin breathed tolerance and open-mindedness. How encouraging to see the former Socialist Revolutionaries and Mensheviks seeking entrance into the Communist Party. The party needed new blood; its leadership was getting old and worn out—look at Comrade Lenin. Hence, Stalin urged expansion of the Central Committee by adding to it "men with independent minds." He could not have known of Lenin's *Testament,* but Stalin's proposed additions were obviously not to be "simple workmen"; rather, they would be trusted functionaries from his apparatus who would help him reduce Zinoviev's preponderance on the Central Committee. The Politburo had been accused of doing some things in secret. Well, said Stalin, you could not reveal everything; the enemy was listening. The party was altogether in splendid shape. How tragic that Comrade Lenin was not there; how proud he would be to see what was going on!

The few critics who somehow felt differently groped for a way to stir up some conflict among the higher-ups, which in turn would encourage the intimidated delegates to loosen their tongues. After a discussion on a sensitive issue had been hastily adjourned, there were shouts in the hall: "Why does not Rykov speak? Let Rakovsky talk about it." But all in vain. "Our Party is healthier than ever," said even Bukharin, the most outspoken and temperamental among the oligarchs.[14]

Strangely enough, the one individual who was attacked most frequently at the Congress was Leonid Krasin. The chief Soviet commercial negotiator delivered what was under the circumstances a very unpolitic speech. He asked the Congress whether they thought that the party could be run then the way it had been ten years earlier, by "agitators and journalists." Those now in power needed professional competence and less politics. "What do you think, you can lead a successful policy by interfering with the recovery of production?"[15] It must have crossed the oligarchs' minds that here was the man whom Vladimir Ilyich, were he in good health, might well have advanced to a high position. But now Krasin could be attacked with impunity; he had no following. Radek ridiculed Krasin as a self-proclaimed candidate for the vacant leadership and, with his typical impudence, implied that the veteran Bolshevik had sold out to Lloyd George. Others poured out their pent-up resentment against this protector of bourgeois specialists. Soon Krasin was to be permanently exiled to a diplomatic post.

And the nationality issue? The Georgian malcontents Mdivani and Makharadze were at the Congress to raise their voices in protest, though they referred gingerly to Lenin's letter to them and to the memorandum. The latter had been shown to some select delegates with the explanation that it would be unseemly and irreverent to Vladimir Ilyich to have it published. The two Georgians had harsh words to say about Orzhonikidze and his brutal behavior in their country, but they were answered by Stalin's other Georgian lieutenant, Enukidze. To the majority of the delegates this was undoubtedly an obscure business, having its roots in the tribal hostilities among the Georgians. As to Lenin's intervention, Enukidze gave plausible explanations: he was "a victim of incorrect information." If someone came to a sick man and stirred him up with tales of people being beaten, humiliated, and the like, it was no wonder that he reacted in a hysterical fashion and unwittingly slandered the people in whom, when well, he had put his full trust. The dissident Georgians' case was valiantly seconded by Rakovsky, the chief commissar in the Ukraine, who attacked the whole concept of Stalin's federalism as leading to Russian domination. Laws and treaties were being signed in the name of Ukraine, Rakovsky said, without its prime minister's knowledge. But here again the delegates must have wondered what suddenly had made the Bulgarian-Rumanian Rakovsky such a defender of Ukrainian nationalism.

The Politburo preserved its united front on the national issue. True, Bukharin kept interrupting when an attempt was made to distort Lenin's attitude on the subject. And he did say, "If Lenin were here he would wash the heads of the Russian chauvinists."[16] But his remarks were in a teasing rather than serious tone. Not a peep was heard from Trotsky on the Georgian business. He absented himself from the sessions of the Congress on the nationality problem, allegedly on the grounds that he was preparing a speech on economics. Stalin promised to make some mechanical adjustments in his scheme for the federation of the Soviet republics. The Congress approved his proposals and passed over the issue. Vladimir Ilyich's last conspiracy had failed.

He himself was now in the final stage of his inexorable disease. The autopsy was to reveal that he had suffered all along from an advanced cerebral arteriosclerosis.[17] To the last, the organism struggled against the inevitable end. In August, with Krupskaya's help, he started to relearn to speak. In September he could walk with a cane. On October 19, amazingly enough, he insisted on being driven to Moscow to the Kremlin and for the last time looked at his office, where so much history had been made. Stories of those last days refer occasionally to Lenin hunting for mushrooms in Gorki or talking with visitors, but evidently his hunting consisted in being wheeled outside the villa, and his speech never fully returned.

The government kept publishing optimistic bulletins, and superficially there was enough improvement to warrant a guarded optimism about his life, but hardly the talk about full recovery, still less of his return to his duties. He tried to learn to write with his left hand, and we do not know whether even in this last phase he attempted to leave a political communication. His wife recalls reading to him about the companions of bygone days: Martov and Axelrod. Lenin was saddened to hear about Martov's illness; his thoughts must have gone to the old times in Munich and London when this lovable and exasperating man would drop in for a chat and stay for five or six hours while Lenin tried to work. Old Axelrod was also ill, also in exile. In 1898 in Siberia, Vladimir Ilyich was thrown into rapture on receiving a letter from this already venerable cofounder of Russian Marxism, in which Axelrod praised the initiate's pamphlet on the labor question. Lenin also listened to and liked an article by Trotsky in which he compared Lenin with Marx. For all of Trotsky's sins of omission and commission, both Vladimir Ilyich and his wife sensed in him a personal attachment and chivalry sadly lacking in the old Bolsheviks. After Lenin's death, Krupskaya wrote Trotsky a heartfelt letter, which is no less moving for the fact that it glosses over the ancient and bitter quarrels and recent disappointments: "The feelings which Vladimir Ilyich showed you when you came to us in London from Siberia did not change up to his death. I embrace you, Lev Davidovich." Another happy memory was of young Trotsky in 1902 banging on the Ulyanovs' door at an ungodly hour in the morning, waking up the whole house and rushing in to ask Lenin about *Iskra*. To Gorky, Krupskaya was to write, "To his very death he was himself, a man of massive will, self-control, prone to laughter and jokes to the very end."

On the night of January 20 Lenin pointed at his eyes. It was thought advisable to summon an oculist, Professor M. Auerbach, who had previously examined Lenin and found that he was nearsighted in one eye. Now he could discover nothing untoward about the patient's sight. He reported this to the doctors in attendance and was ready to return to Moscow when Vladimir Ilyich unexpectedly entered from his room. He indicated—mostly in sign language, one would think—that he was worried about Auerbach returning at such a late hour and that he should spend the night in Gorki. The doctor, touched by this solicitude of the sick man, could only explain that he had to be back in his clinic the next day. He persuaded Lenin to go back to his room, which he did after satisfying himself that the professor was being taken care of. In the morning Lenin suffered his last stroke. The end came in the evening of January 21, 1924.

The next day members of the Central Committee present in Moscow (Trotsky was on a sick leave in the Caucasus) repaired to Gorki to render homage to their dead leader. There began a series of elaborate mourning rites, which would not have pleased the man who with all his other qualities believed in simplicity.

7 | STALIN

Stalin seldom failed to impress foreigners with whom he spoke. The Georgian cobbler's son was in this respect greatly superior to his predecessor. Lenin with a capitalist visitor was always conscious of his own sinful class origins and, by way of compensation, was obsessively doctrinaire and condescending. The father of Communism did not suffer fools gladly, and he placed in this category people like well-meaning Western progressives and Labour politicians. They could always be counted on to ask a silly question —why was terror being practiced? or the like. As for Stalin, "We Russian Bolsheviks have for long learned not to be surprised at anything," he told Emil Ludwig. So when Lady Astor, combining American forthrightness with a British aristocrat's unceremoniousness toward lesser breeds, inquired how long he proposed to go on killing people, Stalin was unfazed. As long as it was necessary, he answered.

Reading his interview with Emil Ludwig, one is struck again by Stalin's intuitive ability to gauge his visitor's personality. Ludwig, a German writer of rather facile biographies then much in vogue, probed into Stalin's family and personal background in a way that would have made Lenin show him the door. But Stalin was calm, courteous, and "one-up" on him. He managed to convey an impression of reasonableness but also just the right touch of mystery and steely resolution, which his visitor would convey to Western readers. He did not lecture, still less orate, in the manner of Hitler. Ludwig kept fishing for some revealing or characteristic clue with which to expose the personality of this mysterious potentate. Did Stalin consider himself a continuator of Peter the Great? No, he was just a disciple of Lenin's, and of course between the maker of Communism and the Tsar there could be no comparison. Lenin was like an ocean; Peter, for all his work in modernizing Russia, was only a drop in the sea. Frustrated in his "Red Tsar" image, Ludwig tried other tacks. He had heard of Stalin's youthful "expropriations"—what then did he think of Stenka Razin and Pugachev ("Stalin, inspired by the Cossack bandit chieftains of yore"). But, Stalin explained patiently, those semibandit, semirebel figures of the tsarist past expressed only a primitive popular reaction to oppression. They had nothing to do with Bolshevism, which pursued humane goals and was based on scientific truth. Sigmund Freud did not help either: Stalin's childhood was quite normal, his parents, though uneducated, treated him well. Ludwig turned to his theological training—what did Stalin think of the Jesuits? Stalin would not swallow this bait. The Jesuits based their system on indoctrination and spying, quite different from what Communism tried to impart to Russia's young. No, this capitalist scribbler would not be able to interpret him according to such Philistine categories. And for his oversubtle visitor he had a sardonic remark: "You in Germany will soon see things you would never have believed possible."[1] The year was 1931.

A perfectly reasonable man, a devout believer but not a fanatic—this was the impression that many a foreigner would carry away from an interview. "I have never met a man more candid, fair and honest," wrote H. G. Wells in 1934, when the tyrant's whims and passions had already led to several million Russians losing their lives.

He could be so convincing and impressive—after all, he impressed such connoisseurs of human nature in politics as Winston Churchill and Charles de Gaulle—because unless something touched off the inner springs of suspicion and rage, he was a most reasonable and perceptive man. A politician's sense of timing and an intuitive grasp of the protagonist's mentality had served Stalin well in intraparty struggles, and they contributed to making him a superb diplomat.

Whatever their respect for his guile and internal maneuverings, his enemies were always sure of one thing: Stalin could never become the leader of international Communism. He had hardly been abroad; he had not mastered a single foreign language; his pretensions as a theorist were ridiculous. How could a man like that step into Lenin's shoes or even replace people with such a cosmopolitan background and outlook as Zinoviev or Bukharin? Yet here again Stalin fooled them. By the early 1930s his mastery over foreign Communism was unprecedented, which was all the more amazing since it extended over people who were not within his physical power. Foreign Communist notables who had argued with Lenin and quarreled with Bukharin and Zinoviev bowed to Stalin. Whatever their private feelings, people as different as Palmiro Togliatti, Mao Tse-tung, and Maurice Thorez echoed the eulogies of him pronounced by Kaganovich or Molotov. The rank-and-file Communist in Paris or New York believed in him as uncritically as the most devout member of the Komsomol (Communist Youth) in Russia. Fastidious Communist intellectuals who later looked down their noses at Khrushchev extolled his name. The emotion experienced on Stalin's death by Louis Aragon, the French Communist bard, made him recall the last moments of his own mother: "She turned towards me those green eyes which had watched over my childhood and whispered against my cheek, 'Stalin . . . What is Stalin saying?' "[2] If one persists in denying Stalin's gift of mastery over men, and the tragedy of twentieth century politics that it epitomizes, one must otherwise explain the behavior of foreign Communists between 1930 and 1953.

To do so, one can resort to a variety of psychological explanations. But the key reason for Stalin's ascendance was the same in foreign as well as domestic politics: he was the "most active" Communist. Beginning in 1925-1928, when the leadership of the Comintern was still in Bukharin's hands and when the recent Chinese fiasco would have led another person in his position to eschew direct identification with international affairs, Stalin stepped to the forefront of the world Communist movement.

Conspiracy was his craft, and power his passion. So with its Sixth Congress in July-September 1928, the world Communist movement took on a new appearance. The last vestiges of autonomy and freedom of decision for the individual parties were dropped. "International Communist discipline must be expressed in the subordination of local and particular interests of the movement and in the execution without reservation of all decisions made by the leading bodies of the Communist International."[3] This was merely a reiteration of the principle formulated in Lenin's time, but Stalin meant it more literally. He argued that the Comintern Executive in Moscow, and thus eventually Stalin himself, must make all the decisions on tactics and policy for the French, say, or Guatemalan Communist parties. There was little point in spending good Soviet money on foreign Communists unless they became disciplined fighting detachments, just as the Russian Communists had. They had to be purged of the last lingering remnants of Trotskyites and soon of Bukharinites as well. The Comintern Executive, hitherto the preserve of the more intellectual and independent-minded Communists, now became staffed by Stalin's servants. After Bukharin's fall it was presided over by Molotov, and when his undivided attention soon became needed on the domestic front, it was turned over to a third-rank Soviet figure, Dmitri Manuilsky. Foreigners, Stalin seemed to say, should get it out of their heads that they needed a Politburo member to hold their hand. Thus, there were no more congresses of the Comintern until the seventh and last one in 1935. Comintern affairs no longer required discussion, but only orders conveyed by Moscow's special representatives, or by party leaders on their return from a pilgrimage to the Kremlin.

It has often been alleged that Stalin did not care for foreign Communists and did not believe in the world revolution. This is certainly overstating the case: foreign Communists were for him a valuable asset that should not be squandered. Certainly the interests of the Soviet state—his state—took absolute priority over those of any foreign Communist Party, or of all of them. But he was not much different in this respect from Trotsky, or from Lenin after his phase of internationalist enthusiasm in 1918-1919, when for a Communist Germany Lenin would almost have sacrificed Communist Russia. Where Stalin was different from many of his fellow Bolsheviks was in his thoroughly unromantic view of foreign Communism. For them, it was an exciting adventure, the stuff of dreams and passions. Stalin was in love with production figures: for an additional millon tons of Soviet steel he would gladly have sacrificed a sizable foreign party. Foreign Communists were advance detachments of the main army, which was the Soviet

Union, and as such, they might on occasion be expendable. Stalin was a true believer: to his mind, capitalism was doomed. But the eventual triumph of Communism abroad would not come through some ridiculous revolutionary adventure and improvisation in Germany or China. It would come through the growing military strength and industrial might of the Soviet Union, combined with the growing debility and chaos of the capitalist world.

Capitalism was the enemy, and in its appraisal of this enemy, whether domestic or foreign, the Communist mind (and not only Stalin's) has always been schizophrenic: the enemy was weak, divided, condemned by the forces of history; yet it was infinitely dangerous and resourceful. The capitalist ruling class was foolish and irrational. Why, for example, had not the capitalist powers combined to choke the infant Communist state in Russia rather than continue to fight over a few square miles in the West? Why did they let the Soviet experiment grow in strength and stability? Why did they recognize and trade with the USSR, and allow their scientists and engineers to help with its industrialization? Yet there was also the constant threat of capitalist intervention. "Objectively" every internal trouble in the Soviet Union was thought to be the result of capitalist plots; every foreigner in the USSR, including every Communist, was a potential spy. Hope and fear were intertwined in this surrealist view of the capitalist world. Vast new conflicts were about to seize the West: Germany against France, Japan against the United States; or—a bizarre notion seriously entertained by otherwise quite sober Soviet international experts—the United States, representing a new and dynamic type of capitalism, would grapple for empire with Britain. But then these pleasurable visions would fade, and their place would be taken by a nightmare: the capitalists were planning a concerted action against the USSR, with the Japanese attacking in the East, Ukrainian and Byelorussian uprisings in the West, helped by a Polish invasion sponsored by the French, while the British from India provoked an uprising of the Muslims of Soviet Central Asia! Sober and efficient Soviet diplomacy operated in the real world of the 1920s, but these phantasmagoric hopes and fears were never absent from the mind of the rulers.

Stalin epitomized the Communist mind at its most realistic and

its most suspicious, in foreign policy as in other matters. This in-
nate suspiciousness as well as a certain lack of subtlety marked Stalin's initial period of guidance of the world Communist movement.
The recent fiasco in China was to his mind a strong argument
against the Communist parties' collaborating with any other radical or, in Asia, nationalist forces. The Sixth Comintern Congress
laid down that the socialist parties were "a particularly dangerous
enemy of the proletariat, more dangerous than the avowed adherents of predatory imperialism." European Communists made
socialism the number-one target of their attack. The propaganda
school for Asian Communists in Moscow had once been called
Sun Yat-sen University, the symbol of that tactic of alliance with
nationalism in colonial areas which, for all the setbacks in China,
had brought Communism such handsome dividends in the past and
would bring more after World War II. But after 1928 the Chinese
Communists were ordered to "eliminate what remained of the ideology of Sun Yat-sen." In India the momentous struggle for independence associated with Gandhi and the Congress Party was in the
eyes of Moscow a reactionary movement. "More and more, Gand-
hism is becoming an ideology directed against the revolution of the
popular masses. Communism must fight against it relentlessly."
Whomever one could not control directly was the enemy: such was
Stalin's unsubtle directive for world Communist parties. It was
only when there was a real and tangible danger to the Soviet state,
in 1934-1935, that this directive was reversed.

With the onset of the Great Depression in 1929 this line was
intensified. Obviously some Western capitalist states were going to
experience a revolutionary crisis. So much the better. As it had
been for many Russian radicals in the nineteenth century, the slogan for Western Communists became, at a signal from Moscow,
"The worse it is, the better." Communists had no reason to shed
tears at the economic and political breakdown in Germany or
France, or to try to prop up those countries' failing bourgeois systems. Fascism? One need not be unduly alarmed at the prospect of
its seizing power in parts of Europe. Soviet Russia's relations with
fascist Italy and semiauthoritarian Poland were correct. National
Socialism in Germany was a beast of a different color, which the

Depression had turned from a sort of lunatic fringe on the right into a claimant for power: after the elections of 1930 more than one hundred instead of twelve Nazi deputies sat in the Reichstag. But the approaching demise of Weimar Germany was viewed by Stalin with more than equanimity, despite all the friendly relations that had prevailed between Germany and the USSR since 1922. Hitler was preferable to the Catholic and Social Democratic politicians who had been seeking a rapprochement with Britain and France. Hitler and his followers might destroy what remained of German democracy, but they certainly could set up a viable and long-lasting regime of their own. A Hitlerian interlude would only serve to radicalize the German working masses and turn them toward the one party that could solve the social and economic problems—the Communist Party. The prospect of a Communist Germany must have been contemplated by Stalin with special pleasure. How much Lenin had hoped and prayed for such a development! Trotskyites and Bukharinites had prattled that he, Stalin, misunderstood and neglected the interests of world Communism. Now, through his understanding of historical forces, he was going to add the country of Marx and Engels, more importantly of the most advanced industry and technology in Europe, to his domain. The German Communists, though they surely did not need much encouragement, were ordered to avoid any common front with the socialists —the "social fascists" in the Comintern's parlance—and were forbidden to try to save the tottering republic.

The realist in Stalin was not entirely absent during those grim years of 1928-1933, when after an illusory brightening of the international political and economic horizon, mass unemployment afflicted the West, and the fragile remnants of the pre-World War I liberalism and rationality in politics were under increasing attack from extremists. In 1931 the Japanese seizure of Manchuria initiated a period of neither-peace-nor-war, which lasted until September 1939. With Japanese "militarist adventurers" now increasingly influential in the government of their country, the Soviet Union faced a real threat, and not merely one of those half-believed, half-imagined dangers invoked in the past which could be countered by denouncing Trotsky and shooting some White Guardists. A real threat for the Soviets had the effect of an electric shock on a patient: it brought them out of the realm of imaginary fears and hopes into a sober appreciation of reality. The Soviet Far East and Mongolia, a virtual Soviet satellite, were vulnerable to Japanese attack. Even a local defeat in an undeclared war might start a sequence of catastrophic events for a country bleeding from collectivization, for a regime hated by the mass of its population, and for the man who had trampled on the party.

The year 1932 saw the beginning of a new look in Stalin's foreign policy. The USSR signed nonaggression treaties with the Baltic states, Poland, and France. This was in the way of protecting her Western flanks, and while the treaty with France could be only symbolic, it was the first step toward eventual alliance. In the same year diplomatic relations were restored with Chiang Kai-shek's China. The man who had massacred Communists in 1927 and was conducting an intermittent civil war against the still obscure Communist chieftain Mao Tse-tung and his "Soviet-republic" in Kwangsi Province now became a valuable potential ally. How desirable it would be if Chiang were to take a forthright anti-Japanese stand and thus make Tokyo forget the vulnerability of the Soviet Far East and become mired in an endless war in China!

In 1933, the Soviet Union became the most vocal exponent of peace, of the inviolability of frontiers, of wide-ranging regional treaties of nonaggression. Even the old Soviet hope-expectation of a new intraimperialist war had abated. In view of the overall international situation, no major war (as distinguished from a local conflict between Japan and China) could be guaranteed not to entangle the USSR. For the next three years, at least, there is no reason to question the Soviet Union's self-estimate as a peace-loving country. The war against the nation had made any war of nations too hazardous to contemplate.

Foreign policy, like everything else in Russia, was Stalin's, but his spokesman and main technician was Maxim Litvinov. Few would recognize in the rotund, amiable, and articulate Soviet diplomat the erstwhile "Papasha," the Bolshevik courier of 1905-1910, the man detained by the French authorities for exchanging the ruble notes expropriated in the 1907 Tiflis affair in which the present dictator had taken a hand. Now this man epitomized the new Soviet policy of peaceful coexistence, of collective security, and soon of antifascism and antimilitarism. The able Foreign Minister became one of the most valuable of Stalin's subordinates. Stalin showed amazing good sense to retain Litvinov, whom he had inherited from Lenin's era (when Litvinov was already Assistant Minister), rather than to replace him with one of his more sinister henchmen, who would never have been able to impress liberal public opinion in the West so favorably or to display such consummate knowledge of European politics. Such was Litvinov's value (at least until as a Jew he would be considered unsuitable for confidential dealings with Hitler) that it could restrain the tyrant's inordinate suspiciousness. An old Bolshevik married to an Englishwoman, Litvinov would have been a logical target in the Great Purge. He himself was well aware of this: for years when in Russia, he went to sleep with a loaded pistol on the night table, determined to take his own life rather than confess to a fantastic tale of treason and "wrecking" in a show trial—a fate that befell his two deputies. But for Litvinov the dreaded knock on the door during the night never came, as it did come to most Soviet diplomats during that period.

It fell to Litvinov in a speech of December 1933 to spell out the new look in Soviet foreign policy: Soviet Russia needed friends abroad. She would seek them among the countries hitherto depicted as sworn enemies of the Soviet Union, as having incited every type of internal trouble, from a kulak uprising to the wrecking of a coal mine. "Any state, even the most imperialist, may at one time or another become profoundly pacifist," he stated. He especially complimented Britain and France. Since he had to educate the Soviet public about the real dangers now facing the country, Litvinov was forthright: "[A] revolution . . . brought a new party to power in Germany preaching the most extreme anti-Soviet ideas . . . Japanese policy is now the darkest cloud on the horizon."[4] The Soviet Union did not deserve such a cruel turn of affairs, continued the Foreign Minister: "Enormous advantages, both for Germany and for us, followed from the political and economic relations between us. Excellent good neighbor relations existed between us and Japan . . . We had such confidence in Japan

. . . that we left our Far Eastern frontier practically undefended.''
After a year in power Hitler no longer appeared as a transitional
figure who, by destroying the Weimar Republic, would clear the
path for German Communism. Perhaps he really meant his anti-
Communist and anti-Soviet rhetoric. As for the Soviets, they were
not really angry with the Nazis: "We understand very well the difference between doctrine and policy.'' The fact that Hitler was
putting German Communists in concentration camps was no bar to
good relations, argued Litvinov: "We as Marxists are the last who
can be reproached with allowing sentiment to prevail over policy.''
So the appeal went out to Hitler to promise not to attack Russia,
not only now but also at such time "when Germany will have
greater forces with which to put those ideas into effect.''

Writing to a friend years later near the end of the war, a Russian
artillery officer made a mildly deprecatory remark about the dictator, which before his elevation to a divinity would have been
laughed off by Stalin and hardly taken notice of by anyone else.
The letter was intercepted by the security organs; and in the prevailing atmosphere of liberalism, the culprit received what by 1937-
1939 standards was a lenient sentence: eight years at hard labor.
Stalin undoubtedly never heard of the incident or of the incautious
officer. For Alexander Solzhenitsyn, this was the beginning of his
calvary, but also of a glorious career as the voice of his nation's
conscience and pride.

Another, more worldly-wise writer deferred his reflections of the
tyrant until he could seemingly be safely criticized.[5] Ilya Ehrenburg
then concluded that Stalin had missed a great chance by not dying
at the end of the war. People would have remembered him as a successful war leader, and the horrors of the past would have been
attributed to others: Beria, Yezhov, and Yagoda.

It is unlikely that Stalin, for all his concern for a posthumous
reputation, would have agreed with Ehrenburg. Though he felt
acutely the indignities of old age, he was far from wishing for or
expecting an imminent departure from this vale of tears. He would
often talk about getting old and about the approach of death, but
this was mainly to register his companions' reactions to such statements and to gauge the intensity of their indignant protestations. In

a 1948 play, which earned for its author the Stalin Prize and which was lovingly edited by its main hero—himself—the theatrical Stalin says that he will live to be a hundred.[6] What a joke that would be on all those scoundrels, his faithful comrades in arms (to give them their press appellation), whose unspoken thought, he was sure, was "When will the old bastard die?" and who were watching him (as well as each other) for any sign of debility. His anguish at getting old took a characteristic expression: he would turn on old servants whose aging appearance reminded him of his own. In a few years not only Voroshilov and Molotov but his personal attendants of long-standing—people like Poskrebyshev and Vlasik, people of no political importance—found themselves in disgrace, with all that that implied in Stalin's Russia.

If his subordinates did not actually wish him dead, they might well have expected Stalin to choose a dignified semiretirement after World War Two. But he strove to rule as ubiquitously as before. People had hoped from the victory an easement of their burdens, but in fact they were going to have to work as hard as before, and Stalin felt that only he could make them. This was no time to "drink a cup, and rest to our heart's desire," as a Soviet poet saw Russian life after victory in a wartime poem. The western regions of the country, including its granary, the Ukraine, had been devastated. The achievements of the Second and Third Five-Year Plans had largely been undone: in 1941, had it not been for the German attack, Russia would have produced over 22 million tons of steel; in 1945 she produced barely over 10 million. People would have to work harder to make up for those millions who had died during the war. To catch up with the West, never mind overcoming it, was as crucial now as in 1930, when Stalin had first advanced the slogan. No one could say how long it would be before the Americans realized their power and were tempted to use it. What if at that moment Russia were still weak and backward?

Other dangers and fears crowded Stalin's suspicious mind. No one could think that the Soviet system or his own power was in danger. But certainly one had to be on guard. People would forget the German atrocities and would suffer their discontents more acutely now that they had been led to expect a better life. In some

German-occupied regions, for example, the Soviet underground had sponsored rumors that after the war collectivization would be either abolished or greatly modified.

Thousands, if not millions, had proved to be disloyal. Unless one dealt with them with exemplary severity and promptly, one was asking for trouble. These included the soldiers who had let themselves be taken prisoner and the population of the Baltic states. There were even regions in the Ukraine where nationalist partisans were fighting the reestablishment of Soviet authority. Millions had seen foreign countries which, though in ruins, must have been impressive for their incomparably higher standard of life. Foreign wars, even victorious ones, have always been dangerous to Russian society. With his sense of history, Stalin must have thought of the First Fatherland War of 1812-1813. At its end, Alexander I was worshiped by the whole country; but within three or four years the Tsar-Conqueror had become hated among the educated classes, and plots and conspiracies were springing up all over the empire. Again in 1825 poison brought from the West had almost taken effect, and the Decembrist plot shook the empire of the Romanovs.

The intellectuals! There was a class that had to be watched even more strenuously than before. Scientists, writers, artists were always prone to go into raptures over foreign ways, and now they obviously hoped that some of the so-called bourgeois freedoms of Russia's allies would rub off on them.

Yes, there was a foreign danger—different from and yet in a way more pressing than the one Stalin had faced before 1941. He now knew enough about the democracies not to fear an imminent war. They would envy and fear Russia's new power. Their governments, especially that of Churchill, would spare no tricks to deprive him of some of the fruits of the victory, but they always reacted so sluggishly—witness how belatedly and ineffectively they had moved against Hitler. Their people lacked a sense of discipline, and once peace was restored, even Churchill would find it difficult to stir them up. But there was this intangible danger of demoralizing ideas and notions seeping in from the West, damaging the sense of cohesion and discipline on which Communist society must rest. Churchill phrased it straightforwardly: "They fear our friendship more than our enmity.'' Saltykov-Shchedrin (Stalin was a devoted reader of the great Russian humorist) once wrote about the nobility of a backwater Russian country that got stirred up by tales of strange institutions and customs in distant America, whereupon the local governor issued an order: ''Shut down America.'' The tsarist government had never succeeded in ''shutting down'' foreign countries, and it had paid for it. Stalin would know how. After the war Russia would be unable to keep up close contacts with her Western allies, Stalin told Ambassador Harriman, in one of those moments of frankness that made it so difficult for people to conceive of him as a master deceiver, she would have to attend to her own problems.

The feeling of his own indispensability for the guidance of Russia, and also, now that the war had been won, of world Communism, was especially strong when it came to foreign affairs. None of his lieutenants was fit to take over this burden. At the height of his generous mood, at the victory banquet on May 24, 1945, Stalin drank to the health of ''our Vyacheslav.'' But even then his appraisal of Molotov was rather modest: a good foreign minister was worth two or three army corps, he said. But *his* diplomacy was at least as valuable as the entire Red Army. Who else could size up foreigners instantaneously, was on to all the capitalists' tricks, and knew their weak spots so well? Could Zhdanov or Molotov be surrounded by so much awe in the foreigners' eyes? Could they or anyone else inspire so much fear, exact the same deference?

The war with Germany was over, but the arrangements for the ramshackle peace had to be completed. Just before the demise of the Thousand-Year Reich, there had been a flurry of diplomatic activity which enabled Stalin to undo much of the damage he had done to his cause during his altercation with Roosevelt. As late as April, Heinrich Himmler tried to interest the Allies in a separate peace. Churchill rejected these overtures and loyally informed Stalin of them. Again, for a moment, the dictator found a way to the Englishman's heart. ''That Churchill is capable of anything,'' he had exclaimed to Zhukov only a month before; but to the Prime Minister on April 25 went this handsome tribute: ''Knowing you, I had full confidence that you would not act differently.''[7] Yet Churchill's attempt to exploit this charmed moment so as to soften the Soviet position on Poland and to reserve some shadow of independence for that unfortunate country met with a harsh refusal: "You, it is clear, do not agree that the Soviet Union has the right to demand for Poland a regime that would be friendly toward the U.S.S.R." Stalin countered that he would not interfere with any arrangements the British might make in regard to Belgium or Greece.

The Prime Minister, with the famous percentages in Eastern Europe melting to nothing before his eyes, thought of another stratagem.[8] After the capitulation of Germany the Anglo-American armies should not retreat to their occupation zones, as agreed previously with the Russians, until and unless the latter became more amenable about Eastern Europe. The vision of Russian and Anglo-American soldiers standing eyeball to eyeball and glaring at each other until such time as the Soviets would behave did not meet with approval among the Americans. President Harry Truman, an admirer of Churchill's, perhaps would have gone along with the policy of pressuring the Russians, especially because at San Francisco Molotov was again making trouble about voting procedures and membership in the United Nations.[9] But the American chiefs of staff, whose advice was now decisive, were against any such confrontation with the Soviets. The Americans' attention was on the Pacific war, and contrary to what has sometimes been alleged, military opinion in this country was nearly unanimous on the need of Soviet assistance against Japan. Quite apart from professional advice, Churchill's scheme was impractical for psychological and political reasons. Public opinion in both Britain and America was eager for peace and continued friendship with Russia. Few would endanger that friendship for the sake of some Balkan country, or because one person rather than another with an unpronounceable name should become the Prime Minister of Poland. The Soviets were well aware of the facts of life of democratic politics. With the war coming to an end, the almost dictatorial powers that the British Cabinet and the American President exercised over their respective countries' foreign and military policies were bound to be terminated. Churchill begged Stalin not to ride roughshod over the "deepest convictions of the English-speaking democracies." But the dictator remembered what Roosevelt had said at Yalta: Congress and American public opinion would not allow American troops to stay in Europe beyond two years after Germany's capitulation. What good were "deepest convictions" without any troops to back them up?

8 | THE USES OF REVOLUTION

What was the Bolshevik Revolution for? Has it been a success? These questions might seem to provide good copy for one of those half-indignant, half-satirical commentaries on Western interpretations of their history with which Soviet writers like to regale their readers. But to the maker of the Revolution this question would not have appeared preposterous. Practically on his deathbed Lenin pondered the meaning of the event that had inscribed his name indelibly on the pages of history.

He did not express contrition or repentance. He was not the man to exclaim, "Plekhanov (or Martov), thou has conquered!" But Lenin was a Marxist, brought up in the tradition that his ideology was a binding picture of social and historical reality and not merely a party program or campaign oratory. Did the Revolution accord with the gospel of Marxism? If not, what could justify this departure from the science of history? Would not the slighted Marxian gods of history take revenge for 1917?

The occasion for these reflections by Lenin was Sukhanov's *Notes on the Revolution,* a garrulous, enchanting chronicle of the events by one who, though considering himself a militant Marxist, could not accept the Great October. Here was an echo of the taunts and warnings that Plekhanov, Martov, and others had expressed before the Bolsheviks embarked on their great adventure: Russia was not civilized enough, the level of her economy was not far enough advanced, for her to start on the path toward socialism; if the Russian proletariat tried to take power prematurely, it would in the end only disgrace itself; and so on. The great strategist of the revolution had then made light of such warnings, but now it was

January 1923, and Lenin was lying semiparalyzed, a virtual prisoner of the Politburo, forbidden to engage in any political activity. A few days before he had written a memorandum containing a scathing characterization of his eventual successor. His illness accentuated his fears for the future: the party he had built up was in the hands of quarrelling oligarchs; bureaucratism and Russian chauvinism were already encrusting the whole machinery of the Soviet state.

Were all those phenomena accidental, or a function of personalities, or was the explanation more fundamental? Was the decision of 1917 somehow responsible for the bureaucratic rot and oppression of 1923? Here is the *cri de coeur* of Lenin's: What else could we have done? He writes almost incoherently, "What if the complete hopelessness of the situation, having by the same token increased the strength of the workers and peasants tenfold opened for us the possibility of laying the foundations of civilization in a different way from all other Western European countries?"[1] But the meaning is clear enough: yes, the Revolution was a departure from the canons of orthodoxy. It was compounded of despair and of a unique opportunity. If spurned by the Bolsheviks, this opportunity might not have come again.

In his memorandum Lenin alternates between scornful references to Sukhanov or his Menshevik ilk as "pedant" and "coward," and snatches of inner dialogue. "Culture" is a word that used to infuriate him in the mouths of his enemies, who said: Russia had not enough "culture" to build socialism; his own tactics in 1917 were "uncultered"; they were those of an anarchist, not a true Marxist heir to the democratic and liberal tradition. But now, intermingled with scorn is Lenin's self-questioning. Yes, we did not have enough culture, we do not have it yet. But was it so wrong *first* to conquer power "and then already on the basis of the worker peasant power and the Soviet system to start catching up with other nations?" Is it not a part of the civilizing mission to begin by chasing out the landowners and capitalists "and then start the movement toward socialism? In what books have you read that such changes of the usual historical process are impermissible or impossible?"[2]

One is tempted to answer: in Karl Marx. But Lenin had other than theoretical reasons for this self-questioning. The gist of his own criticism of his party machine and its current rulers had been precisely that: a lack of culture. That Ordzhonikidze could hit an opponent, that Stalin and Dzerzhinskii could whitewash this and much worse instances of grossness and oppression, had been to him a source of deep humiliation and depression. They in turn could only be amazed by such squeamishness in the man who had sanctioned revolutionary terror, and who, when well, used to quote approvingly that one does not enter the realm of the Revolution in white gloves and on a polished floor.

Lenin succeeds, at least on paper, in reassuring himself. Yes, the decision of October 1917 was the correct one. Napoleon had rightly proclaimed, "On s'engage et puis on voit." And if those Menshevik pedants are shocked by the Russian Revolution, let them just wait. They will see how "new revolutions in the much more populous and socially much different countries of the East will display even more singular characteristics than the Russian Revolution." With this defiant taunt Lenin concluded, except for his subsequent critique of Stalin's administrative methods, his literary activity.

Six years after the Revolution its maker still groped for its meaning and relationship to the creed that had guided his life. If one discounts the circumstances under which the article was produced, written by a sick and embittered man, one is still struck by Lenin's evaluation of the event. The Revolution was not a triumphant entry into the promised land. It was the beginning of a long and tedious process of laying down the cultural foundations on which in turn could be built the bases for the development of socialism. But apart from this attempt to fit the Russian Revolution into the scheme of Marxism, Lenin suggests that, Marxism or no Marxism, we are in the presence of a world revolutionary surge. Other societies, still less ripe for socialism according to the Marxist timetable than Russia had been in 1917, will go through cataclysms the likes of which orthodox Marxists cannot even imagine. That part of his prophecy has certainly been verified and is the source of his successors' most vexing dilemma.

Stalin is not usually credited with a penchant for ideological introspection. But shortly before his death he rephrased Lenin's question and reverted to the then distant events of 1917: "What should the proletariat and its party do in a country—including our country—where conditions favor seizure of power by the proletariat and the overthrow of capitalism . . . but where agriculture, despite the growth of capitalism, still remains so scattered among numerous small and medium owner-producers that there appears no possibility of raising the question of expropriating these producers?" Stalin answers, attributing his solution of the problem to Lenin: "Favorable conditions for seizure of power by the proletariat should not be allowed to slip by; power should be seized without waiting for the time when capitalism contrives to ruin the many millions of small and medium producers."[3] As to the original difficulty, Stalin piously rejects a forcible solution, that is, "expropriating the small and middle producers in the countryside and socializing their means of production." Yet this is precisely what he had undertaken and carried through in his forced collectivization. It is scarcely credible that he could have deceived himself in 1952 to the point where he came to believe that collectivization had been a voluntary process. Yet he then wrote about collectivization by force: "Marxists cannot agree to take this senseless and criminal course . . . since such a course would undermine every possibility of success of the proletarian revolution and would drive the peasantry for a long time into the camp of enemies of the proletariat."

Thus, both the maker of the Revolution and his successor tried to soothe their ideological conscience and to fit the Bolshevik Revolution into the Marxist scheme of things. Their different emphases are interesting. Lenin never emancipated himself entirely from the Social Democratic tradition. His continuous use of "culture" and "civilization" is characteristic. Once the necessary brutal task had been accomplished, the sense of revolution had to be sought above all in changed human relations. This was to be the immediate consequence of the changed power and property structure. In the first days of the Bolshevik regime, his self-delusion on this count was so great that he would often repeat in speeches, "For the first time in Russian history the man with a rifle is not feared." This belief could not withstand his subsequent experience as the ruler of Soviet

Russia. But intermittently to the end he groped for the meaning of the Revolution, not only in great historical but also in immediate human terms. At the very end, when he saw that this element of "culture" was sadly missing in the society he had created, he still projected his dream for the future: at least the foundations for a more humane society had been laid. By curbing the party oligarchs and by introducing simple proletarians into the central party organs, one could save the Soviet system from bureaucracy and corruption. Above all, the Bolshevik Revolution had lit the beacon of hope for those Eastern countries for which the orthodox Marxist would have decreed a patient endurance of further decades of oppression and backwardness. The Revolution had not turned out to be what it had promised in 1917, but it had freed Marxism from a fatalistic bondage to the assumed laws of history and restored to the doctrine, and to the millions of people who followed it, militancy and hope.

For Stalin, the retrospective justification of the Revolution was much more mechanical in nature. There is no heart-searching inquiry into the "cultural" meaning of the event, into its human implications for the rulers and the ruled. One could not let a favorable opportunity of seizing power slip by. Power meant the ability to perform huge tasks of social engineering, tasks that the orthodox Marxists would await dully for history to perform for them. An efficient organization of society and technological progress were the goals that justified the Revolution, just as they justified the "criminal course" Stalin had taken in liquidating the individual peasant holdings. Who could have asked for more at that stage of history? Lenin's musings on "culture" would undoubtedly have been dismissed by Stalin, as were Lenin's strictures on his own personality, for the lapse of a sick man into a sentimentality unworthy of a revolutionary, of a real Bolshevik. Had Stalin expressed himself frankly, he well might have subscribed to the philosophy enunciated by a Red Army commander to Gorky: "Civil War—it is nothing . . . I will tell you frankly, comrade, it is easy to oppress the Russian. We have so many people, everything is in a mess; you burn a village, so what? In due time it would burn by itself anyway."[4]

Both Lenin and Stalin projected in their retrospective views of the Revolution their own self-image: Lenin's being that of a liberator who tried to lead Russia out of oppression and "unculturedness" and save her from a pseudo-revolution; Stalin's being that of a builder of a new civilization who rescued Communism from theoretical and personal wranglings that threatened it with dissolution on Lenin's death and then set it on a course cruel but purposeful. Both men admitted, even if in a roundabout way, that the revolutionary decision of 1917 was against the teachings of classical Marxism. But both, being Marxists, sought a vindication of this non-Marxist beginning in the subsequent Marxist content of the continuing revolution. But to some of their opponents it was this first step that prejudged decisively the future course of the Revolution. Having been conceived in an un-Marxist way, it would never be able to retrieve a real socialist and democratic meaning. Has the experience of subsequent years helped to decide that debate?

Lenin's emancipation from the precepts of classical Marxism was rendered possible by the fact that the Great War had made the whole pre-1914 world of liberal and socialist concepts appear unreal and irrelevant. It is a measure of how far we ourselves have departed from that world that the scruples and hesitations of the Bolsheviks' socialist opponents in 1917 appear to us ridiculous, if not indeed imbecile. Yet being good Marxists, people like Martov and Tseretelli thought mainly in terms of historical precedents and laws. It seems incredible that a man as intelligent as Martov, who had discerned and fought Lenin's dictatorial tendencies long before 1914, would in 1917 consistently proclaim against any measure of repression against Bolshevism. But this contradiction is easily explicable. Before 1914 the Russian revolutionary movement had been in the main a conspiracy and, as such, was always in danger of being seized by a ruthless minority. But in 1917 Russia became a democracy, "the freest country in the world." To suppose that a country of 150 million free citizens could be seized and run by a minority, that the Bolshevik Party, which for all the eccentricity of its leader, was a Marxist party containing many members with genuine democratic feelings, would yield itself to such a design would have meant the repudiation of everything which Martov and others had for decades believed in and worked for. History taught that the main, if not the only, danger to progressive revolutions lay in right-wing conspiracies and plots, in the threat of a Thermidor followed by a Napoleon. The Bolshevik Revolution prevailed largely because its opponents lived still in the nineteenth century, when ideologies were held to be binding representations of social and historical reality and not merely conglomerations of slogans or quasi-religious visions.

The insistence of modern philosophy on the supreme importance of calling things by their right name finds a strong vindication in the story of the Revolution. Was there anything Marxist or Social Democratic about the Bolshevik postulates and activities between April and October 1917? A large proportion if not indeed a majority of those who carried out the October coup and who stood armed guard over the infant Soviet regime during its first weeks professed themselves left Socialist Revolutionaries and outright anarchists of various hues. Yet the allegiance or acquiescence of the working class in the large cities could not have been won by the party of only Lenin and Trotsky. It had also to be the party of Marx and Engels. Most of all, the Revolution could not have been preserved except in the spirit and name of Marxism. Anarchism and pacifism were sufficient to overthrow the old regime, but to retrieve Russia from anarchy and dissolution, one had to have an ideology with a concrete plan for both an ordered society and an international order. The Bolsheviks' anarchism gained them the soldiers and sailors who stormed the Winter Palace and the Moscow Kremlin, and much more important, the passivity of the masses who simply refused to defend any vestige of the established order and its institutions. But anarchism could not have brought to the Bolshevik side the ex-tsarist officers who helped win the Civil War, the engineers and other "bourgeois specialists" who began to restore the Russian economy, and finally those members of the intelligentsia of all political persuasions who simply wanted to work for their country.

Yet as to the concrete meaning of this Marxism within the Communist setting, Lenin and his successors have always been in a quandary. A militant socialist like Rosa Luxemburg, despite all her temperamental affinity for Bolshevism, could not help wondering, at news of the Revolution, what there was spceifically Marxist about it. The very name "Soviet" chosen to baptize the society and regime that they created has epitomized the Bolsheviks' dilemma. It was a word pregnant with meaning in 1905 and 1917, symbolizing to the masses of soldiers and workers that theirs was a direct form of democracy, unlike bourgeois parliamentarism of the West. Yet taken literally, the term was almost meaningless: "Soviet society" means a society of councils, and very shortly it became absurd in relation to what was going on in Russia. No Western parliament was as distant from real decision-making as was the whole network of soviets in Soviet Russia by, say, 1925.

Having seized power and concluded peace, the Bolsheviks could have claimed that their objectives were to put Russia on her feet and to modernize their society. But again those were hardly specifically Marxist objectives, and in achieving them, the Bolsheviks would have had the hearty support of most of the population and no need to set up a one-party state. Was it, then, the "chasing out of the landowners and capitalists" that Lenin represented at times as the "socialist" achievement of the Revolution? But the fact remains that it was Lenin himself who struggled for some weeks after October against what he considered (rightly, from the Marxist point of view) as a premature nationalization of industry, who reintroduced private enterprise in the NEP, and who dreamed of interesting foreign capitalists to invest in Russia. Was socialism then "electrification plus Soviet power," as Lenin explained on another occasion? As with many dazzling slogans, this one will hardly withstand reflection as to what it actually means.

Both Lenin and his successor were much more convincing in explaining what was *not* Marxism. Workers' control of industry, Lenin said rightly, was anarcho-syndicalism and had nothing to do with the precepts of Marx. Stalin was equally correct when he characterized the plea for complete equalization of wages as "petty bourgeois" rather than socialist in spirit. This then was the negative use of the ideology: Marxism was being invoked to strip Soviet society precisely of those quasi-anarchist features that enjoyed the widest popular support, and whose promise had contributed to the Bolshevik triumph in 1917 and in the Civil War.

In fact, much of the content of the ideology was replaced for

Lenin and his followers by a sense of commitment and struggle, accompanied by an almost Nietzschean revulsion against the pre-1914 world. When at a meeting of the Comintern one of the foreign Communists was bold enough to suggest that a revolution, after all, should have the tangible result of improving the welfare of the workers, Lenin exploded: "Revolution should be undertaken only if it does not injure too much the situation of the workers. I ask, is it allowable in the Communist party to speak in such a way? That is a counterrevolutionary way of speaking . . . When we established the dictatorship of the proletariat the workers became more hungry, and their standard of living went down. The victory of the workers is impossible without sacrifices, without a temporary worsening of their situation."[5] It would be hard to imagine a statement more at variance with the spirit and message of Marxism, with its assumption that revolution itself is a rational step designed not to destroy or humiliate the rich and powerful, but to provide a concrete way of rescuing the masses from their poverty and securing the workers, even during the period of transition, an improvement in their material well-being. Communism tears Marxism away not only from its historico-deterministic moorings, but also from much of its materialistic setting. Marx's criticism of capitalism was not that it neglects technology and the development of society's productive power, but on the contrary that its enormous stress on and effectiveness in these respects do not translate themselves into a steady and concrete improvement of the people's standard of living. To assert that revolution in itself and the dictatorship of the proletariat are the supreme goals of socialism is not Marxism.

m The attempt to find out what the Revolution had been fought for provided the background of the political struggle of the 1920s. With the Kronstadt rebellion, the really populistic "soviet" side of the Revolution went down to defeat. From then on, "Central Committee" and then "Politburo" would have been a more appropriate prefix to Russia than "Soviet." Trotsky, then Zinoviev, then Bukharin tried to reclaim Marxism-Leninism as the solid foundation in their opposition to the ascendant current of politics in the USSR, but they found out that instead of solid ground they were standing on a disintegrating ice floe. When in 1927 Trotsky attempted before the Central Committee to invoke the historico-rationalistic arguments that had been the staple of the Marxist discourse before 1917, he aroused general hilarity. As he began, "The worker in 1905 . . . ," there were shouts that Trotsky proposed to read his collected works, that instead of talking of the worker in 1905 he should tell his judges what he had said at the Iaroslav railway station a few days ago, or if indulging in historical reminiscences he should explain how he had "betrayed" Lenin between 1905 and 1914. The only use of history left in Stalin's Russia was that of a police dossier. Not the Marxian categories, but first a majority of delegates, then the command of the secret police were the determining factors in political decisions.

At the Fifteenth Party Congress Stalin assured his hearers that were Engels alive, he would exclaim, "May the devil take the old formulas: Long live the victorious revolution in the USSR."[6] Marxism in Russia had thus suffered a complete attrition. Its use as an official theology reminds one of the cults of those primitive tribes that have forgotten the identity and functions of their gods, but keep worshiping the symbols and objects for reasons they cannot explain. Was socialism achieved in 1936, as Stalin declared? In 1955 his chief collaborator Molotov was publicly reproved for affirming that Russia was *then* entering the era of socialism. Nor was Khrushchev more successful in attempting to warm up the old concepts and enthusiasms. The Twenty-second Party Congress proclaimed in 1961 that in 1980 the USSR would be entering the era of Communism, but beyond a set of statistics the party ideologues exhibited considerable vagueness as to how new this better world would be. Khrushchev's successors, judging by the Twenty-third Party Congress, have already forgotten about the majestic vistas for 1980, preferring to concentrate sensibly enough on the greater abundance of consumers' goods for the 1970s.

Today, after Lenin, Stalin, and de-Stalinization, the prophecy closest to the mark seems to be that of one who disapproved of the Bolshevik Revolution but who also acquiesced in it, though not for ideological or idealistic reasons. Gorky, in his somber assessment of the Russian peasant and of the Civil War, wrote: "and like the Jews, led by Moses out of the Egyptian bondage, so will die the half savage, dumb and heavy people of the Russian countryside . . . Their place will be taken by a new breed of people—literate, smart, energetic. I do not think that they will be the (proverbial) 'pleasant and engaging Russian people' but they will be, finally, businesslike men, skeptical and indifferent to everything which does not bear directly on their needs. They will not think readily about Einstein's theories or about the significance of Shakespeare or Leonardo da Vinci, but probably they will spend money on (biological) experiments and will undoubtedly appreciate the importance of electrification, the value of an agronomist, the advantage of having tractors.'''[7]

Subject to some corrections, this is not a bad picture of the mentality of the average Russian, or for that matter of the citizen of any other industrialized country. But Gorky, who thought that this emancipated Russian nation would be able to take a hard, unsentimental look at its history, would be astounded today to find Russia's past as well as her present still subject to ideological controls by a regime that claims to embody Marxism. To paraphrase what young Lenin wrote about capitalism, many a Russian must feel that he suffers today both from socialism and from the insufficient development of socialism in his country.

This assessment of the work of the Bolshevik Revolution can be subjected to two lines of criticism. One, which would now be classified as conservative but which really bespeaks the point of view of pre-1914 liberalism, argues that the trouble lies with the original ideology and not with the alleged or real abandonment of it by the Bolsheviks. The rigid pseudo-scientific apparatus of Marxism made those who followed it impotent in a revolutionary situation and enabled the others who used it cynically to rationalize their lust for power and oppression. What is worse, the distorted version of Marxism, when genuinely believed in by the first generation of Bolsheviks, was productive of fanaticism rather than a rational and humane approach to the problem of social transition.

The second criticism, which might be called the neo-Bolshevik line, would still adhere to the main lines of Lenin's response to the Mensheviks: whatever pedant or bookish arguments can be adduced against either the Revolution or the development of Communism since then, it is silly to quarrel with history or to expect progress to be achieved painlessly. The Revolution was not a rape performed by a small minority upon a huge nation and eventually upon the whole European civilization. It happened because the old was decayed and incapable of regeneration. Whatever the price, the Revolution lit a beacon of hope for the oppressed masses everywhere, and in that sense it transformed and humanized even its enemies, for the challenge of Communism was largely responsible for capitalism reforming itself and being compelled to emancipate the millions held in colonial subjugation. In the case of Russia, it is granted that the Revolution brought terrible sufferings and abuses, but those have been a by-product of the country's backwardness and hence of the society's inability to perform the needed task of reconstruction under civilized conditions. Yet for all the ravages of Stalinism and the still prevailing lack of freedom, Communism has imparted vitality and purpose and provided the necessary material bases for a future freer life. The work of the Revolution, this argument holds, can thus be criticized in terms of nostalgia for the pre-1914 world or—an argument applicable to all great historical events—of things that could have been done "differently," that is, more humanely. But any rational activity, including the writing of history and projections for the future of politics, must come to terms with reality. And if so, then the October Revolution cannot be treated as a perversion of the "good one" of February 1917, as a huge mistake or a crime, or be subjected to historical nitpicking: this was good, that was bad, this went too far, and so on.

Many in the West would find it difficult or at least embarrassing to question the main lines of this argument, which demonstrates how much the self-appraisal of the Russian and even the Bolshevik Revolution has entered the mainstream of Western thought.[8] But some points of this argument require closer scrutiny. For example, has Russia's advance as an industrial and over-all power been due to Communism? It would be difficult to refute the thesis that, in view of the country's size, resources, and rate of industrial growth for some decades before 1914, it would have been difficult for Russia *not* to achieve the preeminent position she now holds as one of the world's two super-powers. There is something schizophrenic in the regime's boastfulness: the main element in its self-praise has always been that no other system has been able to overcome its own huge mistakes as successfully as the Soviet one, that no other nation could have endured so much in the way of mismanagement and crimes by its rulers as the Russians.[9]

As to the significance of the Bolshevik Revolution for the world at large, one is also constrained to make a few ungracious qualifications. That Communism holds the unique key to the rapid modernization of a Western society is sufficiently refuted by the example of Japan. But the universality of the appeal of Communism requires one comment that may serve also as the final reflection on the Bolshevik Revolution.

Communism was born out of one world war, and it experienced its greatest expansion as a consequence of another. It is strange, in view of Communism's explicit rejection of pacifism, that its most potent attraction was its vision of an eventual peaceful world order. In the wake of the bloodiest of wars, the sacrifices and sufferings of a revolution loomed almost insignificant as against the promise of a world where the extinction of exploitation and imperialism would lead to the abolition of war and the eventual universal confederation of socialist states. Capitalism had led to 1914. The Second International had proved impotent to arrest that development. Hopes for the expansion of Communism after 1921 were often based on the probability of a recurrence of an imperialist war, and people as astute as Trotsky and Radek often postulated the probability and imminence of an Anglo-French or Anglo-American collision. The League of Nations was resented and abused by Soviet spokesmen not only as a possible nucleus of anti-Soviet coalitions but also as a dangerous attempt to recreate a capitalist world order. Even the absolute subordination of foreign Communism to the interests or, rather, commands of Stalin's Russia could be rationalized as the necessary preliminary for the establishment of a supranational Communist world order which, however cruel and destructive its beginnings, would eventually spare the world its greatest scourge.

Beginning with 1948, this most hopeful legacy of the Bolshevik Revolution could no longer be maintained. The Yugoslav conflict showed that Communism possessed no secret formula for dissolving conflicts between states that share its basic assumptions. And with the ripening of the Sino-Soviet conflict, the tenet in which, whatever their other evasions and improvisations of the doctrine, Lenin and his companions genuinely believed—that communism provided the only true internationalism and way of abolishing war —appears as illusory as many other hopes of 1917. In the Chinese Communists' trampling upon old formulas and cautions and their extolling of action over theory, the Soviet leaders might see (though they are not likely to, historical imagination not being their strong point) parallels to the Bolsheviks' adventurous pragmatism and in their own reactions—at times pleading, at times threatening, still half-heartedly hoping for a reunion—the perplexed strivings of Plekhanov and Martov.

9 | TITOISM

It is perhaps insufficiently realized how the movement that received its first organizational expression one hundred years ago has colored our political and sociological concepts and our terminology. Our grandchildren may not live under Communism, but the grandchildren of our political scientists and sociologists, if they should follow the professions of their grandfathers, will most certainly discourse about "revisionism," "Titoism," "Marxism," and all the other "isms" that Communist practice has almost hypnotically induced us to use. We know that there is no such thing as "Bismarckism" or "Disraelism," and that the term "Gladstonian liberalism" represents a more meaningful and somehow more dignified description of an ideology than the various "isms," many of which have simply been taken over from the pejorative terms of Communist propaganda.

As one who has succumbed to the fashion and used "Titoism" in the title of a book, I cannot now dissociate myself from this wretched practice. But we should remember that an uncritical acceptance of a term very often forms an initial barrier to our understanding of the phenomenon under discussion. To digress, one may nevertheless say that to talk about Titoism is certainly not as misleading as to refer to certain pehnomena in the contemporary Communist world as "revisionism" or "neo-revisionism." Eduard Bernstein, that most humane and democratic man, would turn over in his grave were he to realize that he is being lumped together with, or somehow thought related to, a motley company including Marshal Tito and various dissident Polish and Hungarian Communists. He would not be pleased, I think, even with the attempts to connect him with certain theories and practices of avant-garde art and literature that arouse the ire of Communist bureaucrats. Let us then protect the reputation of revisionism for what it was—an attempt to rethink Marx and bring him up to date in terms of social and economic facts of the 1890s—and let us guard this definition like the apple of our eye.

Turning now to Titoism, I submit that the term, if used at all, properly describes certain phenomena in the Communist world centered around the Communist Party of Yugoslavia between roughly the years 1947 and 1953. What happened both before and after in Eastern Europe, although organically connected with the resistance of the Yugoslav Communists to Moscow, is still of a somewhat different character. In brief, Titoism is perhaps a proper name for a historical moment, but not for an ideology or a deviation. For one thing, it is impossible to imagine Titoism without Stalinism, or again, to be pedantic, to imagine Tito's rebellion without Stalin as its target.

But the subject of Titoism, as it is usually thought of, obviously has a broader connotation. This broader meaning might best be translated as resistance on the part of a Communist Party to the domination of the Russian Communists. Another expression, "national Communism," will not do, for reasons that will be spelled out later.

Titoism in this broader meaning has a long and distinguished ancestry. The very foundation of the movement that was to give birth to Communism, the Second Congress of the Russian Social Democratic Party in 1903, witnessed a "Titoist" episode. The representatives of the Bund demanded and failed to obtain a wide organizational autonomy within Russian Social Democracy. That Lenin later chastised those, such as Rosa Luxemburg, who held that the plea for national independence has no place in a socialist program, was to make the future national dilemma of Communism only sharper. When the political and ideological centralism inherent in Communism was combined with the plea for the fullest state and national independence, it became obvious that the two could not coexist without clashes. Eventually one of the principles had to come to express the political reality, while the other one had to atrophy into a mere window dressing and propaganda point.

This paradox was concealed, as were so many during the earlier period of Soviet Communism, by the personality and policies of Lenin. It was also minimized and obscured by the victory of Communism in only one country. Had the Soviets triumphed in 1920 in Poland, or especially in Germany, infant Communism would have been faced with such a Titoist dilemma that its chances for survival as an international movement might well have been fatally damaged. It was well for Communism that the USSR was allowed to grow powerful without any other Communist state being in existence to disrupt this illusion of the compatibility of the doctrine with national independence.

To be sure, even with Russian Communism this issue soon manifested itself. With Lenin on his deathbed, the problem of the domination of Moscow over the affairs of the Communist parties of the Ukraine and Georgia was raised at the Twelfth Congress of the Russian Communist Party in 1923. This Congress is instructive on the issue on two counts. First, it demonstrated the inherent impossibility of solving the conflict of sovereignty between Communism and the individual state within the framework of Communist doctrine as formulated by Lenin. Second, it furnished ample proof that "Titoism" cannot be described simply as national Communism. Titoism was not quite that and at the same time much more than that.

On the first count, among the many complaints heard about domination by Moscow and the Great Russians (and this was in 1923!), not a single one was accompanied by any idea for a solution. They all dwelt on such phenomena as the presence of too many Russian officials in the other republics or the rude behavior of the Moscow authorities. The boldest critic, Christian Rakovski, prime minister of the Ukraine, demanded that nine-tenths of the proposed powers of the federal commissariats (the USSR was not officially proclaimed until the next year) be taken away from them and given to the constituent republics. But how could this have helped? The basic policies and the ideology had to be the same, and nobody could question that without ceasing to be a Communist. All the federal commissariats could be abolished, but the "correct" policies toward the peasants, industry, civic freedom, and so forth still had to be formulated in Moscow.

On the second count, though the pleas were being uttered on behalf of the Ukrainians, Georgians, and all the rest, it is difficult to see in them any pure and simple nationalism (and perhaps there is no such thing). Rakovski became a Ukrainian by assuming the chairmanship of the Council of Commissars of the Ukrainian Soviet Republic. Mdivani and Makharadze, the Georgian dissidents, had worked for and greeted the Russian Soviet Army, which had then destroyed the short-lived independence of their country. Their opposition to Great Russian domination fed upon being dismissed, demoted, or reduced in the extent of their own powers. To be sure, by a simple psychological process they soon became not only disappointed or threatened power seekers, but also spokesmen for some of their constituents' national grievances. Still, their position was logically untenable, and that fact, as well as the strength of the party leadership, made their defeat inevitable.

The existence of the Comintern in the period 1919-1939 provides further proof that there was a complete incompatibility between Communism as fashioned in the Bolshevik Revolution and non-Russian nationalism. One cannot cite a single case of major defection from the Communist ranks in those years based on the rebel's argument that the national interests of his country were being sacrificed for those of the USSR. There were many discussions within the individual parties, notably in countries with a heterogeneous population, as to the most desirable nationality policy to be followed. There were defections based on, or alleged to be based on, such concepts as Trotskyism, Bukharinism, and ultraleftism. But no Comintern congress since the second, held in 1920, had ever considered the problem of the clash of nationalism with Communism. There were no protests heard when at the Third Congress Lenin, in a roundabout and somewhat embarrassed way, suggested that one of the good works the foreign Communists might do would be to follow the activities of the Russian émigrés abroad, something that his "excellent Cheka," as he used to call it, was still not fully prepared to do. The notion of the supranational character of the Third International was already very frail by 1922. When a group of Russian Communists chose to complain to the Executive of the Comintern about the conditions in their own party and cited ample and frightening evidence of the police methods already in use against the opposition, their complaints were brushed aside. They were told that in effect they were helping the Mensheviks and the White Guardists by spreading such slanders about the Russian Communist Party and its leaders.

Internationalism and Communism could not coexist. Soon all Communist parties, whether in France or in Iceland, became part of what Léon Blum called "a Russian Nationalist Party." Nor can this fact be associated exclusively with Stalinism. Many things would have been different had Trotsky, or even Bukharin, emerged as the supreme leader, but no Communist Party would have been less subservient to the interests of the Russian state. Only the appearance of Communism in power in a major state could have challenged this organic connection between Communism and Russian nationalism.

How deep this connection became is well illustrated by what happened at the height of Stalinism, in the thirties. The disgraced and then liquidated leaders Trotsky, Bukharin, and Zinoviev had all been men with enormous followings among foreign Communists, men for whom Stalin was an upstart provincial who knew neither French nor German and was certainly unfit for the leadership of an international movement. Yet at this very time the worship of Stalin among foreign Communists surpassed any previous apotheosis of Lenin. Trotsky, for all his romantic appeal, managed to create only a puny movement, and his own unwillingness to speak more harshly of the Soviet regime, as distinguished from Stalin, must also be attributed to his realization that he would have had no attraction for foreign Communists were he to attack Russia. Yet before 1914 few Russian Marxists hesitated to condemn some national characteristics of their countrymen, or to wish a military defeat on their country, since it would lead to a political liberation. The purges of the foreign parties in the thirties do not alter this general picture. They bore a sympathetic resemblence to the same phenomena within the USSR, and again it would be difficult to find a genuine case of opposition to the Russian character of Communism being given as the reason for the purge of an individual or a group.[1]

This character of foreign Communism, as well as the emotional

Russophilia that became ingrained in every Communist, bore with them a corresponding danger for the future. A less emotionally charged relationship would have prevented some of the violence of the future reactions of disillusionment and betrayal. In the case of Yugoslavia, this emotional nexus was to play a particularly vital role.

It might be asked how aware the Russians were of the danger that was paradoxically inherent in the spread of Communism to other countries. Certainly the limitations of their own dogma did not allow them to ponder the problem, and even now they do not realize the full extent of the dilemma. But as one follows Stalin's policy during and immediately after World War II, one detects some apprehension in the back of his mind as to the possible effects of too rapid a spread of Communism. At one point during the war the Russians evidently considered the possibility of what might be called the Finnish solution for many of their future satellites. These governments would be bound to Russia in questions of foreign policy and would ban the anti-Russian elements from their political life, but the regimes would not be completely or even largely Communist in character. How long this phase was to last is not clear. In any case, after the Soviet conquest of Eastern Europe and the lack of any serious opposition by the West to its sovietization, these plans were shelved in favor of using people's democracies—that is, of imposing Communist rule with or without the pretense of a coalition with other "progressive" parties. In this connection the Soviets also had to deal with the feverish anticipation of power on the part of local Communists, who were extremely unwilling to be sensible and take a long-range point of view. In one case, that of Greece, a satellite manqué, there seems to have been a definite attempt to suppress the more impatient wing of the Greek Communist Party. But though Stalin could do almost everything with the foreign Communists, to persuade them to slow down in demonstrating their loyalty to Russia by taking over power in their own countries was beyond even his powers. In Eastern Europe, the complexities anticipated from the emergence of several Communist states could not have been too great. None of the countries were large enough to offer rivalry to Russia, and none of the Communist parties—except possibly those of Yugoslavia and Czechoslovakia, and the latter did not prove an exception after all—were strong enough to seize power and rule over their countrymen without the presence or the threat of Soviet bayonets.

One wonders in this connection about France and Italy, whose Communist parties were to be accused in 1947, at the founding meeting of the Cominform, of not cashing in on the opportunities that were within their grasp following the liberation. A great deal of research remains to be done in order to determine whether the national and coalition posture of those two parties, which persisted well beyond 1945, was due mainly to the nationalistic impetus they had imbibed during the war, to an expectation of coming to power throught the electoral process, or to promptings by the Russians, who, still incredulous over the ease with which things were going their way in the East, may not have wanted to exhaust Western patience by a too-militant threat of Communism in France or Italy.

There was a period in post-1948 Yugoslavia when the government publicists speculated on and regretted the failure of French and Italian Communists to seize power. It was even suggested that this would have been a deadly blow to Stalinism, and that Maurice Thorez and Palmiro Togliatti would certainly have proved as tenacious in defending their nations' independence and honor as Tito was. This thesis must remain one of the great problems of recent history. Certainly one can speculate that Communist France would not have surrendered her empire but would have transformed it into a free federation of nations on the Soviet model, and that Thorez would have proved a less obstreperous partner for the United States than General de Gaulle. But French cooking would have suffered, Picasso would have painted big glaring canvases, and Simone de Beauvoir and Francoise Sagan could not have written their charming novels. One cannot have it both ways.

Another question, this one having been studied but not exhausted, is how deep the seeds of Titoism lay in the relations between the USSR and Yugoslav Communism in the years 1941-1944. Certainly in Communist politics, as in marriage, there is a great tendency, after the breach has occurred, to go back and maximize the importance of early and trivial dissonances, to which nobody attached much importance in the happy days but which now are clearly seen as the first signs of eventual treachery and collison. I have touched on this problem elsewhere, but it requires a more thorough investigation.[2] Following the break, especially between 1949 and 1952, the Yugoslavs published copious memoirs, pamphlets, and diaries, the gist of which was that they had grown disenchanted during the war with the extent of Soviet help, and that the Russians had disregarded their valiant struggles and were asking them to subdue their Communist fervor. They managed to convey the impression that the Yugoslavs were displeased by the Russians' sins of commission and, especially, of omission in regard to themselves. But in their then flamboyant frame of mind, nothing short of Stalin's personal appearance in Marshal Tito's head-quarters would probably have reassured the Partisans that the epochal and decisive nature of their struggles was being fully appreciated in Moscow. Echoes of the Russian irritation with the posturings of Tito and his group appear in the correspondence of two Central Committees in 1948. There the Russians, with con-siderable justification but with terrible psychology, ridiculed such Yugoslav claims as that they had invented Partisan warfare or that their struggle was a major contribution to the Allied victory. Such early discord did not indicate any thought on either side about the slightest possibility of a future split. It is enough to read Dedijer's diary of Milovan Djilas' record of his first visit to Moscow to con-clude that in addition to their ideological tie and loyalty to the USSR, the Yugoslav Communists had what can only be described as a "crush" on the Russians, and on Stalin in particular. To write "Long Live Stalin" on the walls of the captured towns meant compromising the allegedly non-party character of the Partisan movement at a time when Tito was seeking recognition and support from the Western Allies. But the emotional involvement of Yugo-slav Communists was too strong to allow them to be fully states-manlike. There was the business of the red-star, hammer-and-sickle insignia on some of the Partisan units' uniforms, which even the Russians believed went too far. As Tito said in his report at the historic Fifth Congress of the Communist Party of Yugoslavia: "Our Party did not carry out its role of leader in the Liberation War . . . illegally in disguise."[3]

This brings up another point that is extremely important in analyzing Titoism's earliest phase. The high command of the Yugoslav party was with few exceptions extremely young and cohesive in character. If the few relative oldsters are excluded, such as Moša Pijade, the previous purges and splits are seen to have done their work only too well, which later must have led to some rueful comments in Moscow. Thus, no real barrier existed to building a cult of Tito's personality within Partisan ranks. There were no ancient workhorses of the Comintern who could successfully dispute the leadership of Yugoslavs who had been a part of the armed struggle. Compare the situation with the postwar situation in, say, Bulgaria or Czechoslovakia, or even with a Communist Party like the Polish one, whose leadership prior to 1939 had been decimated even more thoroughly than that of the Yugoslav party. In each case Moscow men were available to be sent in, but they would feel scant solidarity or companionship at arms with the men who had been in their countries during the war. The solidarity of the Yugoslav Communist leadership over the years has been truly amazing. Since the elimination of the relatively few "Stalinists" among them in 1948-1949, practically the same men have ruled Yugoslavia as a team for sixteen years. From young Partisan fighters they have grown into middle-aged bureaucrats, without engaging in one of those bloody and criminal rivalries for power that have characterized the life of practically every other Communist Party in power. Even the obvious exception, the case of Djilas, underlines this uniqueness of the Yugoslav party. For Djilas is the rarest of Communist birds, a man who challenged the ruling faction because of ideological and temperamental differences, and not because he craved the top position for himself, and who only then proceeded to erect an ideology.

Of the Eastern Communist parties after the war, the Yugoslav one must have been regarded by the Russians as the most promising and at the same time the most likely to prove troublesome. Religious enthusiasm, as many churches have recognized, can often be a dangerous thing. It tends to interfere with the quiet and prudent worship that is a greater safeguard for remaining within the communion than flights of ecstasy and excitement. Tito's Communists were especially prone to exhibit unreasoning fanaticism and enthusiasm. Their attitude on the Trieste issue threatened a premature clash with the Western Allies. Their abrupt and rapid sovietization of their country complicated the tasks of Soviet policy in the Balkans. One cannot credit the Soviet charge that the Yugoslav Communists wanted them to go to war on the issue of Trieste, but obviously Yugoslav intransigence and haste were jeopardizing the whole cautious timetable of Soviet policy.

Several more substantive issues of the Russo-Yugoslav disagreement culminated in the final break. For all the voluminous writing on the subject, it is difficult to determine which of them was the straw that broke the camel's back. Grievances on the Yugoslav side and suspicions on the Russian side had been accumulating since the end of the war. The disorderly behavior of Russian troops in Yugoslavia provoked Djilas' tactless remarks that the Russians behaved worse than the British, which were conveyed to Moscow. The inadequate Russian support on the Trieste problem led to Tito's speech in Ljubljana on May 28, 1945, which the Russians morbidly interpreted as an attack on them.[1] A careful reading of the speech leads one to believe that Tito's main purpose was to state that the Russians were not supporting him strongly enough, or were acquiescing in Britain's influence in the Balkans, rather than to make any declaration of independence from the USSR. He merely wanted a Soviet reassurance that Yugoslavia was still the USSR's favorite in the Balkans. But the Russians replied with a strong diplomatic protest, the tenor of which must have astounded the Yugoslav officials: their complaint that they were not being loved enough by the Russians was being interpreted as an "attack on the Soviet Union." According to the Russian version, Edward Kardelj, then Tito's right-hand man, soothed the Russian ambassador by assuring him that the Yugoslav Communists were envisaging their country as a future member of the USSR. By 1945 such views were anachronistic, and if Kardelj in fact made this remark, it must have only increased the Russians' suspicions.

The involved subject of the Yugoslavs' economic plans was also leading to mutual recriminations. Just as in foreign policy, so in industrialization the Yugoslav Communists set their goals unrealistically high. The Russians offered them some good advice on the subject, which again was taken with a hurt lovers' feelings. The

Russian comrades explained that Communist enthusiasm was not enough to industrialize a country or to introduce collectivization in a hurry. But the Russians' advice was given out of more than solicitude; they anticipated and even acknowledged the Yugoslavs' demands for economic help. In those days the only "help" Russia was willing to give to her satellites came in the form of the so-called joint companies, which meant that a country's natural resources would be exploited for the dubious return of Soviet expert help and some negligible provision of capital goods by the USSR. Great though the love of Stalin and Russia was in the hearts of the Yugoslav Communists, their conviction that a self-respecting socialist country must industrialize at a rapid pace was equally strong. The tangible proof of Russian selfishness and duplicity in the matter must have been for them the hardest blow up to that time.

Is it reasonable, one might ask, to use terms like love and betrayal when dealing with political systems, and with seasoned politicians? Even if most of Tito's subordinates were young and naive, was not Tito himself a veteran Communist, who had survived and advanced while foreign Communists were being liquidated wholesale in the Russian purges? An analysis of mine couched in such terms was once criticized for not attaching enough importance, indeed for not taking seriously, the "real" ideological issues and differences that produced the conflict. Communists, it was argued, do not quarrel because of hurt vanity, unreasonable suspicions, or even considerations of power; an interpretation expressed in such terms descends to the level of sensationalism. There *must* have been some ideological grounds for the Russians' suspicions of Tito's regime, some basic disagreement with his economic policies.

I think that although the use of personal and emotional explanations of the conflict can be overdone, it is still true that one cannot understand the conflict without taking them into account. And in a sense they also spill over into the realm of ideology. The Yugoslavs' passion for industrialization and their eagerness to communize the Balkans were ambitions and passions bred by ideology. So too was their belief in the omnipotence of the Soviet Union as the representative of the wave of the future, and their consequent inability to understand why the Russians could "deny" them Trieste. All these things were undoubtedly combined, at least on the part of the more experienced Yugoslav leaders—Tito, Pijade, and Kardelj—with a prudent consideration for their own and their country's position. Unlike young hotheads, such as Djilas, they were probably under no illusion that it was enough to be a good Communist and to love Russia in order to remain in Marshal Stalin's good graces. They initiated plans, evidently with the agreement of some Bulgarian Communist leaders, to provide for a closer collaboration of the two countries and an eventual federation. Tito's diplomatic tours of various East European capitals were apparently intended to broaden this pattern. There was nothing inherently disloyal in these policies and trips; the Balkan Federation had a prior Soviet blessing and so did Yugoslavia's de facto protectorate over Albania. But sooner or later Yugoslavia's strenuous politicking among satellites was bound to arouse the Soviet Union's disapproval. That it did not find drastic expression even earlier was probably because the Soviets saw a more urgent task in Eastern Europe, the final reduction of Poland and Czechoslovakia to satellite status.

To deal with a multiplicity of problems, among them the Yugoslav one, the Soviet Union embarked on the creation of a formal instrument of Communist cooperation—the Cominform. The experiment was abortive. Few international institutions of a comparable kind have had such a brief and disastrous history. It failed utterly in its main objective, which was to create an international veneer for the Soviet domination of foreign Communism. It could not cope with the first and only crisis it was supposed to solve, the Yugoslav defection after 1948. It lingered on as a newspaper and a fifth wheel for a few years, its expiration in the backwashes of Stalinism almost unnoticed.

Yet its original concept and functions are certainly interesting and instructive. Its failure illustrates how difficult it was in 1947-1948 for Communism to assume even the appearance of genuine internationalism. After the Tito affair the Cominform died, one might say, of a surfeit of unanimity and sameness. You could not then create an international Communist body, because the Communists agreed too much. You cannot create one now, as Khrushchev and his subordinates discovered, because they disagree too violently. Here is the pathos of Communist history in the last two decades.

Membership in the Cominform was limited to the prize pupils: the two large Western parties and the parties in power in Eastern Europe. Albania was excluded, probably because of its status as a subsatellite. In China the Communists were still struggling for power, and besides, the Chinese were even then assumed to present a special problem, though it was not realized how much of a problem they would turn out to be. Special reasons accounted for the exclusion of the German Communists. The Finnish party must have felt hurt at its exclusion; most people at the time saw Finland as eventually sharing the fate of Poland, or indeed of Latvia or Estonia. The Russian officials who devised the Cominform were faced with the serious problem of deciding what to give as the ostensible purpose of the new organization. They came up with the humorous notion that the participating parties were to exchange information. You do not pay enough attention to agitation, the Poles might say to the Hungarians, and you to propaganda, the Hungarians would presumably reply; and so both could cheerfully ask how the Russian comrades had solved the problem.

The Yugoslavs' performance at the founding meeting was thoroughly in their pre-1948 style: they threw their weight around and sulked at being put in the same class with such inept pupils as the Poles and Rumanians. On the Russian side, it was probably thought the height of generosity and subtle flattery to ordain that the misbegotten institution should have its seat in Belgrade. Somebody must have remembered how in the earliest and most innocent days of the Comintern there were objections to having its seat in Moscow. Some people might draw the wrong conclusion, they thought, from the fact that the capital of the movement should coincide with that of Soviet Russia.

But the Russo-Yugoslav conflict could not be warded off by such contrivances. There were several major developments as it ripened in 1948. One was the Soviet veto of the Balkan Federation. Another was the anti-Tito intrigue within the Communist Party of Yugoslavia that led to the dismissal and then the imprisonment of two Yugoslav Communists, presumably groomed by the Russians as opponents of Tito and intended to be his possible successors: Andrija Hebrang and Sreten Zhujovich. There were open clashes between Soviet advisers and Yugoslav officials. As a result, Titoism was finally born in the spring of 1948.

Among the contemporary explanations for this phenomenon was the usual simplistic one: it was only a put-up job between two scheming Communist countries, a devious attempt to suck in American money and throw Western statesmen off the track. More seriously, many in the West pondered what ideological deviation the Yugoslav Communists were guilty of. Since many people still believe that the roots of the Sino-Soviet dispute lie in the fact that the Chinese won power by concentrating on winning over the countryside, against Soviet instructions to concentrate on winning over the urban workers, it is not surprising that in 1948 Titoism was being examined in the light of its possible relationship with Bukharinism or Trotskyism. The Russians, it was argued, were displeased with their Yugoslav colleagues because they were not collectivizing fast enough, or, to the contrary, because they were bent upon industrializing too rapidly.

More interesting are the interpretations that were probably made by the two parties to the dispute. The Soviet assumption must have been that Tito's Communists would seek Moscow's pardon. Were they to do so, their position would be compromised and the next step would be a leisurely liquidation of the current leadership of the Yugoslav party and its replacement by persons more amenable to Soviet direction. Whether Stalin said, as Khrushchev later claimed, that he could crook his little finger and there would be no Tito, is at least doubtful; Stalin, for all of his vast vanity, was an astute politician. But it was difficult to see how the Yugoslavs could in fact resist the Russian proposals to lay the whole issue before the Cominform and abide by its impartial judgment. Without Russia, Yugoslavia was isolated. The Western powers had not intervened to save the remnants of democracy in Czechoslavakia; there was therefore little hope they were going to protect one Communist dictator against another. The economic considerations in themselves were pressing enough to force the Yugoslavs to a compromise. Their foolhardy policies would sooner or later involve the country in a disaster, and the Yugoslav Communist Party could not hope to soften it without outside help. The harsh and peremptory tone of the Soviet messages to the Yugoslav Central Committee was undoubtedly meant to dispel any hopes that the Tito regime could maintain its posture and still count on the USSR to save it from disaster.

On the Yugoslav side, the attitude that the Russians would come to realize both their hastiness and the unfounded character of their charges must have alternated with a less naive political calculation. An admission of the Yugoslav "errors," which was all that the Russians demanded in the first instance, would have been only a first downward step toward the eventual destruction of the leadership of the Yugoslav party. There had been misunderstandings since 1945 at least, and they had been cleared up. There was no reason to believe that once the Russians saw the justice of the Yugoslav cause, they would not desist.

Thus, the period of Titoism, from 1948 to 1954, can be divided into two subperiods. The first, which extends to 1950, might be called the phase of innocence. The second phase is that of classical Titoism—a posture of open defiance of the USSR and the creation of an ideology to give it a rationale. During the first phase the Yugoslav leadership faced, reluctantly and incredulously, the prospect of a final break. After all, even at the Fifth Party Congress in July 1948 they chanted slogans honoring Stalin. Then, painfully and slowly, Yugoslavia's foreign policy began to diverge from Russia's. Their attitude of suspicion and hostility toward the only quarter from which they could now expect help, the West, gave way—but again, gradually and reluctantly. Their doctrinaire economic policies were for the most part unchanged.

The ideological distress that the Yugoslavs experienced during that period was best expressed in the writings of their chief ideologue of the time, Milovan Djilas. Gradually his viewpoint shifted to a condemnation of Stalin's personal dictatorship and his ascendance within world Communism. It was then easy to take the next step and to consider Russian Communism as warped, although not hopelessly so, by bureaucratism and chauvinism. Along with other Communist heresies, Titoism embraced the myth that there had once been an innocent and perfect type of Communism, which had been corrupted by the men in power in the Soviet Union and by basic defects in the Soviet Union's governmental structure. Thus, the remedy would lie in a return to the original concept, to Communism unspoiled by great-power chauvinism and by bureaucratism. The term "cult of personality" was not yet being used.[5] But by 1950 the Yugoslav Communists were passing from an enchantment with Stalin to an attitude in which they were ready to see in him the prime source of political evil.

The same period, from 1948 to 1950, was one of what might be called wishful polycentrism. The victories of Chinese Communism were reported in the Yugoslav press with a satisfaction that went beyond mere happiness with the success of their coreligionists. It was argued explicitly that the victory of Communism in a country so vast as China was bound to change the whole picture of world Communism, so that the Russians would no longer be capable of lording it over the other parties. All of which shows that our wishes and fantasies often come true, but sometimes in a strange and unexpected form.

In 1950 Titoism became a self-conscious ideology. There was then little left of the early hopes that the Russian Communists would reform. Stalin's tyranny was clearly recognized, but the attacks began to be more general, directed against the whole Soviet system and considerable portions of the Communist doctrine. Much of the earlier illusion that the spread of Communism would automatically cure its own defects disappeared. Shortly after the beginning of the Korean War, there was an agonizing reappraisal of the Chinese and a discarding of the earlier hopes for them. Then came a definite rapprochement, a virtual alliance, with the West. Finally, an end was put to the ruinous economic policies. Titoism came of age.

What then was this newly fledged system, this curiosity, a Communist country separate from the Soviet bloc? In many ways the Yugoslavs simply lopped off the pathological parts of Stalinism from their theories and practice. Stalin's famous dictum—the

.closer one gets to socialism, the sharper becomes the character of the class struggle—was repudiated by the Yugoslav Communists well in advance of Khrushchev's denunciation of 1956. Terrorism was largely abolished, and Yugoslavia moved closer to the traditional practices of Eastern European police states and away from its fantastic Communist perversion. In many ways the regime could well afford this relaxation, since its struggle for independence endowed it with dignity and popularity even in the eyes of opponents of Titoism and its brand of Communism. The repression of Stalinism did not have to be extensive. There were few bona-fide believers in the old communion with the Soviet Union. Many people purged or arrested for Stalinism were in all likelihood victims of personal rivalries or ancient animosities, which even in the most reasonable Communist dictatorships find their expression in ideological denunciations. The sharp edges of the struggle against religion, and against the Catholic Church in particular, were dulled. The average citizen's life became easier.

In foreign policy, Yugoslavia veered toward the theory of coexistence. This was, in fact, the only policy the Communists in Yugoslavia could, or can, adhere to: coexistence of the two blocs is the only guarantee of the continued existence of their own regime. Were the Soviet bloc to disappear, Yugoslavia could not survive as a Communist state. Were the Western powers still further reduced in their sphere of influence, the Soviet Union, even under the post-Stalinist leadership, would have few reasons not to liquidate the inconvenience that Tito's Yugoslavia represents.

Between 1950 and 1954 the Yugoslavs began looking around for an ideological anchor. What makes a Communist system, even at its mildest, a source of perturbance both to its own citizens and to other states is its inability to stand still. Communism is a classical illustration of Pascal's dictum about the tragedy of human existence, in that man is unable not to thrash about violently. The Yugoslav Communists were not content to do away with the major abuses of the doctrine; they needed an ideology of their own. In this period they made a frantic search in many directions. At one time the doctrines of the left wing of the British Labour Party were examined and found wanting. Efforts were made to study the esoteric doctrines and practices of Oriental left-wing movements. To find a meaning for Titoism, its originators engaged in modest missionary activity among the largely formless socialist and left-wing movements in Asia.

The failure of this effort sheds some light on Titoism in the broader meaning of the term—that is, as an attempt to find a form of Communism divorced from the Russian pattern and not subordinate to Moscow. It became evident to the Yugoslav policy makers, though they would return to a similar enterprise later on, that a country of the size of Yugoslavia was simply not capable of successful ideological proselytizing. For all the sympathy that the Yugoslav stance aroused in countries such as India and Burma, there was little relevance for those countries in the Titoist experiment. Their local Communists, like all Communists out of power, were bound to look to a great Communist country for leadership and inspiration. Their left-wing non-Communist movements could likewise find little in the Yugoslav example. Stalinism has become so firmly imprinted on Communist dogma and practice that if it were to be rubbed off completely, there would be precious little of Communism left.

The truth of this statement must have struck the Yugoslav leadership in 1952-1953, when they began a major structural alteration in their system, which they hoped would give a concrete meaning to Titoism. The changes began—and this is an old technique of Communism—with the application of new names. The Communist Party became the League of Communists, the People's Front the Socialist Alliance. Other name changes were designed to increase the difference between Yugoslav terminology and that of the USSR and the satellites. An elaborate constitutional scheme was designed in 1953. In their frenzied search for innovations that would set them as far apart as possible from the Soviet model, the Yugoslav Communist leaders came up with some devices that bring to mind, ironically, the representative schemes of Mussolini's Italy. In fact, were Yugoslavia not a one-party state, its constitutional and administrative structure would lead to a most appalling political chaos.

The same observation can be extended to the elaborate Yugoslav system of local government based on the devices of communes and workers' councils. It would be unfair to dismiss these as window dressing. They represent an honest attempt to establish what might be called grass-roots Communism, really to enlist the masses in the task of government, and to exercise a bona-fide check on the bureaucracy's powers and privileges. But the tragedy and paradox of all Communist attempts in this direction, from Lenin's time to Tito's and Khrushchev's, is that in a sense they only make more essential the ubiquitous grip of the party on all spheres of political, economic, and social life. The more economic and administrative decentralization there is, the more necessary it will become to assure the unity of political centralization. There are periods when the truth of this is not obvious; but there always comes the moment of reckoning when it is seen that the workers' councils, just like Krushchev's *sovnarkhozy,* can lead to economic anarchy or disorganization, and that the structure must therefore be tightened up.[6] It is difficult enough nowadays to secure or preserve a meaningful degree of economic or social pluralism in a democratic country. In a Communist one it is impossible without giving up the basic tenet of the creed.

What, then, is the essence of Titoism in internal politics? It is really an attempt at depoliticization (horrible word) of the average citizen's life. In the classical Communist pattern, which was Stalin's Russia and to a lesser extent Khrushchev's, the average citizen is made aware of the political importance of every social act. Whether he works, goes to an exhibition, or votes, each of those acts is assumed to have a political meaning. There is no "neutral" picture, no casual attitude toward work, no element of personal or frivolous choice in electing an official. In Tito's Yugoslavia, on the contrary, there is a very elaborate set of devices and institutions designed to persuade the citizen that most of his activities are not connected with politics. In theory, the whole constitutional scheme breaks away from the strictures of Marx and Lenin. In his activities as a producer or as a member of the commune, the citizen is allegedly performing objective economic and administrative tasks, not fulfilling a set of directives laid down by an oppressive political authority. Politics is the business of the League of Communists, and the average citizen is relieved of the presence and pressure of Big Brother; indeed, he is asked not to notice that Big Brother exists. The party officials have become obscured in their state and constitutional roles. The Secretary General of the Yugoslav Communist Party has presumably been swallowed up by the President of the federal republic.

This scheme cannot be dismissed as meaningless. Viewed from the pre-1950 perspective, it implies a considerable broadening of the average Yugoslav's freedom, a considerable release from the tensions that accumulate under a more "activist" Communist regime. The citizen is not compelled to be "alert," "vigilant," and "on guard" against the enemies, be they Mensheviks, Stalinists, revisionists, or dogmatists. He is asked to be a good producer, a good participant in the affairs of his own community, and a good Yugoslav as well as a good Serb or Croat.

The trouble with this scheme from the Communist point of view is that if it succeeds too well, it will present a threat to the regime as such. It is impossible to run a Communist state without a nucleus of devoted and ideologically minded people. Bureaucratized as most Communist regimes have become, it is still necessary to have a periodic influx of indoctrinated and politicized people. Without them, and without intermittent ideological mobilization, a Communist regime would inevitably tend in the direction of an old-fashioned authoritarian state à la Salazar or Franco, in which the original ideology has atrophied and the government expects and receives the tolerant apathy of its subjects but in turn sacrifices its original political and economic dynamism.

Nor can a Communist regime use the current Afro-Asian substitute for an ideology—anti-imperialism. With the direct threat of Russian intervention receding, Titoism has not been able to capitalize on nationalism to the same extent as it did during the heroic days of 1948-1950. Along with the emotional impetus of anti-imperialism, it was deprived of the possibility of indulging in its own brand of expansionism. The harsh realities of the international situation of 1950-1957 turned Yugoslavia into an exemplary neighbor of Greece and Italy. Its previous designs on Albania and Bulgaria also gave way to a sober reassessment. It was a depressing prospect of a quiet life that faced the Yugoslav Communist leaders in 1953-1954. The madcap scheme of collectivization was given up. Helped by massive American aid, Yugoslavia's economy was showing gains, thus vindicating the concept of socialist planning. As early as 1921-1922, Lenin had had the insight that socialism in one country could succeed, even without purges, mass resettlements, and a lowering of the standard of living, if the capitalists would help. Now, what Lenin had not dared to dream about in Russia in 1921—that the capitalists would help without exacting concessions in return—was coming true in Yugoslavia. Titoism represented the only concrete success of the West in Eastern Europe; it was not a success of its own making, but was one that has rendered additional dividends in helping preserve Greece from Communism.[7]

But from the point of view of the leadership of the Yugoslav Party, all the advantages of her position in 1953-1954, which undoubtedly were secretly envied by every Communist leader in Eastern Europe, added up to trouble within the party. In the population at large the modest concessions were bound to produce more ambitious aspirations for greater freedom. Capitalism in our day cannot withstand long depressions. The whole rationale of Communism is in turn jeopardized by a long period of ascending prosperity.

The most tangible symptom of the restlessness within the Yugoslav Communist Party was the Djilas affair. It was entirely logical that this erstwhile fanatical Communist and Stalinist should now have become the most severe critic of the remnants of Stalinism in the party, and that he should begin the evolution which within a few years would lead him to become an exponent of democratic socialism and the multiparty system. One is reminded of G. I. Myasnikov, a ferocious Communist terrorist in the Russian Civil War. After the war he kept petitioning the Communist Party to restore freedom of the press "from the monarchist to anarchist press." After disregarding Lenin's fatherly strictures, Myasnikov had to be expelled from the party, then jailed, and finally sent out of Russia. Djilas, obviously a man of much broader intellectual horizons, chose imprisonment.

With the eruption of the Djilas affair in 1953-1954, the Yugoslav Communists took steps to tighten up party discipline and to curtail baneful Western influences. The regime realized the danger of completely losing support among the younger generation. Insofar as the young were concerned, the party ran the danger of falling between two stools: some were bound to regret the good old bad days when there was a sense of purpose in being a Communist, and when a young party member could shock and terrorize his elders. Others would turn to the new gods, imbibe the teachings of Djilas, and admire such inappropriate heroes for a Communist as Aneurin Bevan. A movement that exists largely on the basis of its appeal to the Young—and the Yugoslav party was a classic case in point—cannot afford a sensible eschewing of radicalism of one kind or another.

It was fortunate for the Yugoslav Communists that their dilemma became apparent just as a great change was coming over Russian Communism. The period 1954-1956 witnessed the first phase, as yet prudent and unpublicized, of de-Stalinization. For all its behind-the-scenes character and its lack of the kind of sensational revelations with which Khrushchev would later regale the world, the period must be characterized as substantively the most "liberal" one in post-Stalin Russian politics. It represented, one can assume, a reasoned consensus of the Soviet leadership as a whole (perhaps including Beria and those other alleged Stalinists whom Khrushchev began throwing to the wolves in hopes of obliterating his own tracks) that the despot's policies had been not only criminal but also mistaken. Insofar as foreign relations were concerned, the 1954-1956 view of the Soviet leadership evidently held that the perpetuation of Stalin's policies would place an intolerable strain on the solidarity of the Communist world, and that more flexibility and a greater autonomy for other Communist countries was also needed from the Russian point of view. It was a period of a genuine, or almost genuine, search for an international formula that would assure the Communist bloc of a united position on basic issues and yet relieve the Russians of constant and troublesome vigilance over the day-to-day activities of their satellites. It is understandable that the satellite leaders greeted this shift with apprehension; they could not be sure that the Russians really meant that they should quietly do away with the Stalinist relics in their policies and personnel, and that they should substitute a search for popularity among their peoples for sheer terror and compulsion.

The Russian gestures toward Yugoslavia, at first coy and then brazen in their cordiality—as when Khrushchev and Bulganin invited themselves to Belgrade—were a key motif in this policy. And they enabled Tito and his party, after the initial bewilderment and reluctance to embrace the Russians again, to retrieve a sense of mission and self-importance. Tito was now seen as a pioneer of de-Stalinization, the man who wisely though perhaps prematurely tried to establish the right pattern of relations among the Communist states. Much as he became excessively entangled with the West, he also pioneered the concept of "separate roads" to socialism, thus avoiding those disastrous errors that marked the satellites' policies and which earned them unnecessary troubles with their own populations, such as the Berlin uprising. To be almost like Tito seemed to be the lesson that Khrushchev and his colleagues were imparting to their satellite lieutenants in their travels (collective leadership in those days implied collective traveling).

For their part, by 1956 the Yugoslavs had thrown themselves wholeheartedly into the game. The Russian advances marked for them a welcome break in the ideological isolation that had bred such confusion within the party. Once again they could claim a degree of primacy within Eastern Europe and assuage their own Communist zealots by pointing out that Yugoslavia was an object of emulation by Hungary and Poland. Marshal Tito resumed his trips.

In 1956 the crisis in the Polish Communist Party and the Hungarian rebellion brought a quick and definite end to this phase. It is important to differentiate between those two events not only in terms of their results but also in terms of their histories. Both marked an end, at least temporarily, to the Soviet hope that de-Stalinization of the satellites could be carried out in an orderly and safe way without endangering the very bases of Soviet influence.

In the case of Poland, the Russians obviously expected that Gomulka and his group would be released and given honorable and minor jobs, that the pre-1956 Communist leaders could be sacrificed to the popular wrath as the tools of Stalin and Beria, and that another group of leaders could be put in charge. This scheme was defeated, among other reasons by the foresight of the Polish "Stalinists": realizing what was in store for them, they became overnight fervent nationalists and forced Gomulka's election, not as the director of a museum or a library, as the Russians had hoped, but as First Secretary of the party. How their guile paid off can best be illustrated by the case of Edward Ochab. Head of the party following Bierut's death, Ochab was instrumental in having Gomulka supplant him in that position. He remained within the inner circle and is today the official head of the Polish state—certainly a better fate than befell Rakosi, Farkas, or Chervenkov, three others who were politically liquidated. The Polish October was greeted by the Russians without enthusiasm, to put it mildly. But they were later to discover that in fact they had unwittingly obtained in Poland what they had been clumsily trying to get all along: a Communist regime adhering strictly to Russian foreign policy and yet enjoying a large measure of popular acceptance and, in the first months, a good deal more than that. From an "imperialist and Zionist agent" Gomulka became Khrushchev's favorite companion and adviser. Just as Khrushchev persuaded himself that in the old days he had fearlessly protected the Ukrainians from Stalin's wrath, so later he undoubtedly credited his own policy with the elevation of Gomulka.

The Hungarian sequel to the Polish events, however, posed a much more basic threat not only to the Soviet position but also to Tito's own position, as he was to realize after his initial doubts. From an intraparty crisis the events turned into a national uprising. An Italian patriot said in the nineteenth century, "We don't want Austria to become more tolerant, we want Austria to go away," and the people of Budapest said the same thing about Russia and Communism. Had the Russians not intervened with force (and the train of events suggests strongly that this decision was not reached without hesitation), the whole Soviet and Communist position in Eastern Europe would have been undermined. The repercussions would have extended in due course to Yugoslavia and Poland, and would have threatened Communism there, "national Communism" though it was. It is clear, then, why Tito—after some schoolmasterish remarks about how the Hungarian situation had been botched both by the local Communists and by the Russians and that it would not have occurred had everybody listened to his advice—accepted the suppression of Hungary, at first with secret, then with public relief.

But the events of the fall of 1956 had to lead to a reappraisal on both sides of Russo-Yugoslav relations. The pattern that had been set just before the Hungarian-Polish explosion could not endure. Yugoslavia was now seen as a demoralizing example for the satellite bloc. Her attempt to rejoin the bloc while preserving a special relationship with the West was held to be one of the indirect causes of the whole sequence of events that had led to Budapest. On the Russian side, the struggle for leadership within the Communist Party of the USSR, which lasted throughout 1957 with Khrushchev's stock dipping and then rising again, postponed any re-evaluation of the Yugoslav problem. On Tito's side, there was no reason to take the initiative in redefining the relationship. The Yugoslav party had every reason to hope for a perpetuation of the pre-Budapest pattern. At the same time, facing the danger of an abrupt return by Moscow to the methods that were employed before Stalin's death, they felt called upon to re-emphasize their independence in foreign policy.

In 1958 the Yugoslav Communists became for the Russians "revisionists." Hints of this development had been dropped earlier, in 1957. Actually, their party program and the speeches at the Seventh Congress contained nothing new or startling. These were in the spirit of the working agreement that they had had with the Russians in 1956. The condemnation of both the Warsaw Pact and NATO was perhaps a bit strong, and so had been their refusal to sign a Soviet-sponsored declaration endorsing the USSR's position in the cold war on the fortieth anniversary of Great October. Yet in both cases the USSR in her post-1956 posture felt compelled to indicate that Yugoslavia's behavior was not ideologically correct. Titoism had now appeared, according to the dicta of the Moscow fashion makers, in a new dress: it was no longer an outpost of imperialism and treachery, as in the Stalin era, nor a prodigal son returning to the bosom of the socialist family of the 1955-1956 periods, but a deviation. The Yugoslav Communists, with the assistance of the satellites and the Chinese, whose attacks surpassed even the Russians' in vituperation, were confined to this convenient purgatory of Communist terminology. There they still are, in the purgatory of revisionism—which has in recent years become a rather comfortable place compared with the hell peopled exclusively by the dogmatists.

In their continuing effort to be different, the Yugoslavs in 1957 discovered a new gambit. The underdeveloped nations of the world have been losing their chains and gaining substantial credits from the two super-powers. It was only fitting that Yugoslavia should make a bid for the spiritual leadership of that vast conglomeration of states, ranging from the undoubted but threatened democracy of India, through such term-defying structures as Indonesia and Ethiopia, to what the American political scientists call by the shameful euphemism of "one-party democracies" of Africa (the latter term—and why not call a spade a spade?—is one that the Yugoslavs probably regret not having invented to describe their own system).

The basis of the new "bloc" can certainly be found in some identity of interests. All of its members have a vested interest in preventing a violent aggravation of Russo-American relations, and by the same token a violent improvement in those relations. The first tendency may lead to war, the second to a considerable reduction, if not elimination, of the economic help that is poured in by the two colossi. All members of this third force—the neutral or uncommitted bloc, whatever it is called—proudly reject capitalism and certain unspecified items of the Soviet ideology. They join in the condemnation of imperialism and neocolonialism. Since sharp disapproval of the Soviet system is liable to have more drastic repercussions than is criticism of the West, the uncommitted nations gravitate ideologically toward a vague form of Marxism, which therefore makes Yugoslavia their logical leader.

But this new attempt to exercise leadership, and to find firm ideological ground under their feet, has not served the Yugoslavs very well either. The underdeveloped third force is too underdeveloped, and too formless to be a real force in international affairs. In moments of stress and danger, its members (witness India) have to forget their strictures about the sinfulness of both sides and the evil of great-power politics. The moral critic appears then in the garb of a humble petitioner for help. Thus, an attempt to export Titoism is once more checkmated by the inexorable realities of international politics, and also by the material weakness of Yugoslavia. Barred from expansionism in the Balkans, shut out of the satellite countries, the Yugoslavs do not find themselves in a much firmer position in trying to exercise political leadership on a wider scale. That their example has been of some influence is indisputable. They have navigated skillfully between the East and West, and they have preserved their independence from either of the two major blocs, perhaps they should now be called three major blocs. In that sense, the lesson of Yugoslavia is worthy of study by each of the new countries. But the Yugoslav Communists cannot provide such countries with any concrete help in achieving their economic or political objectives. And insofar as ideology is concerned, Titoism can impart few lessons to the Moslem socialism of the Arabs or to Pan-Africanism. Ideologies in our own day have become subservient and secondary to the realities of world politics. Capitalist Finland exists within the Russian sphere of influence, and Communist Albania exists in defiance of all her neighbors, both Communist and non-Communist.

Today it is possible to reach certain conclusions about the lessons of the Yugoslav experiment. As an ideology, Titoism, one must conclude sadly, is an optical illusion. A man saying "I am a Marxist" gives a definite indication of his philosophy, the laws of history in which he believes, his belief in the superiority of social over private ownership of the means of production. But what, in that context, is the meaning of the statement "I am a Titoist"? Or, viewing the same problem from a different angle, a man declaring himself to be a Communist can, or could until recently, identify himself with a world movement and with the conviction that the socioeconomic system of Soviet Russia will spread over all the earth. Here again a self-professed Titoist would be at a loss about how to state his hopes and expectations. In essence, Titoism is an amalgam of nationalism and socialism. Here it differs quantitatively from the examples of the same combination encountered in Egypt, Indonesia, or Cuba. The link with Marxism and Communism still persists, as does the attempt to find an institutional expression of those creeds. But the essence of an ideology must be reflected in some quality that transcends national boundaries. And we have not yet seen, and probably never will see, an inhabitant of Africa, Asia, or America saying "I am a Titoist," although there are beginning to be specimens in those areas, including Mattapan, Massachusetts, ready to say "I am a Maoist."

Titoism has another dimension, however, whose importance has been truly historic. This is its significance as a movement of revolt against Stalinism and Moscow domination. It has unmasked the essentially Russian character of Leninism as practiced since the October Revolution. It has broken the connection that many began to believe was an organic one between Russian nationalism and Communism. To reconstruct Communism as an international movement has become increasingly difficult since 1948. Those dogmas of pre-1948 Communism that went unchallenged even by Trotskyism—namely, that Communism implies the support of the Soviet Union and that the Soviet pattern, for all its perversions, must still remain the example for the rest of the world—now lie shattered, and it was small Yugoslavia that first directed a blow at the myth.

The consequences of this unmasking may well have a profound influence on the development of Communism in Russia. For with Yugoslavia's defections there must have been sown the first seeds of doubt as to whether Communist imperialism is worthwhile, and whether there is in fact the identity of interests between world Communism and Russia or Soviet nationalism that has been assumed. To be sure, this lesson has not as yet sunk in. The Russian Communists have gone on propagating their creed, as if the victory of Communism in Algeria or Ghana would still necessarily mean a tangible increase in Soviet power. To men of Khrushchev's generation it must have been extremely difficult to rethink the whole problem of Communism as a world movement, and the same is true of his successors, aged 69 and 71. The current difficulties and dissonances must appear to be temporary in nature, ready to be resolved by some new institution or a joint declaration. But it is difficult to see how the problem is susceptible of a long-range solution. The Chinese are now in effect accusing the Russians of being Titoists, of giving only lukewarm support to the spread of the doctrine, and of being uninterested in the promotion of Communism; and this may in time prove true.

The loss of the messianic and missionary impulse of the Communist Party of the USSR would in turn have profound effects on Soviet society. The rationale of a totalitarian system demands an external threat or a promise of expansion, or both. With the loss of external dynamism, Russian Communism would find it difficult to cope with its own society. The awareness of this dilemma is what makes the Communist leaders push out of their minds any thought of the incompatibility between Communist expansion and the real interests of the Soviet Union. It also provokes them to take the sort of desperate gambles, such as the order for the Cuban missile sites, that had been eschewed by Stalin.

What are the present prospects of Titoism in both its narrower and its wider meanings? On the first count, there seems little doubt that the present system in Yugoslavia will continue, and that even the disappearance of Marshal Tito is not likely to bring about drastic changes in the regime. Yugoslavia's path is determined by the realities of present-day politics. No regime in the immediate future is likely to be doctrinaire enough to cut off its ties to the West, or to become pragmatic to the point of discarding the veneer of Communism in its nationalist, Titoist form. Yugoslavia's main stake lies in the preservation of the present uneasy equilibrium in Russo-American relations. To the best of their abilities the Yugoslav Communists will also attempt to continue in their self-proclaimed role as the champion conciliator and teacher of the Afro-Asian nations. Tito's disappearance from the scene is likely to lead to some contention for power, and quite possibly the factions will range themselves according to the issue of a more versus a less pro-Soviet attitude, but whichever one prevails, it is very likely to continue the traditional Titoist policy (at least since 1958) in international relations.

In its broader sense, the issue of Titoism has become submerged in the present Sino-Soviet dispute. Chinese Titoism, once a dissident voice, has become what its Yugoslav counterpart never could be: a challenge for the leadership of the Communist movement as a whole. At present this attempt is expressed by pressure on the Soviet Union to assume a more militant and expansionist attitude. In due time it will undoubtedly take the form of Communist China's trying to replace the Soviet Union as the leader of world Communism.

The present phase of the conflict is reminiscent in some ways of the old struggles of the Bolsheviks and the Mensheviks. It was Lenin's tactic to accuse the Mensheviks of moderation, of being "liquidators," and thus to achieve the double aim of shaming them into intermittent militancy while at the same time branding them as betrayers of the working class. The current Chinese effort runs on parallel lines: the Soviet Union is to be shamed out of any possible accommodation with the United States, and at the same time any Soviet act of militancy is branded as insufficient. Thus, the Chinese Communists may well expect to expand their clientele not only among other Asian Communist parties but also among militant and impatient Communists everywhere. It takes little imagination to see why a Communist in New Zealand or Norway would look with favor on a more militant policy by the great Communist powers, while those Communists who already rule their countries would have a more sober attitude on the subject. The racial undertones of the Chinese propaganda are also likely to prove a barrier to its acceptance among such large parties as the Italian and the French. But the Chinese viewpoint may well become the dominant one among the "underprivileged" Communists (that is, the nonwhites) and among those who compose only tiny groups in their own countries and who cannot conceivably dream of power without a decisive defeat of Western influence throughout the world.

Yet paradoxically, the Yugoslavs and some other satellite regimes have recently been trying to exert their influence to prevent the Sino-Soviet split from becoming sharper and more definite. The reasons are not hard to find. Just as the Yugoslavs have a vested interest in the precarious balance of power between the Soviet and

Western blocs, for a definite victory of either would threaten them with disaster, so they have come to appreciate that they have a similar interest in a moderate degree of hostility and a precarious balance of power within the Communist world itself. A definite split between the two Communist giants or military action (which can no longer be ruled out) would make a complete shambles of Communism as an international movement. It might lead Soviet Russia to assume "isolationism," to lose interest in the preservation of the Eastern European outposts of Communism. A "secularization" of Soviet society is now seen as a threat, not only in Peking, but in a different way also in Belgrade and Bucharest. Where would the Communist regimes in Eastern Europe be if Soviet Russia decided that her interests might be better served by a real accommodation with the West, and by a policy of spheres of influence that would not necessarily demand ideological as well as political subservience. In the last resort, every Communist regime in Eastern Europe is maintained by the fear of Soviet intervention and the memory of Budapest, and the situation in Communist Yugoslavia is not materially different. It relies not on Soviet bayonets, but on the conviction of the majority of the population of the Federal Republic that, under present international conditions, the only alternative to Titoism is a return to outright satellite status. If that conviction disappears, voices like those of Djilas will not remain isolated and eccentric.

The present turn of events in the Communist world brings Titoism once more into sharper focus. In its broader sense Titoism can be seen as an organic and inevitable disease of non-Russian Communism when in power. Ironically, many of the theses of Marxism-Leninism that were intended to describe inevitable tendencies within the capitalist world have proved to be true of the Communist one. Imperialistic rivalry, for instance, is really the highest stage of Communism. This rivalry in turn enables the satellites and the ex-satellites, like Yugoslavia and Albania, to play an independent if apprehensive role in world politics. It is still an open question whether a formula can be found which will appease their fears and ambitions, which will preserve the formal unity of the Communist world without leading again to its domination by a single power, and which will allow the doctrine to keep some of its meaning and dynamism without increasing the danger of a world holocaust.

It is difficult to see how the Communist world could really become polycentric. Certainly the history of Communism is not encouraging in this respect. Old Russian Social Democracy was polycentric in the sense that a variety of approaches and tactics were advocated within the party. But the essence of Bolshevism from the beginning has been that there is only one correct ideology, one correct road to power, and only one center of power and ideological arbiter. The only departures from this pattern were the result of struggles for succession or drastic external threats. It may well be that the rulers of Yugoslavia, if their ability to improvise a way out of an ideological cul-de-sac is not exhausted, may attempt yet another ingenious solution to the intolerable dilemmas facing world Communism. But the success or failure of such an effort will depend on factors that are not within their power to determine.

PART THREE   INTERNATIONALISM
AND FOREIGN
AFFAIRS

10 | MARXIST DOCTRINE

The existence of continuities between imperial and Soviet Russia's foreign policies does not mean that Lenin's and Stalin's Russia sought simply, under new slogans, the territorial and political aims of the Tsars. The people who captured power in November 1917 were sincere Marxists. No matter how unorthodox from the point of view of ideology was their hurrying the historical process and attempting to introduce socialism into a relatively backward country, they believed that they were acting in the spirit if not according to the letter of their faith. Their mentality was shaped by the doctrines promulgated in the nineteenth century by Marx and Engels and by the circumstances of their long activity as socialists. Thus, what might be called the Marxist element of Soviet Russia's policies has at least three elements. First is the canon of the doctrine: the thought of Marx and Engels. Second is the historical experience of the Bolsheviks in their struggles with other sections of the Russian socialist and revolutionary movement. And finally is the lesson of the years of war and revolution, 1914-1917, when many previous tenets and strategies gave way to bold improvisations and new theories associated with the term Leninism. Impossible though a neat separation of these three components is, it must be attempted, for otherwise it is difficult to see how a doctrine shaped by the circumstances of the mid-nineteenth century came to be the guiding light of twentieth century policies.

The fundamental point to be kept in mind about Marxism is that it is a doctrine shaped by the circumstances and attitudes of the mid-nineteenth century in the West. What might be called pure Marxism could offer little in the way of guidelines for Russia's foreign policies in the twentieth century, and not much more for the strategy of an international revolutionary movement conceived almost exactly one hundred years after the birth of Karl Marx.

A careful reading of the *Communist Manifesto* bears out the fact that Marx and Engels expected revolutions to take place in advanced industrial countries and as a consequence of an internal breakdown of the economic and political system. As to the foreign policies a socialist country might pursue, Marx and Engels have nothing to say. This omission is not fortuitous, any more than is the relative lack of indications in their work as to exactly how the economy of a socialist country should work. The socialist revolution will occur in every country as it reaches a high level of industrialization. This revolution will not be substantially affected by any developments on the international scene. In the *Manifesto* itself is an explicit statement that the materials of international politics—frontiers, militarism, religious differences—are of decreasing importance. The progress of economy and civilization makes nationalism itself of ever diminishing effect on the destiny of peoples. With the economy becoming world-wide, the interests of the two hostile classes, capitalists and workers, also begin to transcend national frontiers. The implication is clear that not only the workers but also the capitalists "have no country," in the sense that no national loyalties can take precedence over what a given class in a given country conceives to be its economic interest.

Thus, the very internationalism of the doctrine is based paradoxically on the assumption that considerations of international politics have become and will continue to be less important. If the capitalists of England and France find their trade mutually profitable, then no considerations of national honor, no territorial dispute will impel them to go to war. And by the same token, socialist France and England will find no reason for war or rivalry: their respective working classes will realize that the fullest development of their internal resources is the only way to improve their countries' economic, and hence general, welfare. War, and with it much of international politics, will simply become obsolete. As to the possibility of a cataclysmic struggle between socialist and nonsocialist nations, that, in the canon of Marxism, is excluded almost by definition. In the first place, the implication is that capitalism, repressive as it is internally, is in international politics a force for peace (a drastic modification of this analysis is what lies at the root of Lenin's philosophy of international affairs). In the second place, the countries entering socialism will be industrially and thus potentially also militarily far advanced, hence will have little to fear from those nations whose obsolete feudal economy and political organization would impel them to warlike and expansionist drives. In brief, Marx's is a socialist version of what was in his time the enlightened liberal theory on the future of international politics— the product of that century of rationalism, of material and scientific progress, and of unbounded optimism in civilized man's ability to eliminate the terrors and distresses of the past.

Such in general is the main view of Marxian theory on the problem of international politics in the future. But this attitude has an important qualification. As publicists and observers of the contemporary political scene, both Marx and Engels wrote voluminously about diplomatic and military problems of the day, and from their insights and arguments emerges a body of observations which, though not contesting their main theory, still represent a different dimension of their thinking on international problems.[1]

In addition, Marx and Engels thought of themselves as politicians and as leaders, at least in the intellectual sphere, who were called upon to advise on the day-to-day strategy of the international socialist movement. In this capacity, Marx and Engels sympathized with most of the revolutionary and national emancipation movements of their day. This sympathy appears quite natural today, as does the whole nexus between the concepts of Marxism and revolution. Yet in fact, few of the other socialist system-makers of the nineteenth century were revolutionaries in the sense of advocating the violent overthrow of existing forms of society. The deterministic character of Marxism would again suggest that it discourages the notion that violence can prevail against the forces of history as expressed in society's economic development. But the founders of the movement were not only socialists but also revolutionaries, and those two strains coexisted and sometimes clashed within Marxism. The approval of various revolutionary movements in nineteenth century Europe, even when some of them bore a most unsocialist mark, was often rationalized in terms of international considerations. Thus, Polish nationalism was warmly supported by Marx, even though at the time its source was found mostly among the Polish upper and middle classes and a Polish proletariat was virtually nonexistent, because Polish nationalism and the abortive Polish uprisings were directed at the three powers—Prussia, Austria, and especially Russia—which were the bulwark of European reaction and were barriers to the development everywhere on the Continent of the modern economic and social conditions that would eventually lead to socialism.[2] Hence, there was excellent revolutionary logic in this virtual alliance between socialists and nationalist-minded Polish landlords. The doctrine of the desirability of some "wars of national liberation" was not an invention of Khrushchev's; it is at least as old as the *Communist Manifesto.*

Of almost equal antiquity, and coming from the same source, is the tactic of what might be called revolutionary patience: the support of a revolutionary movement, even when its strategy and ideology are clearly antithetical to those of Marxism, if this movement is effective in disrupting the traditional pattern of politics in a given country. Marx and Engels viewed with admiration the struggle of the Russian populists against tsarism, much though the ideology and the means of struggle employed by the populists (in some cases individual terrorism) were obsolete and erroneous by the lights of Marxism. The indulgence of the fathers of Marxism extended so far that at times they discouraged the idea of forming a specific Marxist party in Russia, believing that the chances of discrediting or overthrowing the Russian autocracy would only be compromised by internal rivalry within the revolutionary camp.

Nineteenth century Russia was a logical target for the international revolutionary movement because of her backwardness and her role as the main supporter of reaction. But for a militant Marxist, Great Britain, the most advanced capitalist state, was hardly less so. Yet despite the prophecies and assumptions of Marx's doctrine, revolutionary socialism made only insignificant inroads within the British working class, while trade-unionist and reformist tendencies were in full sway. A revolutionary socialist's main source of hope insofar as Great Britain was concerned was the revolutionary stirrings in Ireland, though again these had nothing socialist about them. For in a sense, the fathers of Marxism recognized the danger in taming the class struggle through trade unionism and parliamentary institutions and looked with sympathy on any revolutionary opening, any movement or social problem, that could not be contained within a constitutional and peaceful framework, that would disrupt the state sufficiently to enable revolution to challenge the bourgeoisie.

That the tactics of international socialism have to be flexible, that no weapon—the national or religious question, or even parliamentarism—is to be scorned in weakening capitalism and the status quo, is therefore implicit in the thinking of Marx and Engels. Their commitment to violent revolution per se was never absolute. Marx, some years before his death, granted that in a few states, like Great Britain, the United States, and Holland, socialism might come through peaceful means. Engels, who lived to observe electoral successes of the German Social Democratic Party, enlarged this prognosis still further. In the most advanced European countries, he observed, capitalists were on the defensive: the extension of the franchise was making it inevitable that one day the proletariat would secure a parliamentary majority and with it the machinery of state.

It is tempting to find in these utterances of Marx and Engels a direct source for the policies of the Comintern and the Soviet government. But they had with the later policies as well, major differences. To begin with, the outlook of original Marxism was internationalist, and for Marx it would have been inconceivable that the policies of international socialism should be dictated by one party or one country. Also, for all the flexibility of the tactics prescribed, the fortunes of the movement were for Marx and Engels rooted in factors of economics. Thus, in discussing imperialism, Marx was far from attributing to it the decisive influence on the development of capitalism that Lenin later did. He foresaw the awakening of India and China, but he considered the overseas rule of the European powers as mainly beneficial, bringing industrialization, which in his terms was almost synonymous with progress and civilization, to backward societies. He would not have accepted the thesis that English capitalism could not withstand the loss of its overseas possessions. In fact, despite all of its psychological insights, original Marxism is firmly rooted in the rationalist tradition of the nineteenth century and its economic-determinist underpinnings. Emotional, irrational forces in politics are of importance, yet they cannot supersede the decisive importance of economics. A revolution may succeed in a backward country, but socialism cannot be established until the economic conditions for it are ripe, and no scheme of political organization, no amount of "agitation," can change this fact. In the last instance, the legacy of Marx in international as well as national politics remains ambivalent. Some parts of it can be claimed by what became after his death the main current of European social democracy, but other elements belong to militant socialism, which finally crystallized in Communism. After the failure of the Paris Commune of 1871 the tone, if not the content, of Marx's statements became less revolutionary and more consistent with the vision of a peaceful evolution to socialism rather than of its achievement through violence.

The second part of the Marxian inheritance in foreign affairs is found in the history of the Russian Marxists—or to give the official name of the movement, the Russian Social Democratic Workers' Party, founded in 1898—and particularly in the history of its Bolshevik faction between 1903 and 1914. Since there is a direct connection between the Bolsheviks and the Communist Party as it emerged in 1918, the future policies of the Soviet Union were vitally influenced by the experience of the Bolsheviks before they seized power.[3]

The position of the Russian Marxists prior to 1914 did not offer them much leisure or cause to think about international affairs. They were one branch among many in the revolutionary and progressive movement bent on the overthrow of the monarchy or at least on its reformation into a constitutional monarchy. Even by their own doctrine the day of the socialist revolution in Russia was not imminent. Their doctrine proclaimed that the next revolution in Russia would be a bourgeois-liberal one, and only after a period of

further industrial growth would the country become ripe for socialism. At the time of the 1905 Revolution, this time sequence was
challenged by the thesis of Trotsky and Parvus who, taking up a
term inherited from Marx, formulated the theory of permanent
revolution: since the bourgeoisie in Russia was weak and the proletariat, though not numerous, was the main revolutionary force,
the bourgeois-liberal revolution would soon pass into a socialist
one. But in the main both the Bolsheviks and the Mensheviks
adhered to the orthodox view.

Despite the letter of their doctrine, the two branches of Russian
Marxism were in temperament far more revolutionary than any of
the other major socialist parties of Europe. This was partly the
product of the specifically Russian condition, where even under the
semiconstitutional regime that began in 1906 political parties and
activites were persecuted. Partly it was the inheritance of the Russian revolutionary movement of the nineteenth century, with its
propensity for violence and its belief that a revolution is an act of
will and not a matter of specific social and economic conditions—
the Bolsheviks, under Lenin's influence, having imbibed much of
the ideology of such organizations as the People's Will, with its
terrorist tactics.

The reliance on organization and conspiracy was a natural consequence of the facts of political life in Russia, but in 1902 Lenin
expanded this into a general principle of twentieth century Marxism
in his *What Is To Be Done?* A socialist party could not be a party in
the Western sense of the word; it had to be more like a tightly
organized and disciplined order of revolutionaries. Marx's hope
that the mere growth of industry and the expansion of the industrial proletariat would create favorable conditions for socialism
was reappraised by Lenin. From this primary tenet of Marx's
prognosis, Lenin turned increasingly to the secondary elements in
Marx's thinking: the exploitation of any and all social elements,
rather than just the workers, in the quest for revolution. The socialist party, which after 1918 would be the socialist state, must exploit
every social and political discontent. It must learn to subdue, if
necessary, its ideological scruples. Thus, the peasant's discontent
with his status and his craving for more land were the most serious

threats to the social stability of the empire, but the peasant would turn violently against the Marxists if they urged, as their doctrine required them to, that individual landholdings be nationalized and merged into state-run farms. Hence, already in 1906 Lenin urged that the appeal to the peasant be couched in terms of his craving for more land, Marxism or no Marxism. This policy, much criticized by ideological purists, was the forerunner of the appeal to peasant self-interest that was to serve the Bolsheviks so well in 1917 and which since then the Communists have used with so much success in the underdeveloped areas of the world, most notably in China.

Of even more fundamental importance for the future development of Soviet foreign policies was the evolution of the Bolshevik ideological tactic on the problem of nationality. It brings to mind what one Soviet historian said of Lenin, that he never considered an ideological problem or a policy platform apart from its propagandistic aspect. And to be sure, the ability of Communism to pose as the friend of oppressed nationalism everywhere was to be the key to its most brilliant successes, not only during the Civil War in Russia but especially since World War II. The elaboration of this policy, which again clashed with orthodox Marxism, took place between 1903 and 1912, and its scope was enlarged by Lenin's work *Imperialism,* written during World War I.

Important though social and political problems were as the causes of revolutionary agitation in Europe, they hardly surpassed the rankling oppression and russification of nationalities within the Russian empire. In addition to the suppression of the Polish drive for independence, russification policies were directed by the imperial regime against the nationalities of the Caucasus and the Baltic littoral. The existence of a Ukrainian nation was stoutly denied by tsarist policies, and the numerous Jews in the empire's western provinces were subjected to anti-Semitic discriminations unparalleled elsewhere in Europe. There were other, though less developed, non-Russian nationalisms. The revolutionary and especially the Marxist movement in Russia was always heavily staffed by non-Russians, notably Jews, Poles, and Letts, who were represented in it out of proportion to their number in the population at large.

Lenin saw that even more effective use could be made of the weapon of nationalism if the Marxists would favor the right of every nationality to independence—if, regardless of the character or leadership of a given national movement, whether upper or middle class, or even clerical, Marxists proclaimed that every national group had the right to separate statehood. There were excellent precedents for this policy in the writings of Marx himself. But the orthodox position could hardly tolerate that a Marxist party should make an appeal to nationalism one of its main tenets. The full application of this argument would find the Russian Marxists with some strange bedfellows. Polish nationalism was at the time strongest among the Polish upper and middle classes. An independent Poland would most likely be dominated by the landowners and by Catholicism, strong among her peasantry, and the prospects of her eventual socialist transformation would be indefinitely postponed by her separation from Russia. Among other national groups, especially the Turkic elements and Armenians, the leaders of nationalist agitation were largely motivated by religious issues. Again, from the strict Marxian viewpoint, their independence would be a step backward, the surrender of a largely primitive population into the hands of semifeudal and religiously fanatical classes.

Such a viewpoint was voiced most insistently by socialists of non-Russian background, many of them culturally russified and most of them detesting their own upper classes more fervently than they did the tsarist governors and bureaucracy. But within Bolshevik ranks, Lenin's insistence carried the day. His opponent, Rosa Luxemburg, active in both the German and the Polish Social Democratic parties (the latter had intermittent organizational ties with the Russian socialists), espoused the more orthodox Marxian viewpoint: to the workers, the problem of nationality is a secondary one; what matters is the end of exploitation, whether its perpetrators be Polish or Russian capitalists. Lenin's inherent realism made him see that the appeal of nationalism in the twentieth century often transcended the appeal of class interest, and that socialism struggling for influence (before 1914 he still would not have said "power") in a peasant society cannot make its appeal in purely class terms. That national autonomy was in his eyes consistent with the retention of the frontiers of the Russian state and even with a degree of political centralization is indicated by two pre-1914 developments. He rejected the pleas of the Jewish socialist organization—the Bund—that it should have a more or less autonomous organization within the larger framework of the Russian socialist movement. Also, he envisaged that the future socialist state might be multinational, as indicated by the treatise on the nationality problem that Stalin wrote under his guidance shortly before World War I: separate nationalities within clearly defined territorial units would be given full autonomy if they so desired; but presumably, with socialism established and with exploitation both political and economic abolished, these units would prefer to adhere to a federal arrangement. Militant nationalism was thus seen as a disruptive element so long as socialism was not achieved, but in a socialist Russia there would be no reason for the Georgians or Ukrainians to opt out.

From today's perspective, Lenin's formulas demonstrate a considerable talent for eating one's cake and having it too or, to put it more baldly, for cynicism. In order to defeat your enemy, you have the recourse to the most revolutionary, most disruptive formulas; then when in power, presumably you will rationalize these formulas out of existence. But before 1914 Lenin and the Bolsheviks could feel with some justification that their policies and pleas were well within the Marxian orthodoxy and that they were simply adjusting Marx's precepts to the spirit of the age and to their own society, where emotional factors such as nationalism or the peasants' devotion to the principle of private property were much stronger than Marx, with his Western and rationalist background, had been able to envisage. Neither Lenin nor those closest to him imagined that socialism in Russia was a matter of the near future, still less that it would come in the form of one-party rule.

It is undeniable, however, that the Russian Marxists—and this was hardly less true of the Mensheviks than of the Bolsheviks—felt uncomfortable in the atmosphere of international socialism. In the spectrum of the Second International, both Russian groups were consistently on the left. Much of Western socialism was in their eyes corrupted by the spirit of revisionism and the unwillingness of their German or English colleagues to envisage the coming of socialism as a struggle requiring violent means. Living under a barely reformed autocracy, they could not understand or sympathize with the compromises that Western socialism had made with the bourgeois state, with its occasional tendency to look at parliamentarism as the main means of political struggle, or with the increasing propensity of trade unions in industrialized societies to conceive their task as the securing of economic advantages for the worker rather than educating him in the spirit of the class struggle. For the Russian Marxists, participation in elections and economic struggle did not mean that socialists should dispense with conspiracy or even violence.

Still another element of the Bolsheviks' pre-1914 political experience was to prove of great importance to them once they had become masters of their country and was to color their psychology in dealing with other countries. Except during the revolutionary period of 1905-1906, the Bolsheviks were a rather minor element in Russian politics. Their extremism and, at times, their tactics—as between 1905 and 1907 when they had recourse to expropriations, namely, to armed robberies of state and private funds—brought upon them the disapprobation of their fellow Marxists, not to speak of the liberal elements in Russia. Yet the other branches of the revolutionary and reform movement did not try to excommunicate the Bolsheviks. Until April 1917 the Mensheviks sought unity with their vitriolic opponents. The climate of what was known as the "liberation movement" in Russia was such that it was difficult, even for the most constitutionally minded liberal, to conceive that there could be an enemy on the left or that any means might be illegitimate in struggling against tsarism. The inherently undemocratic character of the Bolsheviks' party organization was noted, but its democratic phraseology was accepted in good faith. In fact, it could be argued that the survival of the Bolsheviks as a political force after 1906-1907 was in the main owing to the tolerance extended to them by socialist and liberal circles both in Russia and abroad. Foreign socialists provided shelter and funds for the Bolshevik leaders within Russia. Liberal lawyers sprang to the defense of accused party members. Non-Bolshevik members of the socialist movement refrained from flaunting too vigorously the Bolsheviks' undemocratic practices and theories before the Russian workers. Such practices were bound to give some Bolsheviks, especially Lenin, the impression of an essential weakness and a lack of self-assurance on the part of liberals and other socialists. Marx's teaching about the tenacity with which the bourgeoisie holds on to power and its ruthlessness in pursuing its aims was thus shown to be no longer fully applicable. By the beginning of the twentieth century, the ruling circles in the West were similarly revealed no longer to possess an unremitting resolve and sense of self-preservation. And in Russia especially, liberals and non-Bolshevik socialists seemed very prone to "fall" for humanitarian and democratic slogans and propaganda, even when they were mouthed by a party that was dictatorial in its organization and that was showing, if at that time still unconsciously, a pronounced authoritarian temper. The lingering effect of these impressions was to be displayed in the Bolsheviks' foreign policies following November 1917. They were to show but little respect for the sense of realism and tenacity of purpose of social democratic regimes and hardly more for those foreign governments and movements that could be called liberal. In world politics, they were to see images of their former domestic protagonists, such as the Mensheviks and the Kadets; in time, their skepticism as to *any* democratic regime's inner strength or sustained purpose was to color the whole course of Soviet foreign policy.

Lenin's and the Bolsheviks' emendations of the original teachings of Marx touched mainly the psychological substratum of politics. The enormous emphasis placed on propaganda and agitation in the Communists' teaching is sufficient testimony to that fact. Marx had believed that the logic of economic facts would by itself educate the working class and bring about socialism. Lenin emphasized preaching and indoctrination. In a sense these were to become the main weapons of the young Communist state when it was being ravaged by the Civil War, then later when it was a backward and devastated society that yet proclaimed its challenge to every other form of government in Europe, and later still when it had become able to withstand concerted economic, if not military, attack and isolation by the Great Powers. One might argue that some of the psychological habits that the Bolsheviks brought with them to the task of ruling their country were, by the same token, to handicap them: extreme suspiciousness of every movement and every government not fully sharing their ideology, underestimation of the staying power of democracy in the Western countries, and a view of international politics as consisting mainly of the clash of economic and military interests. But the reality of post-1914 world politics was to prove closer to the Bolsheviks' analysis than to that which had been shared by the liberals and the more democratically inclined socialists.

It is a truism that World War I changed the tone and content of European politics. But this truism takes on new meaning in light of the change wrought within the Bolshevik Party by the experience of war and the swiftly evolving course of Russian history from July 1914 to November 1917. For all the reservations and qualifications that had previously been spelled out, the Bolshevik branch of the Russian socialist movement considered itself part and parcel of European social democracy as it existed prior to the shots at Sarajevo. Lenin's impatience with the spirit of the Second International did not lead him openly to contemplate the founding of a rival socialist international. The disagreements with the Mensheviks did not mean that the fissure within Russian socialism was deemed irreparable. The Bolsheviks' temperamental dislike of Western parliamentarism did not mean that they anticipated the November pattern—armed seizure of power by their party *alone* and against the opposition of other socialist and revolutionary groups. The official view was still that the overthrow of the monarchy, or at least of the remnants of its absolutism, would be followed by a period under a bourgeois liberal regime, and only then by socialism.

Inherent in these pre-1914 views, absurdly moderate and misguided as they must have appeared to Lenin and his associates in 1917, were certain assumptions about international politics, international socialism, and the situation in Russia, all of which were exposed as hollow by the events of 1914-1917. First, the strength and stability of the European state system were taken for granted by even its most severe critics. To be sure, the apprehension or expectation of a large war was widely shared before 1914, and on several occasions in the preceding decade it did almost materialize. But remnants of nineteenth century rationalism inhibited most people from envisaging the war's devastating and all-embracing character, its duration, or its casualties, both physical and social. The most extensive war within the memory of the living was the Franco-Prussian War of 1870-1871, which, though it had upset the Second Empire and was followed by the Paris Commune, did not undermine the existing social system in either France or Germany. According to the most sophisticated Marxist opinion, it was inconceivable that the ruling classes in Europe—the capitalists in France and England, the ruling houses and bureaucracies in Germany and Russia—would allow the competition for territory or national prestige to undermine their economic and political power. A war would be of relatively short duration; it would not be a total war; and though every good socialist had to hope that it would weaken capitalism, he could not conceive of the destruction of the whole way of life that the war would in fact accomplish after four bloody years.[4] Nor did it seem reasonable to expect the fall of dynasties, the disintegration of empires, and the economic ruin of the defeated nations. The victors' self-interest would urge them to impose a lenient peace, for ruinous peace conditions could lead to a state of anarchy in the defeated countries, and this anarchy in turn might infect the territory of the victors. But such calculations were belied by the intensity of feeling aroused on both sides, which was fed by the wholesale casualties and by the severe privations imposed on the civilian populations. As a matter of fact, internal subversion of the enemy became an accepted weapon of the war. By 1916 it was clear that any accommodation between the belligerents in terms of restoring the pre-1914 framework of the European polity was a forlorn hope. The theory of the essential solidarity of the European ruling circles, and of their will and ability to confine any conflict within manageable limits, was exposed as a myth. The international bourgeoisie, the international order, was much weaker and more disunited than the most revolutionary socialist before 1914 had dared to hope.

By the same token, international socialism as embodied in the Second International was exposed as ineffective. Much as it went against the grain of the Russian Marxists to sit in a body that admitted such nonrevolutionary parties as the British Labour Party or the Zionist Poale Zion, they still had considered the International as the representative of the working masses everywhere and as a power on the international scene. As the war clouds had gathered during the decade before 1914, the International was emphatic that the workers everywhere would not allow a protracted international slaughter at the behest of their capitalist masters. It was freely predicted that the two most powerful socialist parties, the German and the French, would use their very considerable influence over organized labor in their countries to proclaim a general strike should their governments plunge into a war. The International's congress in Stuttgart in 1907 stated, ''It is the duty of the working classes and their parliamentary representatives in the countries taking part . . . to do everything to prevent the outbreak of war by whatever means seem to them most effective, which naturally differ with the intensification of the class war and the general political situation.'' At the behest of the more radically minded delegates, among them Lenin, the congress added: ''Should war break out in spite of all this, it is their duty to intercede for its speedy end, and to strive with all their power to make use of the violent economic and political crisis brought about by the war to rouse the people and thereby to hasten the abolition of capitalist class rule.''[5] The same feeling was expressed even more strongly at the congress in Basel in 1912. The general assumption behind such sentiments was thus that if the capitalists lost their senses and provoked a European war, the socialists would be strong enough to bring it to a speedy conclusion, or at least that if a nationalist madness seized the countries of Europe, good socialists —certainly the leaders of the movement, the great parties of Germany and France—would be able to preserve their sense of proportion and their internationalism.

Yet, a few weeks in the summer of 1914 sufficed to shatter these expectations of the socialists' power and resolve to prevent a world war. None of the major socialist parties in Europe opposed the war. The German Social Democratic Party, the acknowledged leader of them all, presented for a true Marxist the most shocking spectacle. Its parliamentary representation voted unanimously for the government motion for war credits.[6] Even more disturbing was the attitude of rank-and-file German socialists, who appeared to share in the nationalistic fervor evoked by the news of war. Soon, prominent socialist leaders volunteered for war duty, and the party of Marx, Engels, and Liebknecht showed at least during the first two years of the conflict, a loyalty to the Kaiser hardly exceeded by that of the most hidebound Prussian Junkers. Similar developments took place in France, where some previously militant socialists turned into fervent chauvinists and where the veteran left-wing figure Jules Guesde joined the government, in Belgium, and in England (though a number of prominent British Labour Party leaders stuck to the pacifist traditions of their movement).

The effect of this "betrayal" on the more radical of the Russian socialists can hardly be exaggerated. For Lenin, it meant the final jettisoning of whatever there was of the social democrat in his make-up. His writing from the first days of the war is full of fulminations at the whole world of concepts and strategy of the Second International. Even Marx and Engels are criticized in retrospect for implicitly assuming after 1871 that the road to socialism in most European countries could lead through elections and by parliamentary means. Lenin now called for a return to the frankly revolutionary position of Marxism as it had been prior to 1870, as well as for the abandonment of the very name "socialist" and its replacement by "Communist." Insofar as the Bolsheviks and many other Russian socialists were concerned, the democratic and parliamentary encrustation of socialism had been a fraud and mistake. From now on, the emphasis had to be again on revolution and violence.

The dividing line in the Russian revolutionary camp was thus drawn on the attitude toward the war, rather than on any other issue of ideology or tactics. This was to have an incalculable effect on the course of revolution in 1917. Figures like Plekhanov, who associated themselves with Russia's war effort, were discredited within the revolutionary camp. And the previous hostility of such influential leaders as Martov toward Lenin was dulled because they shared the antiwar position.

Not that the revolutionary position was clearly ascendant even within Russian socialism. At the beginning of the war, the parliamentary fraction of both the Bolsheviks and the Mensheviks refused to vote for war credits. The Bolshevik deputies in the Duma were soon sent into exile. But many influential Mensheviks were less uncompromising in their opposition; in fact, many rank-and-file Bolsheviks, far from sharing their leader's position, were enlisting under colors.

The war caused Lenin to elaborate for the first time his theory of international relations. Prior to 1914 he had been a *Russian* revolutionary. Now the focus of the revolution was to become international; the fortunes of the socialist movement in Russia were to be subordinated to the greater task of a European or world revolution. The war freed him from previous scruples and hesitations. He proceeded to elaborate a whole network of theory and strategy for international Marxism. From a pupil of Marx and Engels, he became self-consciously their successor. He became completely emancipated from any reverence for the tradition of the Second International and its German leaders like Karl Kautsky. The argument of prowar socialists like Plekhanov—that Russia was fighting on the side of democracy and civilization against the German threat of militarism and European domination—failed to move him. The war became for him no longer a calamity but a stupendous opportunity for an international revolution.

Thus, as the war progressed and the initial elation in the belligerent countries gave way to apprehension while the toll of casualties grew ever larger and no conclusion seemed to be in sight, Lenin's main target became not so much those socialists who still adopted the nationalist position of their governments but the ones who sought a speedy peace. He wrote: "And objectively who profits by the slogan of peace? Certainly not the revolutionary proletariat. Nor the idea of *using* the war to *speed up* the collapse of capitalism."[7] The idea that war could be the main agency to bring down capitalism was something new in Marxian theory. Previously, Marxism had counted on the "inherent contradictions" of capitalism, its inability to run the very economic system it had created, to bring about its downfall. Now, it was capitalism's inability to preserve an international order, to avoid disastrous wars, that afforded the great opportunity. Lenin drew two deductions from that conclusion. First, the task of revolutionary socialism was to wage a constant revolutionary struggle taking advantage of capitalism's propensity for constant wars, an effort to persuade the armed masses to turn their weapons against, not the external, but the internal enemy: their own ruling class. Second, the stages of economic development so crucial to classical Marxism must be relegated to a position of secondary importance. The war offered socialists an opportunity to take over power in countries that were not yet ripe for socialism. Hence, a world revolution might well have its starting point in Russia, though that country lagged far behind England or Germany in economic development.

Armed with these assumptions, Lenin proceeded to seek both an instrument and a theory for this new form of revolutionary socialism. The instrument had to be a new international. It could not be like the now hateful Second International—a mere confederation of parties, guided only by a shared outlook and negotiating at occasional congresses a general policy that in any case was not binding on the constituent groups. He sought, in brief, to achieve on an international scale something he had tried ever since 1902 to achieve within Russian socialism: part political party and part militant order, ready to plunge into the revolutionary struggle whenever the central authority decided it should. The concept of the Third International was not and could not be fully elaborated by Lenin during the war, for the materials and conditions for it were not as yet available. But he strove to create a new spirit that would detach from the old social-democratic traditions as many practicing Marxists as possible.

The three wartime conferences of antiwar Marxists held at Berne (1915), Zimmerwald (1915), and Kienthal (1916) failed to respond to Lenin's hopes. The main orientation at all of them was pacifist. At Zimmerwald, Lenin's plea that the imperialist war be turned into a civil one was supported by only eight delegates out of about forty. But in many ways Zimmerwald laid the foundation of the Third International that was to be proclaimed in Moscow in 1919. It marked the emergence of Lenin from his position as leader of a faction of Russian socialists, and one on whom most luminaries of world socialism looked with some distaste, to a position as an inter-national leader—of a miniscule group, to be sure, but one that had a concrete and uncompromising answer to the problems of the day.

As the war progressed, the militancy of Lenin and his followers was bound to bring dividends among foreign socialists. All the elaborate schemes of Marx, with the learned emendations of the Kautskys, Hilferdings, and so forth, were to seem less important than a theory and plan to bring the inconclusive slaughter to an end and to liquidate the social and political system that had allowed it to happen. In retrospect, much of the credit gained by the Bolsheviks among their fellow socialists, much of the toleration extended by the most orthodox and democratically inclined Marxists to the Bolshevik Revolution which violated all the canons of their creed, is traceable directly to the fact that the war had dulled people's attachment to the niceties and restraints of the doctrine and put a premium on any revolutionary solution.

The theoretical bulwark of the new position was provided in 1916 by Lenin's *Imperialism*, in many ways the single most important theoretical treatise for the study of the sources of Soviet foreign policy. The structure of the argument was derived from previous works by J. A. Hobson, an English radical, and Rudolf Hilferding, a German Social Democrat, but the tone and conclusions were new. Lenin now proclaimed that militarism and imperialism were organic characteristics of the most advanced type of capitalism. Thus was Lenin able to dispose of Marx's premise of the essentially peaceful nature of capitalism. Marx was right, he said, but only insofar as early capitalism was concerned. Beginning with the 1870s, capitalism passed beyond its constructive and essentially peaceful phase and entered the stage of monopoly capitalism. The drying out of domestic investment opportunities in the most advanced captalist countries led those nations to engage in a competition for colonial territories where they could obtain both cheap labor and raw resources. In fact, Lenin proceeded to state, the rise in the living standard of the English, French, or German worker had been purchased by increased exactions from the masses of India or China. The competition of capitalists was bound to turn into political and then military competition, from which there was no escape short of the destruction of capitalism as an international system.

Lenin drew four important conclusions from his argument. First, the generally peaceful and democratic teachings of Marx and Engels during their last phase, the 1870s to 1895, were no longer applicable. Mature capitalism became once again exacting and oppressive, much more so than at its earliest stage of development, for now the continuation of the system implied not only the misery of the masses but the enslavement of whole nations and gigantic bloodbaths à la World War I. Militant revolutionary activity once more became the duty of every Marxist. Parliamentarism and the peaceful achievement of political power had to be pushed to the second plane.

Lenin's second conclusion was that the whole burden of Marxian activity had to be shifted to the international scene. Marx conceived of the collapse of capitalism as proceeding in a succession of internal overthrows of existing systems, as the given countries reached a high level of industrialization. Now, the Achilles' heel of capitalism was exposed: its international character, the interdependence of the capitalist countries, their dependence on colonial and backward territories, and so on. The crash of British capitalism was not going to be precipitated by what was happening in Lancashire or Glasgow; rather, the collapse of English rule in India and the colonies was going to unchain a series of events that would turn the English worker into a revolutionary. The weakest link in the chain was not the factory at home, but the possessions overseas.

The focus of the revolutionary struggle was thus shifted from advanced industrial nations to semi-industrial or even nonindustrialized countries, according to Lenin's third conclusion. Socialism still could not be achieved in a backward country like Russia, but *socialists* could seize power—a European revolution could be started—more easily in Russia than in England. Implicit in this notion was an assumption that the survival of revolution and the establishment of socialism in less advanced countries was possible only after the flame of revolution had caught on in more advanced nations and with their help. But the starting point was to be in the East. This was the most startling and fundamental revision of classical Marxism, the justification of what the Bolsheviks were to undertake in 1917.

Not only the *geographic* but also the *social* focus of revolution shifted in Lenin's final conclusion. Marx had taught that the only truly revolutionary class was the industrial proletariat. The proletariat was to accomplish the revolution and bring about socialism. Yet in nonindustrialized or semi-industrialized countries, the industrial proletariat was obviously nonexistent or still very weak. Hence, Lenin's *Imperialism* was perfectly correct in appealing to the class interests of the peasant, and the peasant, no matter how poor, if he had land at all, was in the classical Marxian terminology not a proletarian at all but a "petty bourgeois." The tactical consequences of Lenin's rephrasing of the Marxian vision of the world went still further. In colonial areas, the good Marxist should feel no compunctions in allying himself with even the middle or upper classes of the oppressed nationality. No matter how reactionary their social views, their *nationalist* opposition, to British or French rule for example, made them natural allies.

For the moment, Lenin was mainly interested in expanding his pre-1914 tactic of using the nationality problem of the Russian empire as fuel for revolution. Thus, though the influence of Marxism among Ukrainian peasants, say, was almost nil, separatist agitation in the Ukraine would undermine the tsarist regime or that of its bourgeois successors, as it was to do in 1917, and make the task easier for militant Marxists in Moscow and Petrograd. In this way Lenin combatted the ideological scruples of some Bolsheviks who argued that to foment nationalist unrest among the Tatars of the Volga regions or the Turkic peoples of Central Asia was to play into the hands of the most reactionary elements among them, the *mullas* (the closest equivalent to ministers among the Muslims), whose nationalist stance reflected a desire to preserve their religious influence. No allies were to be scorned in the fight against the tsarist regime, no social or national element with grievances against the Russian state was to be excluded from the struggle.

The further implications of Lenin's views were to become obvious once his party achieved power. Communist Russia was not to scorn alliance with the nationalist movements of India, Egypt, or Turkey even though the dominant elements among them were often native capitalists or landowners. At times, this collaboration would require acquiescence in the given movement's or government's suppression of its own Communists. But just as the nationality problem was adjudged to be the Achilles' heel of tsarist Russia, so the colonial problem was seen as the most vulnerable element in the capitalist world order. The thread of tactics implied in *Imperialism* leads through Soviet policy of the 1920s, when it supported such potentates as Kemal Pasha, Chiang Kai-shek, and Amanullah, to Khrushchev's endorsement of "wars of national liberation." Similarly, the tenet that the industrial worker need not be the main instrument of the socialist revolution would find its demonstration in Mao Tse-tung's tactics in the late 1920s and 1930s, when the Chinese Communists based their appeal for power on the aspirations of the peasants and sought to recoup in the countryside what they had lost in the cities of the seaboard.[8] And the current ideological and tactical teachings of the Chinese Communists—when they advocate, in effect, an alliance of the "countryside" (the underdeveloped, mostly rural areas of the world) against the "cities" (the industrialized areas of the world, including the USSR)—is again a descendant of Lenin's teachings as to how imperialism and colonialism can be exploited in the struggle to destroy the established international order.

Thus, Lenin's *Imperialism* provided what was soon to become Communism with a framework of reference on international affairs. Once he was head of state, Lenin would change or modify many of the arguments in *Imperialism*. But it was and has remained, though of late with diminishing effect, the prism through which Soviet policy makers have viewed the outside world and one of the basic premises of their foreign policy. And it was the experience of war that made the Bolsheviks learn the lessons enshrined in *Imperialism*.

11 | COMMUNIST DOCTRINE AND SOVIET DIPLOMACY

Much effort and ink has been expended in the West in pondering over the ultimate aims of Soviet policy. Is it directed to making the world Communist? Is it concerned more with Russia's national interest and security, or with the narrower interests of the ruling group? A more sophisticated approach has recognized that human motivation and political goals seldom, if ever, admit of such simple answers and clear-cut distinctions.

The earliest generation of Bolshevik rulers genuinely believed that they were merely the servants of a world-wide idea and movement and that the interests of the Soviet state could be sacrificed for the sake of a world revolution. Stalin's "socialism in one country" formula represented the rationalization that the cause of the world-wide Communist movement could best be served by strengthening the USSR, that what was good for Russia was good for Communism. Only after World War II was it seen that there could be a basic incompatibility between the two, or to put it more bluntly, that Communist China represents a threat to the USSR largely *because she is Communist*, whereas a non-Communist regime there might well, on the analogy of India, have had the friendliest relations with Moscow.

A question often asked is: Do Soviet leaders believe in the possibility of the peaceful coexistence of different social systems as against the inevitability of war? Here again different answers have been given at different periods. But even the earliest and most pessimistic formulation, that by Lenin, assumed only the long-run tendency toward an inevitable conflict between the two systems. The possibility of peaceful coexistence of socialism and capitalism has, on the contrary, been almost always emphasized as the practical prospect not only for the immediate but also for the fairly long-run future.

Since World War II there has been a somewhat wider gap between what the Soviet leaders have said on this subject and what they actually believe. The growing strength of the USSR, the failure of the United States to exploit its atomic monopoly even for diplomatic purposes, the end of Western empires—all these developments have filled the Soviet leaders with confidence that a major conflict can be avoided. With it has emerged the realization of how all-destructive such a thermonuclear conflict would be. And in their speeches and pronouncements they have allowed as much. At the same time they have been unwilling to scrap the dogma that goes back to the earliest days of the Soviet state: the doctrine of the basic hostility of capitalism to the USSR and of the constant, if not for the most part imminent, threat of a capitalist attack.

This doctrine of the outside capitalist world as mainly hostile has obvious politico-psychological advantages: it preserves the image of the Soviet Union as a beleaguered fortress, thereby justifying the sacrifices and vigilance that the state requires from the citizen whether on the production line or in abjuring the tempting example of the West with its comforts and freedoms. The doctrine justifies interventions in the affairs of other Communist states on the order of the example of Czechoslovakia in 1968. Even to themselves the Soviet leaders probably could not fully admit that they were really afraid of the example of Czechoslovakia; that demands for similar freedoms and eventually for a multiparty system might be raised in Poland or East Germany, for example, and if tolerated there, perhaps even in the Soviet Union. It was easier to allege a capitalist plot to overthrow socialism in a fellow Communist country, and even to hint at the possibility of armed intervention by NATO.

Realistically, no student of world affairs, nobody reading what has been happening in the United States and in other states of the West, could have for at least the last twenty years credited the West with the ability or desire to overthrow Communism by force. But for the Soviet regime, the thesis of the West's basic hostility and evil designs is a necessary psychological crutch. In employing it, the regime has had at the same time to avoid unduly alarming its own people. It reconciles these contradictory requirements by the formula that while the "ruling circles" in the West (and it is seldom made clear whether this expression is supposed to mean the actual governments or the capitalists and their agents within governments) are unremitting in their hostility, the strength and vigilance of the Soviet Union on the one hand, and opposition to war by the people even within capitalist countries on the other, keep aggressive forces in check.

The notion of the basic enmity of capitalism is thus welded into the Soviet creed (still more so into the Chinese Communist one), and it cannot be dispelled even by the most patently peaceful policies of the West, including the periods of collaboration between West and Russia for the attainment of such mutually desirable objectives as the avoidance of an all-out war in the Middle East or a reduction of the burden of armaments. No matter how different American policies might have been at the close of the war, it is unlikely that Stalin could have afforded or chosen a close collaboration with the United States. The need for such collaboration lapsed with the defeat of the common enemy: the continuance of such collaboration was seen, and with some justification, as a danger to the preservation of the Soviet totalitarian system in its full vigor.

Since the war the soviet regime has found itself in a growing ideologico-political impasse on another point of the official doctrine. First Yugoslavia, then much more decisively China, undermined the thesis that the spread of Communism automatically benefits the interests of the Soviet Union. Privately, the Soviet leaders may well have concluded that peaceful coexistence of the United States and the USSR, though attendant with danger, is possible, while peaceful coexistence is far from certain as between Russia and China.

No capitalist power has publicly advanced, as has China, its claims to vast areas of the USSR. Peking has challenged Soviet leadership of the world Communist movement. The present Chinese leadership has made clear that the price of a full reconciliation with Russia must include the virtual subordination of Soviet foreign and interbloc policies to China (the Chinese have not refrained from criticizing Soviet internal policies as well). Moreover, as the

Russians have complained more than once, the Chinese have tried to push them into more risky policies vis-à-vis the United States, perhaps into a catastrophic nuclear confrontation. How feeble, as against these claims on the Soviets, are the alleged plots of the Bonn "revanchists" or the supposed designs of the American "monopoly capitalists."

An outsider might well ask why, in view of this clear and present danger from another Communist power, the official Soviet line is still to picture the Sino-Soviet dispute as a temporary disruption of normally cordial relations between two fraternal Communist countries; why the Russians intermittently seek an accommodation through intraparty or intragovernment talks, as at present; or why Moscow claims that the whole trouble is due to the personalities of the current Chinese leaders, rather than to the basic inability of the two super-powers to coexist harmoniously within the Communist world.

It is difficult to give a clear answer to such questions, and it is probable that different factions within the Politburo view this all-important problem in different ways. Politicians in all societies are adept at rationalizing the really insuperable problems, at believing that something *might* happen to make them tractable, and that in the meantime a compromise, an arrangement, is necessary. The present leaders, for the most part men in their sixties, may well believe that the dispute ought to be patched up, that time is running out on Mao, that his successors might be more amenable or that the Chinese Communists might obligingly engage in a long civil war over the succession. For the next five or ten years the problem might be kept from erupting in a violent form, and afterward it would not be up to *them* to deal with it. Others may well be impatient and believe that time is on the side of the Chinese, hence the Soviets should seek a counterbalance to Peking: actively promote dissension within the Chinese Communist ranks, seek a rapprochement with Japan, perhaps even an understanding with the United States. Actual Soviet policies reveal a mixture of the two approaches: talks are held with China, at the same time as Japanese help is sought to develop Siberia and thus to discourage Chinese ambitions in the Soviet Far East Territories.

Underlying this basic dilemma is the psychological inability of the Soviet leaders to admit to their people, perhaps even to themselves, the true dimensions and dangers of the Chinese problem. To do so would be to reveal how obsolete are the premises of Communism in today's world, to acknowledge unmistakably that the main danger to the security of the USSR comes not from the capitalists but from the growing power of a fellow Communist state. This acknowledgment would in turn challenge the domestic rationale of the Communist regime, the whole structure of the Soviet power, the position of the ruling elite—all this would be put in jeopardy. Thus, the danger the regime would incur would be much greater than that faced through Khrushchev's revelations about Stalin's crimes and errors. For the blame could no longer be imputed to the aberrations of one man and his advisers, but would be linked to the very dogma on which is based the whole Soviet system.

Political and psychological exigencies compel the Soviet regime to persist in this official and unrealistic view of the world: Communist China, while temporarily hostile, cannot in the long run have interests antagonistic to the USSR, whereas the United States, while not an immediate threat to Russia, must be considered a constant danger because of the nature of her system. How long this basic attitude will be preserved will depend not only on events on the international scene but on domestic political developments in both the USSR and China.

The underlying, as contrasted with the official, attitude toward the spread of Communism has also undergone changes in areas other than China. Here again the experience has jarred the earlier ideological assumptions.

It has been seen how a Communist country could actually become a military ally of the West, as has Yugoslavia through her membership in the Balkan Pact; could even, though staying in the Soviet bloc, undertake extensive diplomatic and economic links with the West, as has Rumania, or compel the Soviets to vacate a naval base and sever diplomatic relations, as did Albania. In brief, few of the non-Communist neighbors of the Soviet Union would have dared to display the kind of defiance she has encountered, at times, at the hands of fellow Communists. This must have led to a considerable reassessment of the earlier assumption that the spread of Communism represents, so to speak, so much more money in the bank for the USSR.

On the contrary, it has become clear in the last fifteen years that some of the most valuable allies and clients of the Soviet Union have been non-Communist states. The undermining of Western influence in the Middle East was effected through the exploitation of Arab nationalism. It is doubtful that this effort would have been successful had one of the Arab states become completely Communist. Such a transformation would have aroused the immediate opposition of other Arab states and would most likely have led to a decreased Soviet influence and maneuverability in the region as a whole. The current, generally anti-United States orientation of the majority of Arab states fits the purposes of Soviet policy much better than would special ties with, say, a Communist Syria or a Communist Egypt.

Such ties would also mean, among other things, special responsibilities. Soviet prestige is vitally involved with the fortunes of other Communist countries, even when the given regime, as in the case of North Vietnam, may be under Chinese as well as Soviet influence. But Soviet diplomacy has an obviously freer hand in dealing with Egypt, whose defeat in 1967 could in no sense be interpreted as a defeat for Communism or the Soviet Union. Because of the present unfortunate configuration of events in the Middle East, it may be asserted that the dependence of Egypt or Syria on the Soviet Union is as great, if not indeed greater, than if they were Communist states, while the Soviet stake in them is smaller. This does not mean that the USSR is not strongly interested in the preservation of the current regimes in Cairo and Damascus (indeed, the presence of the Soviet fleet in the Mediterranean may have as one of its purposes keeping watch that the pro-Russian Arab regimes do not change their complexion). But this commitment is not as strong as it would be if Egypt or Syria were Communist.

Doubts about the desirability of further Communist expansion must be reinforced by the consideration that a new Communist regime, especially one in Asia, might turn out less desirable from the Soviet point of view than a previous neutralist one. For some years prior to the defeat of their attempted coup in 1965 the Indonesian Communists had gravitated heavily toward Peking. This explains the rather mild Soviet reaction to the suppression of the Indonesian Communist Party, as contrasted with the violent protests forthcoming from China. The Soviets have striven to maintain normal relations with the governments of Indonesia and Malaysia. It is difficult to see how, from their point of view, it could be a gain rather than a loss if pro-Peking Communist regimes were installed in those countries.

An anti-United States or a neutralist regime in which local Communists play some part, but with whose fortunes the prestige of the Soviet Union is not too closely bound, appears to be the best suited to Soviet needs and desires in Asia. The Soviet Union has given strong diplomatic and economic support to the Congress Party government in India. This, and the Soviet proposals for an Asian security treaty, have led to alarmed ractions on the part of the Chinese communists. Ever since 1958-1959 Peking has suspected the Russians both of trying to preserve the Congress regime and thus working against the interests of Indian Communism, and of trying to build in India a counterforce to the Chinese influence in Asia. These charges go perhaps too far, yet there is no doubt that Moscow would view with apprehension a complete Communist takeover, since whatever faction of Indian Communism would emerge on top, Communist India would most likely tend to be closer to Peking than to Moscow.

An all-out Communist regime presents yet another complication to the Russians. They cannot remain indifferent to internal developments within another Communist country. It is obvious that the whole trend of the internal evolution of Communism in Czechoslovakia from January 1968 was considered to be a danger to the internal cohesion of other Communist countries in Eastern Europe and perhaps even in the Soviet Union. These dangers were finally thought to be serious enought to warrant the risk of an armed intervention. The need to bolster the Czech economy, now deprived of the possibility of the infusion of capital from the West, also places burdens on the Russians. In brief, the pattern of

economic relations between the USSR and the People's Democracies, which in Stalin's time was one of straightforward exploitation, has changed, and in some cases it is the Soviet Union that has
to incur economic sacrifices for the sake of preserving its political
domination.

Were this a more rational world, the rulers of the Soviet Union
might well question the need for, or desirability of, such complete
domination. In her foreign policy, Finland has to be guided by
Soviet desires as much as does Czechoslovakia, possibly more than
does Rumania. However, since Finland is not a Communist state,
her multiparty system and democratic freedoms are not considered
to be a threat and a bad example to the Poles or East Germans. Her
economic problems are of no particular concern to the Soviet rulers
nor a source of expense to the Soviet taxpayer.

Yet ideological exigencies dictate Moscow's continuing policies,
which from the point of view of Soviet national interests either
promise no clear-cut gains or are actually counterproductive. What
has now become a world-wide competition between Russia and
China for the allegiance of Communist and left-wing movements
strengthens the fear of the present Soviet leaders of appearing
either lukewarm in propagating the ideology or overly eager to seek
an accommodation with the capitalists. Thus, ironically, conscious
though they are of the Chinese desire to push them into more risky
policies vis-à-vis the West as well as into more rigid policies at
home, the Soviets cannot help being somewhat influenced by this
psychological pressure from Peking.

In short, behind the apparent self-assurance and sense of direction of Soviet foreign policy, considerable dilemmas and uncertainty are hidden. The removal of Khrushchev now appears to have
reflected, insofar as international relations were concerned, the
decision to hold the line, to stick to the familiar patterns of the
immediate past, and to avoid any dramatic steps such as officially
reading China out of the Communist family of nations and seeking
a basic détente with the West. Instead, the present rulers have
continued an unremitting pressure on the West in areas like the
Middle East where it has been most vulnerable, and have intermittently sought ways of patching up the quarrel with Peking. In

the latter they have been influenced not only by domestic considerations but also by the obvious opposition of many foreign Communist parties to a definite breach between the two Communist super-powers.

Those who are unduly impressed by the Soviets' diplomatic skill and by their ability usually to get their way might well ponder both the Soviet attempts since 1963 to reach some consensus within world Communism on China and the sad record of the world conferences of Communists, conferences that have sometimes aborted, sometimes adjourned, and even when convening have brought no tangible results.

To be sure, there is a definite limit to Soviet inhibitions on account of foreign Communists' views: where the situation is seen to be definitely threatening, as in Czechoslovakia in 1968, no amount of disapproval on the part of such as the Italian Communists will keep the Soviets from protecting their interests. But in the more complex case of China, the views of foreign parties have had some weight on Soviet moves, a situation that would have been unthinkable in Stalin's time.

What is sometimes described as the Brezhnev doctrine, that is, the right of the USSR to intervene in the internal affairs of another Communist country (hardly a novel doctrine and hardly an invention of Brezhnev's), has a counterpart in the as yet timid (except on the part of the Chinese) claims of foreign Communists that their views be considered when it comes to Soviet foreign policy and that they be informed about the reasons for major changes within the Soviet Union, such as the removal of Khrushchev. This tendency could be observed on the occasion of the Twenty-third Congress of the Communist Party of the USSR. There the Cuban delegate argued, in the face of an obviously hostile reception by the congress, that the American bombings of North Vietnam represented such a basic danger to the interests of world Communism that the USSR had to stop them even if it meant "using all the available means and taking the necessary risks." The representative of North Vietnam, in turn, implicitly chided the Russians for their quarrel with Peking, since in view of the Vietnamese crisis the "only correct line at present is unity of all revolutionary forces."

Again, such speeches, or even suggestions made in private, would have been unthinkable in Stalin's time, when foreign Communists were expected to, and usually did, sacrifice their particular interests for those of the Soviet Union, and when any suggestions coming from a Communist source that Soviet policy was not promoting strongly enough the interests of the world-wide movement would have been treason.

To many in the Soviet Union, possibly including some in the ruling elite, their connection with the world-wide Communist movement, and the responsibility for it of the USSR, must then appear increasingly as an encumbrance rather than an advantage. It exposes Russia to dangers of an atomic confrontation with the United States because of the adventurousness and personal ambitions of a Communist chieftain who cannot be entirely controlled by Moscow, or to international complications on account of another chieftain who cannot contain liberalization within what the Soviet leaders consider safe limits. It should not be forgotten how long Anastas Mikoyan had to spend in Cuba soothing Castro's ruffled feelings after the Cuban crisis, nor should the invasion of Czechoslovakia obscure the fact that virtually the whole Politburo of the Soviet party had conferred with the Czechs before the assault, seeking other solutions to the crisis.

Before World War II, international Communism, that is, the presence in virtually every country of a disciplined body of men who were friends of the Soviet Union, obviously brought solid advantages. Now it is no longer so in many cases.

Soviet policies, for all their skill and realism, rest ultimately on a premise that is increasingly hard to describe as realistic: the United States is basically an enemy and a threat, China basically a friend and an ally. The hard and realistic men who run the Soviet Union persist in clinging to this fiction partly because they cannot free their own minds of ideological considerations, or to put it otherwise, because of the habits of thinking and acting of a lifetime. But they cling to this fiction also because probably in their most cynical moments they adhere to a domino theory of their own: acknowledge publicly that one vital element of the ideology is obsolete, and the whole structure, not only of that ideology but of Soviet power, may collapse.

It would be tempting to postulate that the next generation of Soviet leaders will be bolder than these men, who are fearful of departing from the beaten path. But such need not be the case. History shows that political leaders, when confronted with seemingly insuperable dilemmas, have not always followed the most logical path, especially if it involved a drastic departure from habits of long standing. One has the analogy of Soviet agriculture: there is little doubt that the whole economy would benefit greatly if the structure of the collective farm were basically reorganized, probably if the principle of collectivization were gradually abandoned. But so great is the weight of the past and the fear of tampering with a basic ideologico-social feature of the system that such a beneficial reform is not likely to be undertaken for a long time.

With respect to specific issues and negotiations between the United States and the Soviet Union, apart from obvious ideological differences and often clashing interests, we have had, to use a currently fashionable term, a failure of communication. Compared with Russians, the Americans tend to view international problems from either too large or too small a perspective. For the American public—and this has rubbed off even on the most hard-boiled statesmen and diplomats—there have been questions like how to make Russia "collaborate for peace" or, on the contrary, how to handle the "Berlin problem" or "nuclear proliferation." For the Russians, however, the underlying nature of international negotiations is, to borrow a legal term, an antagonistic one. In the very long run the interests of the two super-powers are antagonistic, not only because of their ideological differences but also because of the fact that they are rivals for primacy. This does not mean that they can never reach a mutually profitable and long-lasting accommodation, but that they can never achieve it in the sense of being able to relax their guard completely or to base their relations on, say, the Canadian-American pattern. Negotiations in the American view are occasioned for the interested parties to state their respective positions and to convince their antagonists of their goodwill and reasonability. The Soviet approach is essentially the traditional one of European diplomacy: diplomatic negotiations are a bargaining procedure in which you assess your opponent's strengths and weaknesses and test his endurance.

The Soviet approach to specific points of international disputes is often more elaborate and indirect than is realized on the other side. We speak of the Berlin crisis of 1948-1949 and of the crisis during 1958-1962 period. Yet from the Soviet point of view the pressure on Berlin during those periods was only the means of securing much broader objectives.

The threat to the Western position in Berlin in 1948-1949 was thought in Moscow to be the most efficacious means of making the West abandon or postpone its plans to set up the West German state. When this pressure proved unavailing and a continuation of the blockade threatened dangerous complications, the Soviets simply discontinued it without securing any concessions or declaring what had been on their mind in the first place.

The war of nerves over the same city in 1958-1962 was motivated by similar but even wider objectives: the Russians were eager for a German peace treaty and especially for a guarantee that Bonn would be prohibited from owning or manufacturing nuclear weapons. The most convenient means for extracting from the United States and its allies pledges to that effect was again thought to be to threaten the West in its most vulnerable spot: its rights and access to West Berlin. To appreciate the comprehensive nature of Soviet diplomatic maneuvers, one has to recall that the threat to Berlin was lifted not on account of anything happening there or elsewhere in Germany but as a by-product of the Cuban missile crisis. In the wake of a genuine scare over nuclear confrontation, it was thought too risky and uncontrollable to keep up the pressure and, on the contrary, it was thought desirable to lower the level of international tension. To seize West Berlin was never a Soviet aim in itself, though the cutting off of communications between the two segments of the city had a place, though not a very high one, on the Soviet list of priorities. West Berlin was thought of simply as one area where pressure on the West might extract concessions of much greater importance—and Berlin might again become considered as such an area.

This example shows that sometimes Soviet policies become oversubtle. It seems like common sense, especially in the nuclear age, to be more straightforward about one's fears and objectives and to negotiate more directly, rather than to employ the circuitous route both of veiled advances, veiled to the point of being incomprehensible to the other side, and of threats that, taken at face value, might lead to a confrontation with incalculable consequences. In a rebuttal, the Russians might echo the argument of defenders of militancy on the contemporary American scene: appeals for change and for solutions that seem reasonable from their point of view are seldom heeded unless accompanied by threats and *faits accomplis.*

Another more important reason for the circuitous approach of Soviet diplomacy is that in general the Russians feel it a mistake to divulge fully the nature of one's real fears and the full extent of one's weakness. Had the Western policy makers realized in 1948 how deeply concerned the Soviets then were over the prospect of the West German army, would they not have speeded up its creation and then used it as a bargaining counter to wrest concessions from the Soviet Union? Was not the West deeply impressed how apparently unconcerned the Soviet leaders were between 1945-1949 about the American monopoly of the atom bomb; how they seemed to ignore the dangerous and decisive character of nuclear weapons in any future war? Had the real extent of Soviet fears on this count been realized at the time, would not the United States have acquiesced less readily in Soviet policies in Eastern Europe and in the Far East?

The ability to engage in diplomatic feints and threats is, of course, a natural advantage that any totalitarian regime possesses over a democratic one which has to explain and justify its policies both to public opinion at home and to its allies, and which can seldom engage in forceful policies without alarming its own people and allies as much as its opponents. Yet this advantage carries with it corresponding dangers epitomized in the story of the child who used to scare his elders by crying "Wolf." The nature of Soviet goals was bound to appear to the West so elusive, and the experience of negotiating with the Russians has usually proved so frustrating and exasperating, that for all of its skill, Soviet diplomacy has undoubtedly missed major opportunities for procuring solid advantages and added security for the USSR. Moreover, because of its oversubtlety, Soviet diplomacy has brought about, or helped create, situations of immense danger, as in 1962.

There is a great deal of conjectural evidence that between 1958 and 1962 the Soviet regime under Khrushchev engaged in a most complex political maneuver. The end result was to be a basic détente between the East and West. Its major features were to be a German peace treaty and an agreement on nonproliferation of nuclear weapons, which would have banned any newcomers to the circle of powers producing and possessing such weapons, and thus have prevented or at least postponed Bonn and Peking becoming nuclear powers. Yet the fantastic circuitous and risky path taken by Khrushchev toward the attainment of these sensible aims contributed to the failure of his design. Threats and pressure on the United States were supposed to impress Peking, but they in fact alarmed and finally provoked counteraction from Washington. And advances to and signals for an accommodation with the United States while they failed to be deciphered in America, led first to suspicion of, then to the conviction of, Soviet betrayal in the mind of the Chinese Communist leaders.

By October 1962 the oversubtle policies of the Kremlin had resulted in the most dangerous confrontation yet between America and the USSR. An important consequence of the Cuban crisis was the revelation of the intensity of the Sino-Soviet dispute, and thus with 1962-1963 passed irretrievably the last Soviet hopes of forestalling or delaying China's nuclear armament.

The nuclear test-ban treaty of 1963 meant from the Soviet point of view shutting the barn door after the most valuable horse had bolted. The same went for the nuclear nonproliferation treaty. These treaties are still quite valuable to the USSR, perhaps more so than to the United States, for unlike the United States, the USSR does not like the idea of even a small stock of nuclear weapons in the hands of an ally: few people in America lose any sleep over the fact that Britain and France are nuclear powers, but it hardly requires elaboration that the Russians would not be happy at the prospect of nuclear weapons in the hands of the Czechs or Rumanians. But these treaties do not have the fundamental significance that they would have had in the fifties when the USSR perhaps still had enough economic and political leverage on Communist China to persuade her to forego nuclear ambitions. The Middle East is another area where overdevious Soviet policies may have worked to Soviet disadvantage. A few years ago an agreement between the United States and Russia as to their respective policies in the region would in all likelihood have forestalled the series of events leading to the Arab-Israeli war of 1967. Today it is problematical whether even such an agreement could keep the situation there from further deteriorating with all the attendant dangerous consequences. Does the enhanced position of the USSR in the Mediterranean justify the great risks of deeper and deeper involvement by the great powers in the Middle East crisis? There must be people in Moscow who are pondering over this question.

The motivations and the *modus operandi* of Soviet foreign policy are clearly complex. The Communist regime in Russia emerged not out of an autocratic environment but out of what might be called a disorganized democratic one of March-November 1917. The Bolsheviks, through superior organizational and propaganda ability, were able to outbid and outwit other left-of-center parties and organizations and, through their opponents' disorganization rather than their own strength and popularity, seize power. This experience left a definite imprint on the Communist mentality insofar as dealing with foreign governments is concerned: traditionally left-wing non-Communist regimes have been treated with less respect and considered easier to outmaneuver than conservative or right-wing ones.[1]

Whether in an antagonist or in an ally, the Soviets have traditionally respected a given state's strength—its industrial and military effectiveness and, most of all, its social stability and its rulers' intelligence and political acumen. Hitler's regime prior to 1934-1935, for example, was thought unstable and likely to be overthrown by a conservative reaction or a Communist revolution in Germany. Once he had given proof of internal endurance and an ability to outmaneuver Western powers, Hitler was accounted a formidable enemy but by the same token a potential, even if temporary, ally.

Yugoslavia by 1953 had become, in the eyes of the Soviet leaders, a valuable ally. Tito was courted and appeased not because he was a fellow Communist, but because he had been able to survive and to preserve internal cohesion in the face of Stalin's attacks.

Until 1947 the Russians counted on the Nationalist regime as remaining in power in most of Mainland China, and hence were ready to deal with Chiang even against the interests and pleadings of the Chinese Communists. It was only when they had become convinced that he would be unable to prevent internal collapse and military defeat that they lost any interest in an accommodation with Chiang and acquiesced in the complete victory of the Communists—something that they had not believed possible or particularly desirable prior to the middle of 1947.

It is insufficient to view as the basis of all Soviet actions the national interest, and certainly incorrect to trace such actions exclusively to the desire to propagate Communism. It is also a gross oversimplification to credit the Soviets with some magic endowing them with insuperable diplomatic advantages in any negotiations with the West.

What has been true of Soviet foreign policy in the recent past will continue to be true in the foreseeable future: it conceives of international relations mainly in terms of power politics. It gauges the strength of its opponents and rivals not only by their military effectiveness and industrial potential but also by their social cohesion and the strength of their leadership. Except in terms of propaganda, the ideological character of the government of the non-Communist countries with which they deal remains a matter of indifference to the Russians. They will not be inhibited, if they think it desirable to seek a rapprochement with Greece, by the fact that parliamentary institutions have been suspended there; their policies toward the German Federal Republic will not be appreciably different whether a Socialist or a Christian Democratic party is in power. They fashion their policies according to the specific dangers and opportunities they see and not according to the party allegiance of the governments they have to deal with.

The exigencies of the nuclear age have deeply affected the character of Soviet policies, even if this is not always apparent in statements of the leaders. Their earlier disregard of the fundamental change brought to world politics through the atom bomb was largely a pose. Later on, with both super-powers equipped with a stock of nuclear weapons, Khrushchev still intermittently behaved as if he believed that a nuclear war would be catastrophic to capitalism and not to the world as whole. It was only the Cuban crisis, and then the Chinese Communists' disregard (though undoubtedly also pretended) of the cataclysmic consequences of a nuclear conflict, which made Khrushchev acknowledge the imperative necessity of peaceful coexistence between the world's leading powers. But both he and his successors have held on to the notion that this coexistence still offers ample scope for the Soviet Union to adjust the power relationship vis-à-vis the United States in its favor.

Although they are determined to prevent the outbreak of a major war, Soviet leaders seem as yet insufficiently aware of the need to evolve techniques for preventing small crises from escalating into major ones. On the contrary, they see such small crises as offering opportunities for the Soviet Union to improve its diplomatic and power position. The world, in other words, is for the Kremlin still the stage for a competition between the two systems and for a struggle for primacy between the United States and the USSR. The general tendency of the forces of history, as well as their own superior skill in international maneuvering, afford the Soviet Union, they believe, an opportunity to win those small conflicts while avoiding a major and disastrous one.

George F. Kennan's celebrated paper of more than twenty-five years ago postulated that the Soviets' sense of the historical mission of their own system to inherit the earth would eventually yield to a recognition of the strength and desirability of the economy of the free world. Yet, while in terms of their economic growth democracies have passed the test with flying colors, the Soviets may well feel that, in view of the undeniable loosening of the ties of social cohesion and of the sense of purpose in the West, and in view of the continued political disunity of Western Europe, their own system and country is still bound to win the great race.

Such historico-philosophical considerations probably have only an indirect influence on the Soviet approach to the concrete issues of the day: disarmament, Vietnam, the Middle East. Yet there is no doubt that the current picture of social unrest and political disunity in the main countries of the West is a factor of importance in the Soviet appraisal of world affairs. This situation strengthens Moscow's temptation to exploit the vulnerability and divisions within the democratic camp; it lessens the Soviet sense of urgency about solving or ameliorating the most dangerous situations on the world scene. Though this does not follow logically, the divisions within, and the troubles of, the Western world have in fact made the Soviets more reluctant to admit how serious the split is within the Communist camp, and more reluctant to respond to pressures and tensions within their own society by turning to more liberal policies at home.

12 THE PERILS OF KHRUSHCHEV

On December 12, 1962, Khrushchev addressed the Supreme Soviet and gave for the first time a comprehensive version of the Cuban missile affair. The speech was not notable for its candor: it was the Cuban government that during the past summer had requested the missiles, said Khrushchev, and Russia put them there for the "defense of Cuba," making sure that they were under the control of Soviet military officers. On October 27 of that year, he continued, the Soviet government had received information that unless a settlement was made within two or three days, Cuba would be attacked; once having received a pledge from President John F. Kennedy that Cuba would not be attacked, the USSR had no reason to keep the missiles there. Khrushchev was more honest in answering his own question, "Who won? . . . Prudence, peace, and the world's security have won." He painted a realistic picture of the horrors that had been averted: Russia could have survived a nuclear war, but tens of millions of people would have died. As to the taunts about "capitulationism," Khrushchev in his turn became sarcastic: the Albanians "and those who support them" chided Russia for her withdrawal, yet no one called the Chinese cowardly because they tolerated the foreign occupation of Hong Kong and Macao. Or take the Chinese withdrawal to a cease-fire line after their Indian campaign: some might say this was done because China was afraid of the United States and Britain, but Khrushchev thought it was wise moderation.[1] In further defiance of Peking, he stressed Russia's warm relations with Yugoslavia (whose leader was in the audience).

Though Khrushchev continued to insist that the problem of West

Berlin must be solved and a German peace treaty signed, he stated these requirements without giving any time limits or making bombastic threats. One passage in his speech gives a clue that his internal position was now more vulnerable: the party would continue to denounce Stalin's errors, he said, but would acknowledge his "historical merits." It was a sober speech, in which relief and a degree of zest were balanced by awareness that there were no quick solutions to the most perplexing problems facing Russia in her relations with the outside world.

The events following the Cuban crisis did not justify the fervent hopes expressed at the end of those anxious October days that an important milestone in American-Soviet relations had been reached, marking the beginning of an era of real coexistence. This was because of many factors, but mainly because of China. The missile crisis marked the collapse of the last attempt by the USSR to control in any meaningful way the foreign policy of the other Communist giant. Attempts at a détente with China were made again in the spring of 1963 and following Khrushchev's ouster in October 1964. And in a sense, the ever more violent dispute between the two countries still does not rule out the possibility of such an attempt being made again or even being, for a time, successful. The harsh words exchanged so often between the USSR and Yugoslavia have not prevented those two nations from drawing together at other times. But it is precisely this example that is instructive. Never after 1948 was the USSR to regain full control of Yugoslavia's foreign policy—despite the vast disproportion of power between them. And never will an agreement between China and the USSR restore the relationship that had been based on Soviet domination and which was ceasing to exist even before Stalin's death.

This change in the basic relationship with China was to inhibit Soviet foreign policy in other areas. The primary reason was not, as is sometimes argued, that the Soviet leaders were so afraid of being denounced as fainthearted by the Chinese that they had to be especially pushy; nor that they had to be sure that the New Zealand, North Korean, and other Pacific Communist parties would not line up against them. When the interests of the Soviet state are at stake, a united chorus of all the Communist parties of the world against them would not make them budge. But the Soviet leadership considered the fiction of unity of purpose in the world Communist movement to be of importance for the survival of the Soviet Communist regime. Hence the problem of either containing China within the Communist camp or somehow expelling her has absorbed the Soviet policy makers to the point where other issues have become secondary. Were the Kremlin to confess what it undoubtedly feels —that the major threat to the security of the Soviet Union is China and not the United States—it is not what foreign Communist notables would say but the Soviet citizens' reactions that would be of concern.

This unhappy dilemma thus curbed the Soviets' freedom of movement in making foreign policy. On the American side it was fondly hoped that the resolution of the Cuban missile crisis would be followed by Soviet willingness to meet at a summit conference or at least to make far-reaching proposals on disarmament.[2] But in fact his passion for summit meetings temporarily abandoned Khrushchev. On disarmament, the hopeful prospects failed to materialize, and discussions settled down once again to such problems as on-site inspections; much of the previous Soviet zest for such an agreement was now lacking. Indeed, at least half of the original Soviet motivation was gone, for now the Chinese would never agree to stop their nuclear weapons development. There was a faint hope that maybe a test ban agreement would somehow shame the Chinese into a form of compliance, but common sense told the Soviet leaders that this was wishful thinking. Was it then worth signing an agreement with the United States and Britain and bringing down upon themselves the inevitable violent outpouring of Chinese abuse? A test ban agreement might have an inhibiting value in regard to West Germany, but the Americans, for all their talk, were apparently not going to give Bonn nuclear weapons after all. Still, there were cogent secondary reasons to have an arrangement that might slacken the pace of the armaments race. The Soviet economy was in difficulties throughout 1962 and 1963, and a reduction in the defense budget was highly desirable.

One form of nuclear proliferation that the Russians viewed with concern was the proposal for a multilateral nuclear force in NATO (the MLF), with which Washington planners hoped to appease the French and German ambitions for nuclear weapons without at the same time adding new members to the "nuclear club." Anything involving German participation in the disposition of atomic weapons, however "internationalized" the decision making, aroused the Russians' deepest fears.

All these considerations entered into the series of negotiations that led to the agreement of July 25, 1963, in which the United States, the Soviet Union, and Great Britain agreed not to test nuclear weapons in the atmosphere, in outer space, or under water. The unsolved problem of how inspections would be carried out made it impossible to extend the ban to underground testing. The Russians would agree to no more than three on-site inspections per year, any presence of foreign observers on Russian territory going against their grain, and the Americans insisted on more. The dilemma was solved by exempting underground testing from the treaty and by abandoning the whole issue of inspection, since atmospheric explosions were detectable without it in any case.

Negotiations over the test ban treaty in Moscow overlapped with Russo-Chinese discussions held, allegedly, to explore the possibility of the two nations resolving their disagreements.[3] There is probably a reason for this coincidence. The likelihood of reaching an agreement with the West, the Russians may well have thought, would make the Chinese more amenable. But the most that could be hoped for was a papering over of the continuing disagreements and a moratorium on mutual public abuse. Since at least March, Peking and Moscow had made accommodating noises to each other. The Chinese expressed interest in having Khrushchev visit them; the Soviets in return extolled the beauties of Russia in spring and summer—would not Comrade Mao take this occasion to travel in the USSR and acquaint himself with the people? Both leaders spurned the invitations. If, as was to be alleged in Peking in 1966, Mao was at this time engaged in a desperate struggle to preserve his hold on the party against the faction headed by Liu Shao-chi, Soviet solicitations for a lengthy visit may well have been motivated by reasons other than the desire to show him the beauties of their vast country. But the main reasons for the refusals were the question of prestige and the strong personal aversion that Khrushchev and Mao held for each other. The conversations were therefore conducted without the participation of the top men—the Chinese delegation being headed by Teng Hsiao-ping, the Soviet one by Suslov—and were adjourned without any tangible result on July 20. Five days later the test ban treaty was initialed, and Khrushchev entertained Averell Harriman and Lord Hailsham with ostentatious cordiality.

The theatricalities of hostility both before and after the breakup of the negotiations somewhat obscure the fact that the Soviet leadership had been careful not to burn all their verbal bridges to China.[4] Ambassador Harriman's hint that the test ban treaty should be supplemented by one forbidding the transfer of nuclear weapons from one country to another was, no doubt sorrowfully, rejected by Khrushchev. The Chinese were going to raise a storm, he knew, over the test ban; to include a nonproliferation provision would drive them to frenzy and into making the kind of revelations he feared. But even after the failure of the Sino-Soviet talks and in virtual certainty that new public displays of controversy would issue from Peking, Khrushchev refused to discuss China with Harriman. The American diplomat kept probing: "Suppose we can get France to sign the treaty. Can you deliver China?" Khrushchev replied cryptically, "That is your problem." Harriman tried again. "Suppose their rockets are targeted against you?"[5] The usually voluble Soviet leader was silent. Not only was the problem insoluble, but he was now probably under some constraint from his Russian colleagues. It would be fantastic to suppose that a "pro-Chinese faction" existed in the Presidium, but many of its members probably wished that the dispute would cease to be publicized and that Nikita Sergeievich would stop aggravating the already difficult situation by constantly popping off.

But Khrushchev's unusual discretion did not improve the matter. Neither China nor France was to sign the treaty. That West Germany did sign was a gain.[6] There was scant consolation in the fact that about one hundred other countries did sign, since a vast majority of them could not produce a jet engine, much less a nuclear bomb. On the American side the treaty was hailed by the administration as a major breakthrough in the cold war.[7] But in Moscow it could arouse neither elation nor deep apprehension. The major objective of all the Soviet maneuvering on nuclear disarmament during the past five years was still out of reach.

Khrushchev's delicacy about China—his desire to propitiate her by not attaching explicit nonproliferation provisions to the treaty— availed Russia but little. What the Chinese had had to say about their Soviet comrades before the treaty was now surpassed with a cascade of abuse unequalled in the intra-Communist epistolary tradition since the memorable correspondence between Yugoslavia and the USSR in 1948. Much of the Sino-Soviet correspondence bears on relations between the two parties and countries since 1956. In all fairness, it must be admitted that in the exchange the Chinese come out better. For all their recklessness and alleged madness, the correspondence reveals the Mao circle as shrewd analysts in foreign policy matters; it is thus reminiscent of Stalin's foreign policy in the 1930s, which was usually based on quite rational considerations, at the same time that elements in internal politics must be traced to clearly pathological aberrations. The Chinese pitilessly dissect the selfish and nationalistic motivations hidden beneath the Soviets' language of international solidarity and devotion to the socialist camp. The Russians, they point out, were always ready with offers of help *after* an emergency, as in the 1958 statement of support for China over the crisis in the Formosa Straits. Equally shrewd is their appreciation of the Soviet government's predicament in the face of the Frankenstein monster it had helped to create. "The Soviet Government . . . is insolent enough to say that we are able to criticize them only because China enjoys the protection of Soviet nuclear weapons. Well, then, leaders of the Soviet Union, please continue to protect us awhile with your nuclear weapons. We shall continue to criticize you, and we hope you will have the courage to argue the matter out with us."[8]

To be sure—and again the parallel with Stalinism is striking— this shrewdness occasionally shades into obsessiveness; a realistic view of international politics leads at times to pathological suspiciousness. Already in 1963—and here they are striking a theme that will be magnified by 1965-1967—the Soviet leaders are not merely pursuing their own power interests but actively plotting against China with the connivance of the United States, and the Yugoslav Communists are not merely revisionists but agents of imperialism. Khrushchev cannot take a vacation in Yugoslavia without some deep ulterior motive.

On their part the Soviets all too readily show their fear of the Chinese. The leitmotif of the main part of the correspondence is, "Why do you need nuclear weapons? We are protecting you anyhow." Goaded to fury by Chinese taunts on this count, the Russians go to great lengths to prove the Chinese nonchalance and irresponsibility on nuclear war, citing Mao's famous words about 300 million Chinese surviving the holocaust, or "asides" made by Chinese officials that if "small nations" such as Czechoslovakia and Italy disappeared entirely, it would be in the interests of the socialist camp as a whole! But here the Chinese could have retorted, as they almost do, that such statements were intended to unnerve the *capitalists*; indeed, Khrushchev himself had indulged in pretty much the same game. The Chinese argument in essence is: it pays to be tough when talking with the capitalists and to be unyielding in one's principles; this does not mean that one should not be prudent in action and flexible on concrete problems.

In what sense, then, is the Sino-Soviet dispute ideological? Communist habits of thought do not allow major disagreements on policy to be merely accidental or products of differing national interests. Thus, both sides have groped for deeper explanations for their dispute, but the basic one is that Russia is now highly industrialized, while China is not but has 600 million people.[9] The Chinese view Russia's intermittent attempts to reach accommodation with the United States as expressing not only personal cowardice and treason on Khrushchev's part, but also an un-Marxist and un-Leninist revisionism on the part of the Soviet elite. From this point of view, the root of the trouble goes to the original denunciation of Stalin, which the Chinese believe—quite logically, from their point of view—lowered the prestige of Communism in the international arena and opened the door to the evolution of Soviet society and policies on the pattern of Yugoslavia. The fact that Stalin would have been much harder on them than his successors, and that in all likelihood he would not have confined himself to verbal attack, is conveniently overlooked.

The Russians, on their side, have seen in the Chinese grievances an equal departure from the Marxist-Leninist orthodoxy. What was the Chinese experiment with communes, their stress on personal asceticism, and their encouragement of adventurist revolutionary attempts but left-wing dogmatism and sectarianism? China's unwillingness to subordinate her policies to those of the Soviet Union was both evidence for and the substance of a many-sided heresy.

This proneness of practical, often cynical men to rationalize a quarrel in terms of ideology has not been without its uses. It has enabled both sides to eschew the agonizing question: Does Communism, or any other universalist ideology, make sense in today's world? It has enabled both sides to keep alive hopes of reconciliation. Nothing can change the *facts*—that Russia is a generation or two ahead of China in industrialization and military power and that there are many more Chinese than Russians. But it is always possible to hope to bridge an *ideological* gap: "Khrushchev's clique" might be removed, and then the Soviet Union would acknowledge the correctness of the Chinese interpretation; or the Chinese "might come to their senses" and realize that it was they who had departed from the 1957 and 1960 declarations. Here it might be interjected that the trouble with international politics since 1914 has been precisely this tendency of statesmen to universalize their aims and to couch their objectives in ideological semantics. On this count the West, with its slogans of "making the world safe for democracy," "preserving the free world," and so forth, should display more understanding for the dilemmas of the Maos and the Khrushchevs.

The public eruption of the Sino-Soviet dispute had serious effects throughout the Communist world. To some parties, especially those most vulnerable to the threats of the "capitalist" world (Cuba and North Vietnam), the dispute was a grave embarrassment, if not an outright danger. Other parties lined up on one side or the other, depending on their proximity to or dependence on the giants. It is not surprising that the East Germans followed Moscow or that the North Korean and Japanese parties at least initially drew toward Peking. Elsewhere, the temperaments and prospects of local Communist leaders have influenced their allegiance. Because a miniscule Communist Party such as New Zealand's has no earthly prospect of coming to power in a peaceful world, its leaders respond favorably to Peking's militancy. So do the Albanians, because of their fear of Yugoslavia. And in all Communist parties and movements, there are adventurous spirits yearning for action, chafing under pro-Moscow party bureaucracy, and drawn to the exciting new variety of Chinese Communism.

The Soviets have accused the Chinese, with some justice, of giving a racist tinge to their variety of Communism. Certainly Peking's "splitting activities," to use the Soviet expression, have been most noticeable in Asia, Africa, and Latin America. And especially in the last few years Peking has in some ways been trying to portray Soviet Communism as "the rich man's Communism"— cautious, sedate, working in an informal, or perhaps even formal, alliance with imperialism; as against which Peking extends a helping hand to the *real* wretched and underprivileged of the world, or at least to the parties purporting to represent them, which have nothing to lose but Soviet subsidies and invitations to Moscow. The long reach of Chinese propaganda extends even to the Communists in "overdeveloped" countries. According to a choleric statement of the Communist Party of the Soviet Union in 1963, "The leadership of the [Chinese Communist Party] is organizing and supporting various anti-Party groups of renegades who are coming out against the Communist parties in the United States, Italy, Belgium . . . In the United States support is being given to the subversive activities of the left opportunist 'Hammer and Steel' group."[10]

Another aspect of the Sino-Soviet dispute revealed by the publication of the 1963 correspondence is the matter of disorders and sporadic troubles along their common border. The Chinese allege that in the spring of 1962, the leaders of the Russian Communist Party used their organs and personnel in Sinkiang China to carry out large-scale subversive acts in the Ili region and enticed and coerced tens of thousands of Chinese citizens into going to the Soviet Union."[11] How a few consular officials could coerce "tens of thousands" of people is left unexplained, but what occurred, evidently, was a mass flight of Sinkiang Kazakhs to the USSR. On their part, the Soviets alleged more than five thousand border violations by the Chinese in 1962 alone. The implications of this aspect of the dispute are obvious.

The best comment on the 1963 outbursts between Russia and China is unwittingly provided by a quotation from Lenin given in a Chinese statement: "Abuse in politics often covers up the utter lack of ideological content, the helplessness and the impotence, the annoying impotence of the abuser."[12] Neither side could budge the other. In a different world, even a few of the grievances aired would have led to war. To paraphrase a saying, if one has such "fraternal parties," one does not need bourgeois imperialists. But both parties had to go on making sounds and gestures about possible accommodation, exchanging increasingly cool greetings on their respective national and Communist holidays, and expressing "unshakable confidence" that in due time the dissonances would be overcome.

However, as long as the Gordian knot of Sino-Soviet disputes remains uncut, Soviet freedom of operations in foreign affairs is severely restricted. The Soviet Union must compete with the United States and at the same time with China for the allegiance of Communist parties and national liberation movements all over the world. She must try to coexist with the United States, in the sense of avoiding a nuclear war and at the same time with China, in terms of avoiding a definite breach. A Stalin might have been able to cut this Gordian knot by formally renouncing the Sino-Soviet alliance and securing an official condemnation of China from the majority of the Communist parties of the world, thus casting the Chinese Communists and their allies out of the Soivet-controlled Communist bloc. But these options were not within Khrushchev's power.

The predictable effect of the Sino-Soviet conflict was that it made a partial American-Soviet détente more possible but a far-reaching one impossible. The test ban agreement was accompanied and followed by a series of measures, hardly momentous in themselves, indicating the Soviet leaders' continuing interest in lowering the level of tension with America: the "hot line" established in the summer of 1963 permitting instantaneous communication between the Kremlin and the White House; in October the Soviet Union's adherence to the United Nations resolution asking all states to refrain from orbiting nuclear devices in outer space.

The Soviets would have liked to accompany the test ban treaty with a nonaggression pact between the Warsaw Pact powers and NATO. This proposal was never enacted, owing to United States fears of the possible difficulties with West Germany and the all too actual ones with France. The latter, or more properly General de Gaulle, refused to sign the test ban treaty. Though they severely criticized France's decision to acquire atomic weapons, the Soviet leaders refused to view it with the seriousness they attached to this possibility in the case of West Germany and especially China. Khrushchev chose to joke about it: "De Gaulle has said that he wanted his own 'nuclear umbrella,' but to construct a nuclear umbrella is not such a simple thing. One may end up both without one's pants *and* without the umbrella."[13] Like practically everything else he was saying at the time, this was supposed to be read and pondered in Peking. But within three years, de Gaulle, who had acquired a modest atomic force while keeping his trousers, was to be a cordial friend of Khrushchev's successors.

A nonaggression treaty would have meant the West's implicit recognition of East Germany and of Poland's territorial gains under the Potsdam decision. Though the Russians do not take such treaties terribly seriously, it would have strengthened their case against the Chinese indictment that they were appeasing the United States without getting anything in return. As it was, Khrushchev had to give a warning on the eve of signing the test ban treaty: "This of course does not mean, comrades, that one should let oneself be prey to illusions, that the dawn of new relations between us and the United States has already risen. No."[14] It is quite likely that further concrete measures of détente with the United States would have strengthened Khrushchev's personal position though Nikita Sergeievich cannot be made into a warm friend of America, it is clear that following the Cuba fiasco he was readier than most of his colleagues to improve Russia's relations with the United

States. And he was badly in need of tangible successes and a vindication of his position.

Between July 1963 and his ouster, Khrushchev's position as leader of international Communism was to be gravely compromised by domestic setbacks and difficulties. He could have survived the reverberations of the Cuban crisis and the worsening relations with China if his domestic plans and policies had been succeeding. But 1962 and 1963 were years of considerable economic difficulties and shortages. The contrast between Khrushchev's boasts and the reality was shatteringly revealed following his ouster. Said a member of the Presidium: "We heard the slogans [that we must] catch up and overcome in the near future the United States in per-capita production of meat and milk. We heard slogans about fulfilling the Seven-Year Plan in three and four years, [slogans] that we live well now and tomorrow we shall live even better. But what did we have in fact?—Bread lines!" [15] In his attempt to overcome the difficulties, Khrushchev had recourse to various administrative improvisations, which disturbed his hitherto faithful bureaucratic followers. His temper grew short. A few minutes' conversation with Khrushchev, a ruffled bureaucrat was to lament, and an important party official was fired or transferred (the speaker did not reflect how much more serious the results of an interview with Stalin had often been).

The dilemmas and dangers involved in a simultaneous rapprochement with the United States and conflict with China were vividly illustrated in a Central Committee meeting held shortly before the signing of the test ban treaty to discuss the ideological tasks of the party. The theme of the report delivered at the Plenum by a secretary of the Central Committee, Ilichev, was the absolute impermissibility of confusing the desirable principle of peacful coexistence among states of differing social systems with the subversive notion of coexistence of ideologies: "To call for the peaceful coexistence of Communist and bourgeois ideas is to act as scouts of the enemies of socialism, to sell out the basic interests of workers, to work in the interests of our enemies, who want to exploit even cultural ties between nations for subversive purposes." Ilichev went on to reveal the leadership's fears about ideological erosion in the Soviet Union and especially about the yearnings for greater freedom expressed by the intellectuals and students. Khrushchev himself, in the concluding speech, acknowledged a petition from a number of party members calling for greater freedom ("straightened out" by the leaders, those comrades then withdrew their petition).[16] The whole tenor of the meeting testified to the party's serious concern with the potential dangers of this intellectual unrest. The outstanding sinners mentioned in this context were people like the writer and journalist Victor Nekrasov, who liked too much what he had seen in the United States and Italy; the abstractionist sculptor Neizvestny, the sight of whose works threw Khrushchev into a veritable tantrum; the young poet Andrei Voznesensky, who had given an incautious interview to bourgeois journalists; and "unvigilant" movie producers and magazine editors.

The proceedings of the Plenum, though they contained no secrets and could hardly be a revelation to even a casual reader of the Soviet press, were not published as a whole until one year later, which underlines their connection with international politics.[17] In the international context of mid-1963, the call for ideological vigilance was bound to be confusing: was a loyal Soviet citizen to feel closer to his coreligionists in China, who poured vile abuse upon his leaders, than to the Americans, with whom a friendly agreement had just been reached? Did not perhaps those comrades who argued for greater intellectual and artistic freedom allege the Chinese danger as a reason for their position? How could one deprecate a degree of ideological coexistence with the bourgeois world, when ideological unity with the largest Communist state was clearly a sham?

These bewildering questions must have been asked repeatedly in the Presidium of the Central Committee. Since there was no easy way of answering them, Soviet policy went by fits and starts until the ouster of Khrushchev in October 1964. At one point the leadership pressed for another conference of Communist parties, where presumably the Chinese and their allies would be condemned and isolated, if not indeed expelled from the international movement. At other times it proposed an end to the public polemic and a further exploration of the possibilities of reconciliation. But the image of Communism as a united movement was visibly crumbling. Among many parties still loyal to Moscow the idea of a conference met with little enthusiasm: it was bound to advertise the internal dissensions, perhaps cause an irreversible split. In the Communist states this might well lead to a repetition of the troubles in East Europe of 1956, perhaps on a larger scale. In non-Communist states the influence of the orthodox, Soviet-type Communist Party might also weaken, fickle intellectuals and adventurous youths being drawn to the Chinese "Marxist-Leninist" parties, or many people might simply abandon a divided movement that no longer promised to be the wave of the future.[18] The vision of high officials of the Communist Party of the Soviet Union haggling with their counterparts in the New Zealand and Danish parties, imploring the Italians, being snubbed by the Rumanians, would have brought a smile to Stalin's face. He had said, "You will be lost without me."

China's "subversive" activities were not limited to world Communism. That profitable sideline exploited by the Soviets since World War II, the national liberation movement, now became the locus of keen competition between the two Communist super-powers. Superficially, all the advantages here might appear to be on the Soviet side: the Soviet Union had power and resources dwarfing those of China; she could provide economic help that China could not match. But the Soviet Union had to move more cautiously and sedately, while China could proffer reckless advice and encouragement to the ambitious heads of new states. In the underdeveloped world the Soviet Union found herself competing with China under disadvantages somewhat similar to those the United States experienced in competing with the Soviet Union. For figures like Sukarno or Nkrumah, Soviet policies were beginning to sound as "square" as the tedious American insistence that the best course was to concentrate on economic development. The billion or so dollars expended by the Soviet Union on helping Indonesia were an almost complete waste; the mercurial Sukarno drew closer to Peking, and the Indonesian Communist Party cautiously but distinctly ranged itself on the Chinese side.

The Chinese moves were made in a deliberately provocative manner, Soviet Communism being pictured as not only the "rich man's" but the "white man's" Communism. Mao himself authored the theory of the "three spheres" of imperialism (the United States and her allies), of the Soviet Union, and of most of the rest of the world where presumably China was destined to lead (Asia, Africa, and Latin America). In December 1963 Chou En-lai toured Africa propagating the Chinese brand of revolution; Soviet representatives were reduced to undignified haggling and protests over China's demand that they be excluded from the conference of Afro-Asian states.

It might be thought that Soviet sensitivity over the Chinese tactics was excessive, if not ridiculous. The notion of the Third World being united in any meaningful way is sufficiently refuted by the fact that its constituent parts are usually found in the most acute conflict with each other rather than with the former colonial powers: India versus Pakistan, Somalia versus Kenya, Algeria versus Morocco—this melancholy enumeration could be carried further. The idea that one could capitalize on the revolutionary potential of African nationalism also flies in the face of the fantastically unstable nature of politics in that continent, of which the fate of Nigeria provides the most vivid illustration—the very state which, it had been assumed, had the most solid chances for stable economic and political progress. But the Soviets' sensitivity revealed an awareness that their old monopoly in exploiting the strains and stresses of decolonization and underdevelopment was at an end. At the very moment when the West's weaknesses and confusions presented Soviet Communism with the opportunities it had dreamed of since its foundation, the anti-imperialist game could no longer be played with the old zest and self-assurance.

The Chinese challenge was the specific subject discussed at a special session of the Central Committee of the Communist Party of the Soviet Union held on February 14-15, 1964. Published two months later, the proceedings constitute the first public report of the Central Committee's deliberations devoted to the Chinese problem. Moreover, since the Plenum of the Central Committee was held in the presence of a large number (hundreds if not thousands) of party and government officials, the gist of the discussion and the seriousness with which the leadership viewed the problem could not but become known immediately to every party and government official.[19]

The main part of this Plenum was taken up by a lengthy report given by Suslov. Two aspects of the report and the subsequent discussion deserve special attention. The first is the violence of the personal attacks on Mao Tse-tung. He was unabashedly portrayed as another Stalin desirous of establishing personal dictatorship over the entire Communist movement: "The leadership of the [Chinese Communist Party] is trying to propagate the cult of personality of Mao . . . so [that he], like Stalin in his time, would tower god-like over all the Marxist-Leninist parties and would decide all questions of their policy and activity according to his whim."[20] But what was once tragedy repeats itself in history only as farce, said Suslov with bitter sarcasm. The Communist Party of the Soviet Union has finished with the cult of personality once and for all. Yet in China, said another speaker, silly verses written by Mao in a free moment are presented as a historic event in the nation's life.

The nature of these attacks leaves no doubt that if there was any hope of re-establishing some modus vivendi with China, the Soviet leadership had definitely abandoned it as long as Mao was at the helm. This in turn leads to the possibility that the Russians knew of the dissensions within the Chinese party that came to light with the cultural revolution and were encouraging and abetting the efforts to remove Mao. Knowing the man, they could not think that he would ever forgive or forget these scathing attacks and ridicule.

The second striking aspect of the debate was the great stress—excessive, one would think—on the devotion and attachment of the Soviet leadership, party, and nation to Khrushchev: "Our nation knows well and trusts without reservation its leaders, and it knows well and has boundless confidence in Nikita Sergeievich Khrushchev, a passionate revolutionary, outstanding continuator of Lenin's tradition, indefatigable fighter for peace and Communism . . . We the Soviet people credit our successes to the untiring efforts of Nikita Sergeievich for the benefit of our nation, for the welfare of all toilers in the world . . . He expresses the deepest thoughts and dreams of the Soviet people." Letting the cat out of the bag, Suslov perorated, "the Chinese leaders, and not only they, should get it through their thick skulls that our Central Committee, headed by this faithful Leninist Nikita Sergeievich Khrushchev, is more than ever united and monolithic.''[21]

Eight months to the day after this statement was made, the Central Committee fired the "universally acknowledged leader of our party and nation." If to the Soviet leaders Mao's person became the primary obstacle to renewed negotiations with the Chinese Communists, the Chinese felt the same way about Khrushchev.

Substantively, Suslov's report added little to the known sins and derelictions of the Chinese as they had already been catalogued. Their leaders were once more accused of "adventurism in foreign policy, attempts to preserve the atmosphere of the 'cold war,' sectarianism, putschism." It was ominously pointed out how closely their ideas paralleled Trotsky's, how leaders of the Trotskyite Fourth International applauded and helped Peking's activities. But above and beyond the tortuous ideological formulations and parallels, Suslov had to acknowledge the underlying national hostility: "Strange as it may seem, the education of the Chinese nation in the spirit of hostility to the USSR and the Communist Party of the Soviet Union has become practically the main concern of the Central Committee of the Chinese Communist Party." In a seeming refutation of his presentation of the Chinese leaders as fanatics, however, Suslov admitted that in deed as distinguished from word they were fairly realistic. And he delivered an unwitting commentary on the inflexibility of American foreign policy: "With a stubbornness worthy of a better cause, the Chinese leaders attempt to prevent the improvement of Soviet-American relations, representing this as 'plotting with the imperialists.' At the same time the Chinese government makes feverish attempts to improve relations with Britain, France, Japan, West Germany, and Italy. It is quite clear that they would not refuse to improve relations with the United States *but as yet* do not see favorable circumstances for such an endeavor."[22] As against the Chinese fear of Soviet-American collusion, the Russians were already nurturing a modest nightmare of their own: what if the Chinese and Americans ganged up against *them*?

"Where do we go from here?" the lesser participants at the

Plenum must have wondered as they dispersed to their ministries, offices, and kolkhozes. Short of a complete breach of relations, if not indeed war, there appeared to be no way out. However, in the short run the trouble hinged on the personalities of the top leaders. If they could be got out of the way, perhaps a temporary solution might be found, or at least the dispute might proceed under conditions of greater decorum. And it could not have escaped the attention of people sensitive to such details that for all the avowals of love for and solidarity with Nikita Sergeievich, only one other full member of the Presidium chose to repeat Suslov's endearing remarks about the First Secretary.

The split within the Soviet leadership must have been acute. The "usual" crises of 1964 in the Congo and Cyprus evoked the usual Soviet responses. In the Congo, the Russians provided arms for the rebels against the central Congolese government, and official protests were lodged about American help to the latter. Since the rebels were strongly supported by the Chinese and since the whole movement was of a most primitive tribal variety, this Soviet response was based on the traditional need to react adversely to any "imperialist" initiative rather than on great hope and solicitude for the rebels. In Cyprus the Soviet Union was simply happy to collect the dividends of the quarrel between two allies of Washington, Greece and Turkey. The latter, once the stanchest ally of the United States in the Mediterranean, now became friendlier to the Soviet Union, as a result of what the Turks considered to be American indifference to their grievances in Cyprus and despite the fact that the Soviets continued to supply and support Archbishop Makarios' regime.

Such small successes—as well as the visible disintegration of NATO consequent upon General de Gaulle's increasingly anti-American stance and the customary impasse of American foreign policy in a presidential election year—could not really make the Soviet leaders rejoice, beset as they were by aggravating internal problems and baffled as they were by the Chinese problem in foreign policy. Both an attempt to set up a Communist-parties conference and half-hearted attempts at some sort of détente with China continued through the spring and summer. Were it not a matter affecting the lives and fortunes of hundreds of millions of people, this phase of Sino-Soviet relations could provide rich material for a comedy. Letters bristling with invective—to choose a mild example, "you are telling a whopping lie"—would conclude "with fraternal greetings" by the given Central Committee. Attempts to mediate were undertaken by such unlikely go-betweens as the Rumanians. A few years back a frown by a minor Soviet official had the power to bring down the entire Central Committee of the Rumanian Party. Now its representatives argued with the Russians, were consulted by the Chinese, and successfully strove to establish a degree of independence in foreign and economic policies. Any "expert" who would have predicted such developments a few years before would have been stripped of his kremlinologist's epaulets, if not consigned to a lunatic asylum.

Further shocks were in store. In August 1964 Palmiro Togliatti, leader of Italian Communism and long a faithful follower of Stalin and then of his successors, succumbed to a heart attack while vacationing in Russia. A sizable Russian town was renamed in his honor, the Soviets not having learned the lesson of how troublesome such practices had been in the past, but it soon came out that Togliatti had left behind him a memorandum critical of Soviet internal and external policies. He criticized Soviet leadership for not taking more resolute steps to liquidate the backwash of Stalinism and for not allowing more cultural and even political diversity. On foreign policy he warned against any attempt to deal drastically with the Chinese. His "testament," as it became known, was the product not of any sympathy for the Chinese position, but simply of his realization that a permanent split would injure Communism everywhere. Hasty attempts were made to prevent the publication of this embarrassing document, but Togliatti's successors were obstinate. That a man with his record would write such a memorandum was palpable proof of how low had fallen the prestige of the Soviet leadership in the Communist world; now at the height of her industrial and military power, the Soviet Union was incapable of even approximating that absolute control of the movement which the weak and backward Russia had held in the 1920s and 1930s.

Nothing, however, could have prepared the Kremlin for the shock it received in August when the Japanese press published a report of an interview given by Mao to a group of Japanese socialists. Diplomatic efforts were made to have the interview declared spurious, but they were unavailing. On September 2 *Pravda* published a summary of its text, together with a full page (one-fourth of the issue) devoted to a commentary on Mao's startling pronouncements.

Mao classified the USSR as an imperialist state. In Europe, she had "appropriated" part of Rumania, taken East Germany for Poland after taking eastern Poland for herself, in both cases chasing out "local inhabitants." "The Russians took everything they could." But Mao was only warming up. How about the territories taken from China in the nineteenth century? And Mongolia, which he, Mao, had reclaimed for China in 1954 when Khrushchev and Bulganin were in Peking? On these issues the Chinese leader graciously conceded: he was willing to wait. But the Kurile Islands should be returned to Japan forthwith. The Soviet Union had more territory then she needed for her population, in comparison to Japan, say, crowded on her little islands. (Other interesting parts of Mao's interview praised Japan as a great nation, the proof being the Japanese conquests in World War II!)

The average Soviet reader must have rubbed his eyes in disbelief. What Mao said about the Soviet Union surpassed the most ambitious statements of the late Secretary of State John Foster Dulles about the need to "roll back" the Soviet sphere. The "German revanchists" at their worst, reported the Soviet editorial, would have been incapable of the insolence and provocation contained in every sentence of Mao's interview. He proposed an eventual partition of the USSR! He claimed for China enormous territories of more than 1.5 million square kilometers, inhabited by millions of Soviet citizens! In the past, a claim for a few miles of Soviet territory brought forth declarations from the Soviet government about the readiness to strike with missiles, "the mighty Red Army," and so forth. Now, for all its length, the editoral on Mao was noticeably weak in tone, plaintive rather than threatening. Khrushchev, currently in Prague, made noises about Mao's theories of *Lebensraum* and compared him to Hitler. But the provocation was so huge that any verbal response had to be anticlimactic. The Chinese Chairman had had his revenge: *now* let them laugh at his poems.

Time was growing short for Khrushchev. There were obscure signs that his colleagues were reaching the end of their patience. At a reception for the President of Indonesia on September 29, 1964, Mikoyan, as head of state, was put ahead of Khrushchev on the list of Soviet leaders. On October 2 the Presidium of the Central Committee and the Council of Ministers held their joint meeting in the presence of many other officials and activists: this fashion of holding Central Committee meetings had long enraged the members of the oligarchy, since the mass of uninitiated party members, for whom any criticism of the First Secretary would have sounded like treason, prevented them from voicing their objections and reservations. Now Khrushchev evidently proposed to use the same technique in respect to the Presidium. It is not known whether this was the last straw, or whether Khrushchev had other "harebrained" proposals that his colleagues could not stomach. In a few days he took off for a vacation in the Crimea. The press was full of the doings of the Soviet cosmonauts: a three-man team was orbiting the earth. The Central Committee members began to assemble for their triumphant reception, to which Nikita Sergeievich was scheduled to fly from Sochi.

On October 14, Osvaldo Dorticos, President of Cuba, arrived in Moscow. He well might have wondered at the sparsity of the dignitaries greeting him—only a few Presidium members—and possibly also at their preoccupied air. To Mikoyan, Dorticos divulged the purpose of his trip in a little speech: he came principally to exchange his "impressions and views with dear Comrade Khrushchev." Alas, this was not to be. On the same day the Central Committee "acceded to the plea" of Khrushchev that on account of his advanced age and ailing health he be released from his numerous state and party duties. So ran the announcement on October 16. Brezhnev and Kosygin were to succeed him, and the man who had dominated the Soviet Union for ten years, and who had shaken the world with his threats and designs, became overnight an obscure emeritus.

13 | THE 1966 CONGRESS

Apart from his relatives, it is the Western kremlinologists who have suffered most through Nikita Khrushchev's abrupt departure from power. Under Khrushchev, they had grown accustomed to anticipate eagerly that vast gathering of the ruling elite, the Communist Party Congress. Each was almost guaranteed to bring further revelations of Stalin's crimes, a growing list of former leaders who had collaborated in them, and more engrossing details of intrigues by remaining Stalinists against the First Secretary, Comrade Khrushchev. Khrushchev, to be sure, would invariably crush the latter with the help of the Central Committee of the party and the unanimous support of the great Soviet people.

Apart from such fascinating tales, the First Secretary would intermittently threaten the West or speak in honeyed words of coexistence, implying a virtual Soviet-American alliance. Thunderbolts would descend, sometimes on the heads of "dogmatists" and sometimes on those of "revisionists." Even in discussing inanimate objects, Khrushchev was dramatic and unpredictable. No sooner did his passion for steel production cool off than it was replaced by an infatuation with reinforced concrete. Kolkhozniks who have been urged by Nikita Sergeievich to plant corn, corn, and more corn were abruptly told to drop practically everything else and grow beans.

No such pyrotechnics were to be expected at the Twenty-third Congress, concluded on April 8, 1966, Khrushchev's two successors, Brezhnev and Kosygin, have practiced what might be called the cult of nonpersonality. They are much more the products of the Stalin era than was Khrushchev, who had joined the party in 1918 and who retained to the end the Leninist belief in the power of oratory and dramatic improvisation. Brezhnev and Kosygin, in contrast, have always operated in the Stalinist bureaucratic fashion, unobtrusively and behind the scenes. Where Khrushchev went in for bluster, they have ushered in what they hope to be the age of discretion and circumspection.

At the Twenty-third Congress, as speaker after speaker pronounced the ritualistic formulas of praise for the Central Committee's policy and its proposed Five-Year Plan, many delegates must have wondered whether and when the name of *that man* would be mentioned. Yet through an amazing display of self-control, none of the procession of party secretaries and ministers ever did utter Stalin's name. The reasons are as complex as they are instructive about the current dilemmas and style of Soviet politics.

Before the Congress took place, it had been public knowledge that the rulers intended a partial and circumspect rehabilitation of Stalin. Khrushchev's obsessive serialization of his crimes was held to have had a profoundly unsettling effect, especially on the younger generation. More damaging than Khrushchev's constant harping on the terror and sufferings of the Stalin era, which the middle-aged party oligarchs believed the younger generation ought now to forget, was his portrait of Stalin as a fool and a coward: "He was afraid to go into the city, he was afraid of people," the First Secretary had announced in 1962.

The Twenty-third Congress was scheduled to be treated to a better balanced view, more in keeping with the original and subdued period of de-Stalinization which had lasted from 1953 to 1956. At that time, the dead despot was depicted as a man who had rendered great services to the party and the country, but who had regrettably strayed from the Leninist path in his later years. As part of this program of rehabilitation, it was decided to restore the names of two Soviet institutions that have definite Stalinist associations: Secretary General of the Communist Party, and the Politburo. Since 1953 the highest party official had borne the name of First Secretary; until 1965 Stalin was the only Soviet leader to have been named Secretary General of the party. The Politburo had been rechristened Presidium in 1952 with the explanation: "It expresses better the nature of its functions." At the Twenty-third Congress the name was changed back again with exactly the same explanation.

The projected rehabilitation of Stalin evidently encountered a good deal of determined opposition. A number of leading intellectuals addressed a letter to Brezhnev imploring him not to revive old fears and painful associations. There are grounds for believing that even in the highest party councils fears were expressed that the move would be untimely and unfortunate. Plans for a broad historical reassessment of the Stalin era were dropped, and all that remained was the restoration of the two names. This led to awkward circumlocutions at the congress. In proposing the restoration of the term Politburo, Brezhnev explained that this was the word used "under Lenin and later." And in proposing the re-establishment of the post of Secretary General, Nikolai Yegorychev, the Moscow party head, found it expedient to mention that this title had been established "in 1922 on the initiative of Vladimir Ilyich Lenin," while skipping any reference to the only man who had actually carried the title.

More significant was the fact that, though several local party secretaries mentioned approvingly the restoration of the Secretary-ship General and the Politburo, other leading delegates limited themselves to a mere general statement of support for the party line. A totally new precedent was set when several members of the highest party body—the Presidium Politburo—did not take the floor at all. It is risky to read meaning into such developments, but in the ritualized process of Soviet politics such omissions cannot be accidental. They testify to a deep division of opinion among party leaders as to whether and to what degree the Stalin era should receive a new varnish of respectability.

One omission inevitably led to another. If Khrushchev had sinned by his denunciations of Stalin, how was it possible for the congress, even in good cause, to denounce Khrushchev himself? Obviously it was not. Instead, the party leaders resorted to their limitless vocabulary of circumlocution. In October 1965 they unanimously approved as wise and salutary the decision of the Central Committee to condemn sins of subjectivism, voluntarism, boastfulness, and "from aboveness." They undertook to correct these errors in a spirit of objectivity, with strict regard for scientific laws and an unhurried and principled consideration for the needs of the people.

Behind the dreary and repetitive jargon it was possible to glimpse the causes of Khrushchev's downfall. One could sense the oligarchs' dull hatred of a leader whose constant innovations disturbed their bureaucratic slumber, a man who, as one anguished delegate exclaimed, would on the basis of a single brief interview fire a party leader or have him transferred thousands of miles away —the speaker did not reflect that in Stalin's time one brief interview could cost considerably more than a job. Another speaker implied that through his newspaper henchmen, including presumably his son-in-law, Khrushchev undermined respect for the mainstay of the Soviet system, the local party secretaries.

Khrushchev's critics at the congress were the very same people who had come to his rescue in 1957 and helped him to eject Stalin's hated lieutenants—Malenkov and Molotov, among others. But since gratitude is no more a characteristic of Soviet politics than of any other, the party leaders chafed in turn under Nikita Sergeievich's unpredictable moves and moods, his attempted projection of himself as the national leader over and above the party. There were other and substantive reasons for the shift. At the Twenty-second Congress in October 1961, Khrushchev had pictured tremendous advances in economic growth and a definite cure for the perennial Soviet problem of agriculture. Then he had jokingly asked: "What fantasies, if you please, does Khrushchev conjure up about the agricultural growth?" His joke, alas, turned out to have been a prophecy.

In the course of the congress both Kosygin and Brezhnev described the sad state of Soviet agriculture during the past five years: the production of grain, though generally increased, had failed to keep up with the growth of population. The year 1963 was a particularly disastrous one, in which the number of cattle and pigs, as well as milk products per cow, fell substantially. No one at the congress sought to minimize the grave defects of collectivized agriculture or to revert to Khrushchev's boasts that within a few years Russia would overtake the United States in the production of meat, butter, and milk. Other boasts and promises were exposed as equally hollow. Steel production for 1970 had been projected in 1961 as 145 million tons; current estimates ranged between 124 and 129 million tons. By 1970, Khrushchev had promised, the average workweek would be reduced to thirty to thirty-five hours; in the present mood of sobriety the party promised a five-day, forty-one-hour workweek.

Khrushchev was not solely responsible for these wildly exaggerated forecasts. His present critics, most notably Kosygin, had been his closest collaborators in 1961. They too had prophesied that Russia would surpass the United States in many respects by 1965 and that it would enter into the era of real Communism by 1980. But as his targets receded, Khrushchev took exasperated recourse to fantastic administrative improvisations. The vast Ministry of Agriculture was suddenly ordered out of Moscow and told to move closer to the soil. In 1962, in the most renowned of his "harebrained schemes," he tried to split the whole party apparatus into two separate sections, agricultural and industrial, a measure that, if fully carried out, would have led to hopeless chaos.

Khrushchev's successors, Brezhnev and Kosygin, learned at least to be more modest and realistic in their goals. They were also more determined and consistent than Khrushchev in tying increased growth to a greater flow of consumer goods. For the first time in the history of Soviet five-year plans, the projected rate of increase in the production of consumers' goods was to be almost equal to that of heavy industry: the 1970 rate of production of automobiles, for example, was to be four times that of 1965. The social security benefits and the guaranteed wages enjoyed by the industrial worker were to be extended to the kolkhozniks. The very structure of the kolkhoz was to be revised in a further attempt to make the peasant appreciate that collective farming is not simply a new form of serfdom.

Did these reforms, together with those already announced allowing individual industrial enterprises more autonomy and incentive, amount to creeping capitalism? Seldom had the party shown itself so sensitive to foreign criticism as on this count. It is a vile slander, said the Soviet President N. V. Podgorny, to talk about 'liberalization' of [our] socialist society which is supposed to be developing, if you please, in the direction of convergence with the so-called 'free world.' "

The reasons for this sensitivity were obvious: the charges of "liberalization" came not only from Western capitalists but also from Communist China, and the attempt to rebut them was connected with two other issues that were paramount at the Twenty-third Congress: the growing disunity in the Communist world and the need for a sterner cultural policy at home.

The post-Khrushchev leadership tried to be tactful and conciliatory on the subject of China, and this policy reaped at least superficial dividends in all Communist parties represented at the congress (China and Albania of course were not there; neither was Japan or New Zealand). In a rare mention of China, Brezhnev pledged that the Soviet party would do everything in its power to heal the breach and proposed a conference to settle all outstanding differences. Yet indirectly but firmly the Soviet leaders also indicated that they would not let the Chinese determine Soviet foreign policy and push the Soviet Union toward a fateful provocation of the United States.

On two other counts the Soviet leaders demonstrated that they did not propose to appease the Chinese beyond certain limits. Tito's Yugoslavia, which was hated by the Chinese even more fervently than "the Khrushchevite revisionists," was treated at the congress for the first time since 1948 as a full-fledged member of the family; and Brezhnev went out of his way to express Soviet friendship for India. Constant condemnation of American aggression in Vietnam and the need for a settlement based on terms laid down by Hanoi and the Vietcong were paralleled by an equally insistent stress on the need for coexistence and the Soviet readiness for a post-Vietnam rapprochement with the United States. The plea of the Cuban delegate "to make North Vietnam a cemetery of American planes" and to prepare for similar risk-taking in other parts of the world was greeted in silence. Both Brezhnev and Foreign Minister Andrei A. Gromyko clearly indicated that Germany still stood at the heart of Soviet foreign policy concern. They spoke with genuine indignation about the possibility of West

Germany's gaining access to nuclear weapons. There was no mistaking their earnestness in this matter.

As to the Sino-Soviet split, some foreign delegates implied that they would be delighted to have the Chinese thrown out of the international Communist movement once and for all. Premier János Kadar of Hungary spoke of left-wing adventurism and shameful attempts to stimulate anti-Soviet feelings. The Argentinians proposed an international conference with or without China. From Australia and Peru came indignant stories of how the Chinese had tried to promote party dissension. But officially such outbursts were dampened to avoid disturbing delegates, including those from North Korea and North and South Vietnam, who were unwilling or unable to face the prospect of a permanent split. On top of this there was the overriding consideration that the Soviet Union could ill afford, either at home or abroad, to acknowledge even by implication that the international unity of Communism was simply another myth.

This deep concern for the preservation of the regime's ideological raison d'être also characterized the discussion of culture and the arts. Long before the Twenty-third Congress, certain party bureaucrats had bewailed the consequences of the de-Stalinization in literature. P. N. Demichev, then and in '66 party secretary, had said in 1961 that only a few writers had fallen victim "to the noxious bourgeois influence" but that if "an illness is not nipped in the bud, it can become dangerous." Khrushchev himself had frequently if inconsistently made similar noises. An added warning was conveyed a few weeks before the congress by the severe sentences imposed on Andrei Sinyavsky and Yuli Daniel. But despite a good deal of railing against writers who had dared to depict the grim Stalinist past, the congress stopped short of reinstating a strict Stalinist surveillance of the arts.

The most virulent attack on literary freedom came from Mikhail A. Sholokhov, the dean of Soviet writers. Unmellowed by his recent Nobel Prize, embittered by his lack of acceptance by the younger artists, Sholokhov raved and ranted that in the old times Sinyavsky and Daniel would have been stood up against the wall and shot. He told the delegates that he was ashamed for those literary figures who had petitioned the authorities for more lenient sentences. Though Sholokhov's outburst was interrupted by cheers, some of those in the audience must have remembered that Sholokhov himself had once been the target of similar attacks. In fact, the author of *Quiet Flows the Don* had come to resemble one of his main characters, a paranoid and sadistic Communist who turns a previously friendly Cossack village against the Soviet power. In essence his attitude was that of the middle-aged party bureaucrats: people should be grateful to the party for making things better than they were rather than complaining and asking for more.

On balance, the congress did little more than underscore the leadership's determination to follow a steady course, without the shifts and histrionics of the Khrushchev period. The new leaders would not, if they could help it, please the West by a noisy quarrel with China. Nor would they appease the Chinese by turning over to them the direction of Soviet foreign policy. They would not seek to disarm critics in the West or even in Western Communist circles by condoning what they considered license in literature and the arts. They would not relax their monopoly of political power in Russia or their claim to primacy in world Communism.

At the conclusion of the congress Brezhnev epitomized their creed: "everybody" understands that strengthening the economy and power of the Soviet Union is the greatest contribution that can be made to the world Communist and liberation movement. Under Stalin the simple idea that what is good for the Soviet Union is good for world Communism was thought to be self-evident. For all their caution and determination, however, the post-Khrushchev leaders would find it increasingly difficult to defend this creed either to their own people or to the impatient Communists in other lands.

14 THE POST-KHRUSHCHEV ERA

In 1967 the Soviet Union entered its fiftieth year. The Revolution had been made by young men. At forty-seven, Lenin had loomed over his followers as an aged and venerable patriarch. Now, appropriately enough, the Soviet Union in its middle age was ruled by men in their fifties and sixties. Not only for ideological reasons did they look disapprovingly at the impatient young man in Havana and fearfully at the terrible old potentate in Peking, trying to recoup his revolutionary youth by stirring up fanatical youngsters. Unable to solve the major dilemmas inherent in the condition of world Communism, the Soviet rulers fell back upon the easy premise that these would at least be ameliorated by the passage of time. For middle-aged men in power, it is natural to stick obstinately if anachronistically to the things one learned in one's youth, and Karl Marx had taught that history creates no problems it cannot solve.

For people who have also been taught that history is on the side of Communism, Marx's dictum is an incentive to go on doing what in general one has been doing virtually from the beginning. Thus, in the fiftieth year of the Soviet state the average Russian may have sensed that the existence and policies of a fellow Communist state presented the greatest long-run threat to his country's well-being and security, but in official propaganda "imperialism" was still the enemy, just as it was in the days when Lord Curzon presided over the foreign relations of the British empire and Mao Tse-tung was an obscure official in the Chinese Communist Party. And while official policies are infinitely more complex than official propaganda, it is still true that, though the revolutionary impulse is no longer so simple and zestful as in former days, the main thrust of Soviet foreign policy, as if by a momentum imparted long ago, is being exerted to reduce the power and influence of the greatest capitalist state.

Thus, in 1967, as in previous years, the United States sins of omission and commission were capitalized upon by alert Soviet statesmen. In the measure that Franco-American relations grew frigid, Franco-Soviet relations became cordial. Premier Kosygin would gravely consult de Gaulle on the Arab-Israeli crisis, for example, and since even the most astute statesmen are not immune to flattery, the French President must have appreciated that his country was being treated again as a great power and that a "hot line" now connected the Kremlin not only with the White House but also with the Elysée Palace. In Nigeria a civil war disrupted what from the Western point of view had been the most hopeful attempt at nation building and the most promising force for stability among the new African states. Immediately, though unobtrusively, the Soviets proffered their help to the central government in its struggle against secessionist Biafra. In Yemen republican forces struggling for the control of that primitive land were assisted by Soviet arms, supplies, and instructors. With the British about to move out of Aden, Soviet influence was reaching into the Red Sea. In practically every corner of the world the departure of Western rulers or the eruption of civil strife was followed by the arrival of Soviet advisers, economic "developers," and offers of economic and military aid. Even the stanchest of America's allies, regimes that in the past had been saved with American help, such as Iran and Turkey, were vigorously wooed by the Russians. Washington policy makers could remind these imprudent and ungrateful countries of the United States' long-standing record of anti-imperialism, could warn them that they would be sorry for all their cuddling-up with the Russians, could quote the story of the young lady who set out for a ride on a tiger, but the fact remained that every misstep of American diplomacy, every crisis in a pro-Western country, was followed by the appropriate Soviet move. The Russians, American statesmen and global strategists proclaimed, were not playing "fair"; as one of the world's superpowers, it behooved Russia to behave responsibly, to try to

decrease rather than enhance international tensions in this dangerous world. But the Russian statesmen (though they themselves were
making somewhat similar allegations about the Chinese) showed no
signs of putting a stop to this game. Undoubtedly the disintegration
of the Western alliance and the collapse of Western influence provided welcome psychological reassurances on the fiftieth anniversary of the Revolution.

The other side of the coin, undoubtedly recognized as such by
some Soviet statesmen, was that the Americans' complaint, disin-
genuous as it was and reflecting as it did exasperation with their
own clumsiness in international affairs, still contained an element
of truth. Under contemporary conditions power politics, whether
in its traditional or Communist form, has certainly lost much of its
original rationale. The old imperialism at least in theory implied the
economic exploitation of dependent territories. Now, to gain political influence in underdeveloped areas, even the USSR must make a
considerable economic sacrifice in order to satisfy the new states'
lust for industrial development. It often means, too, underwriting a
dictator's schemes for aggrandizement and his misuse of money.
The fate of Sukarno, who fell from power in 1965, was a melancholy lesson in this respect. Was the game still worth playing?

As to the further expansion of Communism, the Soviet rulers
harbored very real, if secret, doubts on this count. In Vienna in
1961 Khrushchev had exploded angrily when Kennedy suggested
that the USSR should refrain from expanding her ideological
sphere of influence and thus upsetting the balance of power: was
Russia supposed to sit like a schoolboy with his hands on the top of
the desk and not take advantage of the opportunities presented by
the decline of capitalism? But Khrushchev's rage surely reflected
serious inner doubt on this subject, and in 1967 the dilemma was
more acute. The case of Yugoslavia could be rationalized as having
its origin in a political and psychological error made by Stalin.
China was a "very special case." But when Rumania began to
create trouble, the most obtuse and ideologically indoctrinated
Soviet citizen had to question the whole premise of Communist
expansion. It was no longer creating satellites; it was even doubtful
whether it was producing allies. In May 1966 Nicholas Ceausescu,

First Secretary of the Rumanian Communist Party, more than hinted at the injustice of the Soviet Union's annexation of Rumanian territories in 1940, declared that all military blocs should be liquidated, and asserted his regime's determination to trade and develop friendly relations with all countries, irrespective of their social systems. It was vain to expect that Rumania's example would not one day be followed by Czechoslovakia or Poland. Communist countries, even small ones, loomed as future liabilities rather than assets.

An observer in 1967 might well have thought that each of the two super-powers was pursuing policies which, apart from any moral or ideological considerations, were anachronistic. In the main the Soviet Union was still behaving, though with increasing doubts and reservations, as if accession of yet another country to the Communist bloc would represent a gain in real power, something that had been certainly true before 1950 but which events since then had first thrown into doubt and then refuted. By the same token the United States, though her leaders now appreciated the existence of devergent strains in world Communism, considered the prevention of a Communist takeover of a small Southeast Asian country of such decisive importance that she was pouring into the task men and resources on a scale surpassing her effort in the Korean War. Each great power was becoming a slave to its past commitments, to a rhetoric that no longer corresponded to its national interests rationally defined, to a fear that jettisoning obsolete foreign policies would have dangerous domestic consequences. It was exquisite irony that only from Peking came voices alleging what, if it existed, would have been a rational policy: united by their fear of China, the Chinese said, Soviet revisionists and American imperialists were in collusion to end the war in Vietnam and isolate China.

Even if there had been men in the Soviet Politburo capable of such super-Machiavellian schemes, it is unlikely that they would have thought it wise thus to involve the United States. The painfully public character of American policy making, the notorious inability of American politicians to keep a secret if by revealing it they could improve their "image" or garner political support, made intrigue with them well-nigh hopeless. It was not only false pride that kept Khrushchev from unburdening himself about China to Eisenhower and Kennedy; it was also the realization that inevitably the news would find its way into newspaper columns and television, become the subject of hearings before Congressional committees, and so forth. The United States simply did not qualify as a partner for a grand historical intrigue in the style of the Nazi-Soviet pact.

The shared concern about China in Washington and Moscow thus could not by itself lead to any meaningful collaboration. In the abstract, it might appear, as it did to Chen Yi, Chinese foreign minister, that this shared interest dwarfed the significance of Vietnam to either nation. But in practice, since the defeat of Communism in South Vietnam had become the primary American policy objective, so the frustration of that policy had to become a primary aim of the Soviet Union. A French proverb has it that even saints should not be tempted. How could the far from saintly leaders of the Soviet Union pass up the opportunity of exploiting the American involvement in Vietnam? Compared with the enormous American outlay, Soviet aid to North Vietnam came relatively cheap. The cost of Soviet military supplies to Vietnam in 1967 amounted to about $700-800 million; no Russian lives were being lost; and while the psychological repercussions of the war had a divisive effect in America and all over the West, in Russia they undoubtedly bolstered the regime, for those elements that could become most restive and desirous of further reforms and liberalization would be most sensitive to the moral and political discredit that the world's greatest democracy was incurring by its actions in Vietnam. The United States' prodigious expenditure was blunting her economic superiority over the USSR. By 1967 the Soviet Union was able to reduce considerably American superiority in nuclear and missile armament, still so pronounced at the time of the Cuban crisis in 1962, and to mount an impressive naval force. Such advances did not make the prospects of a nuclear war less suicidal, but the psychological effect of near parity in nuclear weapons was of enormous importance. For all its ultimate dangers, the American entanglement in Vietnam was of immediate and solid benefit to the USSR.

Paradoxically, the very disunity of the Communist camp could be turned to Russian advantage. They could not force Hanoi, the Soviet leaders could claim, to arrange peace negotiations with the United States. Insofar as one can gauge, they recommended moderation to North Vietnam. In the nuclear age a super-power's decisive defeat in a "brushfire war"—a somewhat ludicrous description of the Vietnamese conflict—can be as catastrophic as decisive victory. So with somewhat studied vagueness the Soviet leaders repeated that American bombing of North Vietnam was the main stumbling block to negotiations.

It is not to be imagined that without Vietnam the course of Soviet-American relations would have run more smoothly or that Peking's apprehensions would have been fulfilled. But it is reasonable to assume that without the war the strains and stresses of world Communism would have become more serious, the foreign policy dilemmas of the Soviet Union more obvious to her rulers and people. But, as for individuals, so for whole societies: awareness of real troubles, and the desire to solve them in a fundamental way, are often dulled by the comforting reflection that others are confronted by problems of equal or greater magnitude.

The common concern of the two powers to avoid a nuclear war and to prevent the proliferation of nuclear weapons remained, to be sure, as strong as ever. But a purely negative interest in avoiding the worst eventuality cannot alone form the basis of a working arrangement. From the Soviet point of view, prevention of further nuclear proliferation was no longer as important as it was when China was still without atomic weapons. Now that the most dangerous proliferation of all had taken place, much of the original Soviet urgency in barring the spread of nuclear weapons was gone. To be sure, there still remained West Germany, but the Soviets concluded that Washington was not likely to furnish nuclear weapons to Bonn. Prudence still dictated that no efforts should be spared to prevent further proliferation. But the issue was not now of such an overwhelming urgency and importance to secure Soviet-American collaboration on a number of issues rather than just this one. It could not escape Soviet notice that the government in Washington, absorbed as it was in Southeast Asia, was willing to meet the Russians, who now appeared relatively sedate and responsible, more than halfway on other issues. "Taught a lesson" by the Cuban missile crisis, worried about China, the Soviet leaders were not likely to do anything "rash."

But one should not believe everything the Chinese say about their Soviet comrades; the image of a peaceful and reasonable Soviet Russia, bent, as in her Tashkent mediation between India and Pakistan, on averting dangerous international crises, was seriously shaken during the Near East war in 1967. For all its long-standing guile and newly acquired caution, Soviet foregin policy can, because of previous commitments and a well-nigh irresistible temptation, become involved in a very riskly gamble.

This is not to say that the USSR actively precipitated the events that led to Egypt's proclamation of a blockade on Israeli shipping in the Gulf of Aqaba in May, which in turn resulted in Israel's attack on the neighboring Arab states on June 5. But it is certain that had the USSR warned sternly her Syrian clients and Egyptian ally against actions that Israel would interpret as a threat to her very existence, those actions and then the war itself would not have taken place. It is less certain, but probable, that had the USSR not been interested for a long time in maintaining a state of what might be called controlled tension in the Near East, this tension would not have risen so uncontrollably in the late spring of 1967. The situation in the eastern Mediterranean demonstrated the dangerous limitations of the doctrine of coexistence as currently defined and practiced by the USSR. Peace cannot be assured simply by both great powers striving to avoid a big war. They must also develop techniques of avoiding or localizing "little" wars, which by accident or commitment could grow into big ones.

The Soviets may well have felt that the United States had broken one of the unwritten "rules" regulating the conduct of the cold war by its attacks on North Vietnam. The temptation must have been strong, then, to demonstrate the limitations of American power by letting a crisis in another area reach the boiling point and then watch the United States commit herself to still another political-military venture or draw back in discomfiture.

The central figure in the Near Eastern crisis, as in practically every previous one since 1952, was Nasser. Nasser's relations with the Kremlin were not, despite the usual assumptions in the West, constantly harmonious or purely those of client and protector. In 1958 and 1959 serious tension had developed between Nasser and the Russians, and Khrushchev in a moment of anger called the ambitious Arab leader "a hot-headed young man." As a matter of fact, the main Soviet worry between 1958 and 1962 had appeared not so much the prospect of Nasser's overthrow as of his succeeding too well. Had the Egyptian dictator been capable of achieving a considerable degree of Arab unity under his leadership, his need for dependence on the USSR would have been considerably reduced or altogether removed. By the same token Nasser was the only man in the Arab world with enough prestige and political sense to achieve even temporarily a modus vivendi with Israel, the main reason for Arab hostility to the West and for its continued dependence on the USSR. Therefore, the Egyptian leader had to be fed a carefully adjusted diet of Soviet aid designed to keep him in power but to deny him ultimate success. The peculiar conditions of Arab politics helped this Soviet design. Prospects of unity would appear, only to dissolve next day. Nasser's most successful achievement, the union of Egypt and Syria, collapsed one day in 1961, its demise discreetly assisted by the activities of Syrian Communists. The United Arab Republic, as Egypt illogically continued to be called, then found itself involved in a protracted military adventure in Yemen. Here the Egyptian army, equipped with modern (but one suspects not too modern) Soviet arms, found itself unable to dispose of the resisting tribesmen aided by Saudi Arabia. Because of his inordinate ambition and impatience, the Egyptian dictator found himself more and more dependent on the Soviet Union.

By the same token, the Soviet stake in the Mediterranean and Near East grew. The Soviet Union's military and economic help to her Arab friends—mainly Algeria and Iraq, in addition to Egypt and Syria—grew in volume. Given the economic importance of the region and the chance of denying its wealth to the West, the prospect of losing this great investment was distasteful. At the same time, conditions in the Arab countries hardly warranted complete equanimity. A coup could overnight change the political complexion of any of the pro-Soviet Arab states and bring to power somebody like Tunisia's Bourguiba. The overthrow of Ben Bella in Algeria was an object lesson in this respect, even though Boumedienne modified but slightly his friendly policies toward the Communist bloc. Apart from the ghost of the CIA there was also the fresh danger of the "wrong kind" of Communists seizing power. The Arabs were beginning to develop undesirably close relations with Peking.

To minimize such unpleasant possibilities, it would be useful to develop a Soviet "presence" in the Mediterranean. To the traditionalist Russians, this would mean the consummation of ambitions dating back to Catherine the Great. One recalls Stalin's passion for a base in Turkey, at Potsdam, Molotov's subsequent plea with the obdurate Byrnes for the "promised" trusteeship in Tripolitania. A base at one time had materialized in Albania, but then the Sino-Soviet unpleasantness had led that Liliputian Communist state to request the Soviet navy to leave. In 1966 on a visit to Egypt, Kosygin brought with him the commander-in-chief of the Soviet navy, and it is unlikely that Admiral Gorschkov came to admire the pyramids. A sizable Soviet fleet in the Mediterranean would have had a healthy effect on political stability in the pro-Soviet Arab countries and offered interesting possibilities in the case of political upheavals elsewhere.

Yet another coup in Syria in 1966 brought to power a strongly pro-Soviet regime, some of the members of the new government being avowed Communists. The new government stepped up its border warfare with Israel, and here again one is forced to conclude that while the Soviets were not directly responsible for this enhanced bellicosity, they took no determined steps to stop or contain it. Border incidents increased in number and intensity. Significantly, the Syrian press baited Egypt for an alleged unwillingness to confront Israel and for hiding behind the shelter of the United Nations Emergency Force stationed on Egypt's side of the frontier with Israel. It is hard to believe that this policy did not at least enjoy Soviet acquiescence; the USSR continued to provide Syria with arms and instructors.

The other aspect of Russia's policy in the Near East concerns her attitude toward Israel. Here the picture is equally involved. Anti-Zionism has always been a strong element in Bolshevism, even in the days when leadership of the Communist Party and state included many Jews. In Stalin's era, especially toward its end, an element of outright anti-Semitism entered official circles and evidently lingered on after the tyrant's departure. Still, it would be a gross oversimplification to attribute Soviet hostility to Israel to sheer anti-Semitism. Zionism is seen as a threat to the loyalty of Soviet Russia's more than two million Jews. Traditionally, the Soviet state abhors any suprastate loyalty among its citizens, is suspicious of emotional ties with a foreign center, be it the Vatican or Jerusalem. Diplomatic relations with Israel, restored after Stalin's death, were never close, and Russia's wooing of the Arabs precluded any but the most formal relations. The renewed agitation by international Jewish bodies concerning instances of anti-Jewish discrimination in the USSR and the denial of religious and cultural facilities to the Jewish minority there was greeted with irritation. It was viewed as a provocation to force the Soviet authorities to license the mass migration of Soviet Jews. Isolated, usually elderly Jews were permitted to leave, but there was no chance of a real migration. Apart from the loss of valuable human material, it would have clashed with the official philosophy: Soviet Jews, alongside their fellow citizens, already lived in the Promised Land. The main lines of Soviet policy toward Israel were no more based on anti-Zionist sentiment than was Stalin's recognition of Israel in 1948 on a pro-Zionist one: in both cases it was a matter of cold calculation.

What were the Soviet objectives in allowing the crisis in the Middle East to reach such dangerous proportions? The first phase was spurred by Soviet intelligence reports, fed to Cairo and Damascus, that Israel in the wake of repeated border incidents with Syria would deal a major blow to that nation. This story is substantiated by a column in *Pravda* on May 22, which claimed that the imperialists were up to new tricks in the Near East: "Their main objective is Syria, whose anti-imperialist policy is disliked by Washington. It cannot be excluded that there would be new provocations against Syria." To what degree responsible Soviet officials believed this, and whether they thought it was, to use their expression, a "provocation," is difficult to determine. But in view of the rumors and the taunts from Damascus and other Arab capitals, Nasser felt compelled to concentrate troops on Israel's frontier and to request the United Nations to withdraw its emergency force. The Secretary General complied with this request, rapidly and possibly more completely than Nasser desired. On May 18 U Thant ordered the withdrawal of the entire United Nations Emergency Force, including the tiny detachment guarding the Strait of Tiran, which enabled Israeli shipping to navigate the Gulf of Aqaba and to reach Eilat, a port of great importance to Israel since it was convenient for trade with Asia and Africa and partly offset the disadvantages of the Egyptian embargo on Israeli shipping through the Suez Canal. On May 22 Nasser, now carried forward by the momentum of his own oratory, declared the Gulf of Aqaba closed to shipping by or to Israel, thus rendering Eilat useless. Were Israel to acquiesce in this step, it was clear that she would become the subject of further Arab encroachments and attacks.

At this point the element of design (or at least of temptation) unmistakably entered Soviet policy. Whatever the rationale of Russian policies and intelligence reports before May 18, after that date, had the Soviets desired to relieve the tension, they could have warned their Arab allies not to institute the blockade or indulge in provocative oratory, or, if their warnings were not heeded, they could have made plain their disapproval of the blockade or demanded a great power conference to head off a war. In his speech to the United Nations on June 19 Kosygin was to say that if Israel had a grievance, she should have come to the Security Council. But obviously, between May 22 and June 4 no remedy for the blockade was being provided by the Council. On May 30, in a typically fruitless debate the Soviet delegate, Fedorenko, without specifically endorsing the blockade, supported the Arab position and stated that the USSR stood ready to help Arabs fight any would-be aggressor. The head of the Syrian regime had arrived in Moscow on May 29. What he was told there clearly did not stop the Arabs' provocative oratory, typified by Nasser's statement that whether in one or ten years, Israel would have to be definitively crushed.

There were certainly some members of the Soviet government

who felt that the crisis should be allowed to "ripen." The United States, Britain, and France had pledged to guarantee free navigation in the Gulf of Aqaba. Now, with France pulling out of the agreement, and Britain weak and irresolute, the American government, already overcommitted in Vietnam, had to contemplate either another military venture (perhaps occupation of the Strait of Tiran) or a virtual withdrawal, either course destroying its remaining assets in the Arab world.

In brief, one must conclude that the leadership of the USSR lapsed from its usual caution into a gamble reminiscent of Khrushchev's. It undoubtedly believed that the risk for the USSR was small. The greatest danger would be a war in which Israel suffered an initial defeat, something that would undoubtedly bring about American intervention and thus put the USSR on the spot. But as the course of events was to show, the Soviets thought the prospect of an Arab victory was slim, even if they did not expect a rout. All other contingencies appeared manageable. The United States might attempt to force the blockade; then the USSR would call for an immediate conference and a peaceful solution. Or the United States might implore the Soviet Union to help; then the Russians would be able to exact concessions in other areas in return for helping the United States. Or, when the crisis had sufficiently ripened—and this seems to have been in the offing when the war actually broke out—Nasser might offer a compromise: he would let shipping through the Gulf of Aqaba to Eilat, provided the ships were not under Israeli flag. This, if accepted, would mean a diplomatic victory for Egypt and Russia, and a humiliation for the United States and Israel. In the meantime, while assailing the imperialists' evil schemes, the Soviet government piously asked the United States to restrain Israel, truthfully asserting that *it* was urging the Arabs not to start the war. Headlines in the Soviet press, as contrasted with those in the West, conveyed little of the urgency and seriousness of the crisis. The eventual outcome of the crisis—Israel's attack and the Arabs' catastrophic defeat—shook for awhile the Soviets' position in the Near East, but they recovered it within a short time. Their subsequent policies were to contribute to further crises culminating in the war of 1973.

15 | MOSCOW PLAYS THE BALANCE

The concept of the balance of power originated in an era when monarchs and cabinets made foreign policy with only scant consideration for public opinion. It is, in other words, a game which, for all the recent attempts in this direction by Nixon and Kissinger, cannot be easily played by a democracy, especially a democracy in the current condition of the United States. For the USSR, on the contrary, the balance of power has been the stuff of international politics virtually from the beginning. Even in the era of Soviet isolation and the alleged capitalist encirclement, the USSR profited by what the Communists call the "inherent contradictions of the capitalist world." In fact, the Soviets expanded and used the concept far beyond anything meant by the balance of power in the days of Metternich and Canning. The Rapallo phase of the Soviet foreign policy, the era of the Popular Front, then the Soviet-German Pact of 1939, offer instructive examples of this technique. From being a concept designed to deal with policies between states, it has been expanded by the Soviets to take account of social and political forces within the given states, and of worldwide movements and phenomena such as anti-imperialism and pacifism. The rulers of the Soviet Union may justly feel that it was largely their skill in manipulating and recognizing conflicts and conditions in the outside world that has enabled their system—at the beginning a weak, devastated, and backward country founded on a principle hostile to that of every other state in the world—to grow into one of the two super-powers, the leader not only of a worldwide movement but also of a sizable group of states. As recently as 1945 the Soviet Union, though victorious, was confronting a world that every criterion, whether of economic or military power, solidity of the internal regime, or universal attractiveness of its political philosophy, *should* have been dominated by the United States. Yet it has been the dynamism of Soviet foreign policy, and the diminution in both America's influence and America's self-confidence in her world role, which have been the outstanding features of world politics since World War II. President Nixon's visit to Moscow, the treaties signed with West Germany, the Soviet-Indian alliance, are vivid illustrations of the change that has taken place in one generation. Not a bad record for a country which emerged from the war with its economy in ruins, more than 10 percent of its prewar population destroyed, and a political system held together by internal repression unequalled in modern history.

And yet, though they may feel justifiably proud of the Soviet record in world affairs, Russia's rulers must also be apprehensive that in some very important respects they have become victims of their own successes, that paradoxically the very extent of Communism's triumph and of the disarray in which the capitalist system finds itself presents a danger to the USSR and to their power. There is, first of all, the enormous success turned into danger—China. The rule of present-day Russia, now a super-power, over world Communism can never again be as secure as was that of the backward and weak Russia of the 1920s. Likewise the military danger that then existed from the capitalist states was never as realistic as the one which, if it does not exist now, will in another generation when the fellow Communist giant is industrialized and furnished with a multitude of nuclear weapons in addition to her awesome manpower.

The disarray in which the capitalist world has found itself ever since the early 1960s, with the United States overcommitment in Southeast Asia and the collapse of the until then promising momentum for European political unity, while pleasing to the Kremlin, has been far from constituting that steady decline of Western and especially United States power for which the Soviets have been hoping. It has presented the USSR with unexpected opportunities but also threatened unexpected dangers. In this age, and especially if one's opponent has a sizable nuclear arsenal, you have to wish for a degree of social and political stability even in that opponent. And so the American mining of the North Vietnamese waters, combined with the desperate mood in this country about the war, made the Soviet leaders more rather than less anxious to talk with Nixon.

The present international era will probably enter the history books as the Age of Paradox. The massive American intervention in Vietnam was prompted by a belief that this was the place where Chinese Communism had to be stopped and taught that wars of liberation do not pay. Yet seven years later the Present of the United States went to Peking, thus acknowledging China's role as a great power, largely in an effort to help America extricate itself from Vietnam. For years the Soviet leaders have avowed that China's aim was to push them into a confrontation with the United States, a not too unrealistic apprehension. Now their eagerness to negotiate with America is to a large extent prompted by a fear of the United States providing sizable economic and technological help to China. Much of the traditional meaning of terms like détente, alliance, ideological interests, and military security has been eroded by the swiftly moving current of political and technological change.

The same fate, though not to the same degree, has befallen the concept of the balance of power. It can no longer be used as a technique through which one power can protect its interests and secure an equilibrium of potentially hostile forces by moving its support from one side to the other. For the arithmetic of military-diplomatic strength can no longer be confined to such simple calculations as the number of divisions on each side, or even the relative production indices of steel. Such criteria have been proven fallible in the case of Israel, North Vietnam—and the United States and China. Nowadays, it is necessary not only to count nuclear weapons and estimate the gross national product, but also to try to assess the more intangible elements of strength: will Japan translate her enormous industrial power into a political—not to mention military—one? Will the current American mood of exasperation with world affairs pass, or will the United States tend more and more to reduce its commitments? Will Western Europe recoup its momentum for political unity? Will the spirit of nationalism and reform in East European Communist states continue to be inhibited by the memories of Prague and Budapest, or will it soon confront the USSR with a new challenge?

Such, then, are the complex assessments on which one must base any conceptualization of the balance of power in today's world. There is every indication that Soviet official thinking has for some time run along these lines, just as, belatedly, Washington appears to have shifted from a vision of international affairs as a morality play to a view of it as a more realistic calculation of existing facts and future probabilities.

To the Soviets, the desirable balance of power for the foreseeable future includes a parity of nuclear strength with the United States, the growing influence of the USSR in Europe, and the containment of China. On the first two items Moscow feels it has made considerable progress. The armaments agreement signed in 1972 by Nixon and Brezhnev is an acknowledgment in Soviet eyes—and never mind the technical details—that for the first time since 1945 the United States and the Soviet Union are on terms of nuclear equality. Its symbolic importance was emphasized by Brezhnev who, against all protocol precedents, signed it himself though he was not a government official; Stalin when only General Secretary would never put his signature on an international agreement. The agreements with West Germany recognized something that John Foster Dulles and Konrad Adenauer were ready to risk a confrontation about rather than concede: that the status quo in Central Europe is permanent and German unity no longer a question of current politics.

This last success is not without possible drawbacks: it diminishes Moscow's opportunities to use the alleged "Bonn revanchism" and the ghost of the Wehrmacht as a weapon against Polish and Czech nationalisms. Yet at the same time it reduces in the Kremlin's view the level of tension in Western Europe, increases the opportunities for profitable political and economic intercourse with the West, and throws open the further perspective of the American withdrawal from the area. There is now the seductive vista of an eventual "Finlandization" of Western Europe, of neutralism in a new guise becoming the dominant tendency in Paris, Rome, and even London. And while the Soviets no longer desire, or even very strenuously pretend, that Communism should become the ruling creed in any large country—the experience of China has been too instructive and painful in this respect—they would not be displeased if coalition governments including Communists should take over in Italy or France.

In Asia, any Soviet hopes for a balance of power must hinge on internal Chinese developments as well as on the general international configuration. Khrushchev schemed and with his manner made his purpose apparent, at least to Peking, to have India act as a counterpoise to China. His successors scored an undeniable success in this direction: Pakistan can no longer offset India's role as an Asian power. But it is still obvious that India's influence, not to mention her military power, cannot in itself neutralize China's. The Soviet hopes still hinge on an event that cannot be far off: the disappearance of Mao and what is described in the Soviet press as his clique. Further than that, the Kremlin must secretly wish for a prolonged period of internal turmoil to make new rulers or factions in Peking more agreeable to a decorous modus vivendi with their senior Communist power. In the long run the Chinese problem, certainly by the premises that have guided Soviet policies since the beginning, is intractable and fearful. But as Lord Keynes said, in the long run we shall all be dead.

The middle-aged rulers of Russia may well feel that in view of the increasingly complex world situation they have not done badly and have established what might be described as a floating balance of power, which will remain, with shifts in their favor, for the next decade or two. They may reflect with some complacence how much more stable and prestigious the position of their country has become in comparison with what it was under their predecessors: the almost unbearable level of international tension that prevailed in Stalin's last years, and Khrushchev's "harebrained schemes" intended to deny China nuclear arms and to arrive at a division of the world into spheres of interest between the United States and Russia. They may also recall complacently how those schemes misfired: China becoming openly hostile, the USSR and America coming almost to the point of a nuclear confrontation. The world from the Kremlin no longer looks full of grandiose opportunities and terrible dangers. There is now a much more sober realization that the dangers which remain must be minimized through prudent and conciliatory policies, while gains that can be secured are not to be sought through dramatic improvisations and thrusts but through patient diplomacy and careful assessment of world realities.

16 | THE SOVIET UNION AND THE INTERNATIONAL GAME

The Russian Revolution marked the opening of a new era in modern history. This is one of those rare platitudes that needs to be repeated rather than eschewed. Consider the European State System, which for the period between 1648 and 1918 was virtually synonymous with the world state system. During that period the ideologico-religious character of a given state was at most of secondary importance insofar as its role in world politics was concerned. There were only occasional and short-lived exceptions to this rule. The First French Republic between 1793 and 1800 constituted a challenge to every other major state system in Europe, and ideological proselytizing was an important element in its drive for expansion. But beginning with the Napoleonic phase, these ideological pretensions of the French state became, if not completely eradicated, then subdued by other elements. The expansionist thrust of the First Empire came to reflect not any specific ideology but French nationalism and, even more than that, Napoleon's personal and dynastic ambitions. His bid for European domination was no longer coupled with an ideological challenge to every other form of government. Eventually the French armies were defeated by the same principle and emotion that had led to their dazzling successes: nationalism. Between 1815 and 1914 no state had declared itself to be the carrier of a universal ideology or sought the overthrow of other forms of government. To be sure, Nicholas I's Russia was a self-proclaimed defender of the principle of legitimacy or, as it might be called anachronistically, of counterrevolution. But this stance, just as was the Holy Alliance of Nicholas' predecessor, was designed for the preservaton of the status quo rather than for the propagation of a specific ideology, and in any case both attempts at "freezing," so to speak, the political system of Europe of 1815 soon met with failure.

In brief, any citizen, not to mention a statesman of nineteenth century Europe, would have deemed fantastic the thought that there could be a state which would demand and enjoy all the international appurtenances of "normal" statehood and membership in the community of nations at the same time that its professed aim and ideology was to subvert all other existing forms of government. Nothing resembling such a situation had existed since the religious wars of the sixteenth and early seventeenth centuries. Even the First French Republic did not explicitly seek destruction of nonrepublican forms of government in countries with which it was not at war. Paris was not the center of an international movement with adherents in Vienna or Saint Petersburg plotting the overthrow of their governments. "Friends in peace, enemies in war" was the ruling maxim of international relations of the era that came to an end on November 7, 1917.

It is startling to reflect that the people who carried out the Bolshevik Revolution had, only three years before, shared in this concept of international relations. The vision of an eventually socialist world enshrined in the Second International did not include the notion that the state which first became socialist would have any international obligations on that account. One can search in vain in the Russian radical literature prior to 1914 for any hint as to the foreign policy of a socialist Russia. To be sure, the prospect of such a Russia appeared quite distant. It would have been fantastic to think of backward Russia as the standard-bearer of militant Marxism. And if such a vision ever passed before the eyes of Lenin or, for that matter, Martov, they must have thought of revolutionary Russia's role as that of an example to the rest of Europe rather than as the center and directing force of a disciplined international movement.

With the outbreak of the European war, Lenin repudiated the social democratic tradition of the Second International and made his celebrated appeal for a return to the earlier militant essence of Marxism. Implicit in this appeal were two assumptions: that the European state system as it had existed since 1815 had broken down, and that the moving force in international relations was to be class struggle, which would at once replace and absorb the national question as the main element of world politics. The new role of the Soviet state was to arise from the fact that the first assumption turned out to be amply justified, the second only partially so.

In the first flush of their enthusiasm after taking power, the Bolsheviks believed, indeed, that a completely new revolutionary era had dawned over Europe. If their country of the "half savage, stupid and heavy people of the Russian villages and countryside," to quote Gorky, became the stage for the first Victorian socialist revolution, if her relatively small and backward working class seized power, could one doubt that before long the workers of Berlin, Paris, and London would follow suit?[1] All the cautions of the old social democracy, the schemes of stages of historical development carefully worked out by Karl Marx, had suddenly become obsolete. With the World War, capitalism had committed suicide. In Lenin, as in most other Bolsheviks, the revolutionary had triumphed over the historical determinist. It was foolish, then, to worry about foreign policy in the old sense of the word, or about other appurtenances and trappings of traditional statehood. The Commissar of Foreign Relations, Trotsky, a man normally of the most practical cast of mind, explained to a petitioner for a job that there was hardly anything worthwhile to do in his department: "I myself took this job so I would have more time for the party work. All there is to do is to publish the secret treaties, then I will close shop."[2] There was a messianic feeling of the irresistible wave of revolution surging throughout Europe, weary of the economic system and civilization that had brought forth the frightful bloodbath.

This feeling received its first check at Brest Litovsk. The ratification of that humiliating and disastrous treaty marks the true beginning of the Soviet state. Before it, Communism can be described as enthusiasm that seized power. With March 1918, this revolutionary enthusiasm became embodied in a state which, apart from its self-professed mission to carry out the world revolution, had to perform the traditional tasks of statehood: collect taxes, build roads, engage in diplomatic negotiations. After their victory the Soviets addressed German, French, or other workers over the heads of their governments. But at Brest Litovsk, their emissaries affixed their signatures to the treaty along with those of His Majesty the German Emperor, His Apostolic Majesty the Emperor of Austria, and the King of Hungary. This was the first and most fundamental lesson in political realism that the rulers of the infant state absorbed.

Revolutionary enthusiasm lingered on and did not receive a definite check until the days in September 1920 when the defeated Red Army reeled back from Warsaw. Only then did the vision of the world kingdom of socialism give way to the weary resignation to the purgatory of capitalist encirclement. Russia, Lenin acknowledged, would have to exist within a system of states, would have to coexist with capitalism.

The very nature of this coexistence was from the beginning to have a profound influence on the character of the Soviet state and in the longer run, even before the USSR became a world power, on that of other states. The uniqueness of the Soviet regime proceeded not only from its Communist ideology but also from what might be called its existentialist nature. One may today observe how the character of a state—Israel is the example that comes most readily to mind—can be shaped not only by its political structure but also by a challenge to its very existence by hostile forces surounding it. The external threat is not an occasional one, it does not touch on a territorial dispute or rivalry over spheres of influence or trade; it is directed at the very essence and existence of the political organism. In some ways this threat can become an element of strength for the regime; the mentality of the state of siege endows the given society with cohesion.

The Soviet regime has developed the exploitation of external danger to the level of an art. This is not to argue that at times the danger was not real or felt as such. Still, capitalist encirclement has been much more than an occasional propaganda weapon in the armory of Soviet Communism. It has been a continuous theme in Soviet internal and external politics, an invaluable means in the hands of whoever holds power in the USSR to suppress opposition and dissent. There was perhaps some superficial logic in the argument around 1921-1922 that the weak and isolated Soviet state could not afford the luxury of free political debate and that not only other Marxist parties but an organized attempt at dissent within the Communist one had to be suppressed. The erstwhile capitalists and landowners were just waiting for internal divisions and chaos to attempt, with foreign help, to fasten their yoke on the people of Russia. But even today, with Russia a world super-power, and with the last of the pre-1917 capitalists moldering in the grave, a similar argument is being used to justify the ban on dissent in the arts, the refusal to publish a novel by Solzhenitsyn, and the jailing or expulsion of those who claim liberties spelled out in the Constitution of the USSR. The "enemy" is always there, waiting a change, unreconciled to the existence of the state that first in the world enshrined socialism as its ruling ideology.

There is no question that a masterly exploitation of this motif was what enabled Stalin to erect his edifice of tyranny. At crucial points in his struggle for absolute power, he invoked the foreign danger in order to cow his opponents and silence the scruples of his own partisans. It is difficult to understand how the rank and file of the party would have acquiesced in the "defeat" of Lenin's companions who were led by Trotsky, except for Stalin's ability to persuade the party between 1924 and 1928 that his rivals were "objectively" working for the enemy. One decade later he was able to physically destroy such rivals by "proving" that they were in fact the agents of Berlin and Tokyo. And many of those who recoiled from his schemes of social engineering, which brought famine, death, and destitution to millions, had their hand stayed by the dictator's argument that the sufferings of mass collectivization were necessary if Communist Russia was to survive. The existence of foreign danger, the permanence of international crisis, thus became a fixed principle of the Soviet philosophy of government and, in fact, might be described as a principal working tenet of current Communist ideology.

How, in fact, is this tenet of Communist faith regarded by its high priests? In their own innermost thoughts, do they perceive foreign dangers to be as concrete and constant as their oratory has led many to believe? Even in their public pronouncements Soviet leaders have given a hint of their basic ambivalence on this point. Speaking at one of the most danger-fraught times for the Soviet state, Lenin could still give this amazingly sober and optimistic appraisal: "We are in a situation in which the raging waves of imperialist reaction which appear at any moment to overwhelm the small island of the Socialist Soviet Republic, time and time again break against each other."³ Uncompromising hostility to the Soviet system is a basic tendency of world capitalism. But so are rivalry and inner conflict. The first tendency requires of the Soviet Union never to let down its guard, never to assume that permanent peace is achievable as long as capitalism remains. The second bestows on the Soviet Union an attribute no social system or regime possessed in the past: indestructibility. The very forces of history preclude the possibility of Communist Russia being attacked by a superior combination of powers. This, then, was the counterpoint of the Soviet philosophy of international relations—at least until nuclear weapons and the rise of another Communist, but potentially hostile, power called for a reexamination of these basic tenets, just as they challenged the whole ideological basis of the Soviet state.

Throughout most of the existence of the USSR, its rulers have defined its role in international relations quite differently from that of any state in the past. Owing to its ideological character, Soviet Russia had different obligations and faced different dangers from those which confronted a "normal" state. Therefore, the USSR claimed and, rather amazingly, achieved a special status in international relations. It was to be treated as a regular member of the community of nations; yet unlike other states, its rulers never made a secret of the fact that they sought and hoped for an overthrow of other forms of government. To be sure, Soviet diplomacy worked strenuously to maintain the fiction that there was a definite distinction and separation between the Soviet leaders in their capacity as governors of their state and as guides of international Communism. But already in the beginning, and against the advice of his more timid diplomats, Lenin refused to lend any plausibility to this fiction by having government figures keep away from the Comintern. "There can be no question of me and Trotsky leaving the Executive Committee," he wrote to his Foreign Commisar Chicherin.[4] Soviet leaders who were pleading for diplomatic recognition and foreign credits thus continued as members of the body that issued inflammatory revolutionary appeals, drew scurrilous characterizations of bourgeois politicians in France or Britain, and in general interfered in the most flagrant manner in the internal politics of countries with which the Soviet Union sought normal diplomatic and trade relations. The very fact that neither Lenin nor his successors really tried to conceal their roles as spiritual and political directors of a world revolutionary movement again throws an interesting light on the fact that as politicians the Communists discounted the alleged danger which as ideologists they incessantly invoked. Had they been really convinced of the imminence of a capitalist attack from abroad, it is reasonable to assume that they would have chosen to be more hypocritical, to try to disguise more effectively their role as international revolutionaries. But as Lenin wrote in the same letter to his Foreign Commissar, for Soviet dignitaries to resign from their Comintern posts would only create an impression of weakness. And to this very day the Soviet regime has observed the principle which has served it well, that to create the impression of weakness among foreigners is much more dangerous than to maintain the posture of ideological hostility.

By 1933 the Soviet Union obtained what it had sought so persistently and unflinchingly since 1921: a special status in the community of nations, according to which other major states virtually acknowledged that the USSR had the right to all the usual appurtenances of statehood and diplomatic and commercial intercourse, even though its professed philosophy was one of hostility to every other form of government, and despite the fact that an international movement centered in and directed from Moscow had as its professed aim the spread of Communism to all corners of the world. The major powers which recognized the Soviet regime as the legal government of Russia, concluding with the United States in 1933, often demanded and sometimes exacted that the latter renounce formally its interference in their internal affairs. But except in the case of America, it is difficult to believe that such assurances were sought seriously rather than as a gesture. Certainly by 1933 it was almost humorous to expect the Soviet government, as Litvinov pledged in a formal note to the United States Department of State, "to refrain, and to restrain all persons in Government service and all organizations of the Government or under its direct or indirect control . . . from any act overt or covert, liable in any way to injure the tranquility, prosperity, order or security of any part of the United States . . . Not to permit the formation or residence on its territory of any organization or group . . . which has as its aim the overthrow or the preparation for the overthrow . . . of the political or social order of the whole or any part of the United States."[5] That such pledges were sought could in itself be taken as proof that the old diplomatic order had disintegrated beyond any hope of reconstruction.

But by the time the Soviet Union took its place as a full member of the world community of states, its status as such was still more paradoxical and, by the pre-1914 standards, scandalous than had been the case in the twenties. Until roughly 1925-1926 it could still be claimed with some superficial validity that the Soviet Communists were members of a world movement in which their country played the leading but not absolutely dominant role. By 1933, however, it was clear that the rulers of Russia were not mere participants in a world revolutionary movement and did not simply enjoy a special status among their fellow religionists, but were their absolute masters. With Stalin at the helm, foreign Communists were now obedient servants of the Soviet Union, foreign Communist parties an extension of Soviet power. A decision made in the Kremlin was after 1928 or 1929 as binding on the party organization in Paris and Prague as it was in Kiev or Minsk. With the Sixth Congress of the Comintern, even the tactics as well as the personnel policies of foreign Communist parties passed under the direct control of Moscow. Official recognition of the USSR thus amounted to a virtual acknowledgment by the major powers that they could have normal diplomatic relations with a state which both claimed and received from a number of their own citizens a loyalty superior to that which they acknowledged to their own government.

Ironically, it fell to the country that has traditionally been most jealous of the principle that the loyalty of its citizens should be rendered exclusively to their own government to recognize most vividly the universalistic pretensions of the Soviet state. On a visit to Moscow in 1935 following the signing of the Franco-Soviet Pact, the French Foreign Minister Pierre Laval sought and received Stalin's approval for an internal policy of the French government, a formal declaration which was thought necessary to make the French Communists support their country's defense effort: "Comrade Stalin expressed complete understanding and approval of the national defense policy pursued by France with the object of maintaining its armed forces at a level consistent with its security requirements."[6] Thus a right-wing French government pleaded with the leader of the world Communist movement that he should sanction its internal policies and thereby make them acceptable to a number of its own citizens!

Even at the time when the growing fascist threat made the Soviet Union anxious for allies abroad, its government refused to play down its role as the directing force of the world Communist movement. The farce that Foreign Commissar Litvinov chose to enact before American Ambassador Bullitt in 1935 speaks for itself. According to Bullitt, he expostulated with Litvinov that the approaching Seventh Congress of the Comintern would, in view of the participation in it of the American Communists, constitute a violation of the Roosevelt-Litvinov agreement of 1933. "Litvinov said: 'What, is there to be one?' I answered, yes, on the twentieth of this month. Litvinov replied with a broad grin, 'You know more about the Third International than I do. The other day when I was talking with Stalin I said I had heard there was to be a meeting of the Third International on the tenth of this month. Stalin replied, 'Is there?' He knew about it no more than I do.' "[7]

The reasons that the Western powers accepted such an unprecedented state of affairs are found first of all in the destruction of the European state system wrought by World War I. The cornerstone of this system was the principle of state sovereignty. The Treaty of Versailles failed to restore the old system. In fact, by imposing on the defeated powers, notably Germany, severe restrictions on their sovereignty, Versailles helped establish the notion that state sovereignty was *not* the basic foundation of the international order. The Western powers' intervention, sporadic and ineffective though it was, in the Russian Civil War further weakened legally and, even more, psychologically the case for holding the Soviet Union accountable to the normal rules of international intercourse. If capitalist powers had tried to overthrow the infant Soviet state, could one by any logic deny this state the right to have special friends and partisans abroad?

More basically, after 1918 the democratic ethos became a powerful force in international relations. This sounds paradoxical, for that date also marked the opening of an intense challenge to democratic and liberal institutions throughout the world. But it was precisely in the name of democratic principle that the forces inimical to democracy were to score their greatest gains. The doctrine of national sovereignty became unavailing in face of the democratic one. Public opinion in democratic countries found it difficult to resist the argument that the feelings of the majority of Germans in Austria and Sudetenland possessed a higher validity than the legal rights of the Austrian and Czech states. It was equally difficult for the French or British governments to suppress political organizations or opinions in their own countries merely because they reflected the wishes and served the interests of a foreign power. By the same logic the Soviet Union could not be blamed for the fact that a number of British or American citizens shared the ideology and political premises of its rulers. In fact, acquiescence in the Soviet Union's unusual role in international relations preceded the toleration of local Communist parties by the democracies. Persecution and chicanery against those parties by many democratic governments could be traced to their ostentatious hostility to democratic institutions, especially in the twenties and early thirties, rather than to their link with the USSR. Weimar Germany found no incompatibility between its virtual alliance with the USSR and political and legal measures directed against the German Communists. And fascist Italy, which relatively early established diplomatic ties with Moscow, was not inhibited by this fact from suppressing the Communist Party within its borders and imprisoning its leaders.

The challenge that the Soviet Union represented to the world order, then, was unique in nature. The response, or rather the lack of response, of other powers to this challenge contributed to the final demise of that world order in the thirties. For it was then that the ideological principle finally prevailed over state sovereignty as the strongest element in international relations. The initial considerable successes of Hitler could be traced to his masterly exploitation of the changed rules of the game signaled by the Versailles Treaty, but brought into full prominence by the existence of the new type of state, the USSR. Anti-Communism was more than Hitler's propaganda stock in trade; it was a technique that enabled weak and isolated Germany to obtain allies and, most important, time for rearmament. It is often alleged that Hitler "got away" with his trampling over Germany's treaty obligations and his aggressive posturings between 1933 and 1938 because of fears of Communism in the West. This is true enough. But a large part of his success must be traced to the breakdown of the general principle of international obligation and of norms of international comity that had occurred before and largely because of the USSR. It would have been an international scandal and quite possibly a *casus belli* for the Tsar of All Russias to express publicly Russian territorial claims to Eastern Galicia on grounds that the majority of its inhabitants were Little Russians, as the Ukrainians were referred to in tsarist Russia. But Hitler's public claims to foreign territories, whether rationalized on grounds that the Germanic race needed *Lebensraum* or that the territories in question were inhabited by Germans, did not automatically brand him in the eyes of the other powers as the enemy of the European order, as Louis XIV and Napoleon had been branded for advancing similar expansionist claims, or even as Nicholas I of Russia had been branded on the occasion of the Crimean War. Hitler's claims were no more shocking than those advanced by the Soviet Union by virtue of its role as the fatherland of socialism; in fact, to some conservative circles in the West, even to people who had little sympathy for fascism as such, Hitlerism appeared as a welcome counterforce to Communism.

A world order, even a rudimentary one such as prevailed prior to 1914, must be based on the assumption that legal norms, such as national sovereignty, are superior to considerations of nationalism or ideology (this distinction is itself awkward, since integral nationalism and racism, as in Hitler's creed, are a species of ideology). However ridiculous or immoral the "little wars" of the nineteenth century may appear to us, they were limited and of brief duration because none of the contestants sought the overthrow of its enemies in the name of a "higher" principle. What kept the Crimean War "small," for example, was not its limited scope—it involved, after all, three of Europe's five major powers at the time —but the limited objectives of the contestants. One can readily envisage that had this war taken place some fifty years later, it would have turned into a total war, not so much because of changes in the nature of warfare as because it could not have failed to assume an ideological character. The French and the British would have proclaimed it a war against tsarist autocracy; the Russians would have evoked—as in fact they tried intermittently and ineffectually to do throughout the century—the principle of national self-determination, though to be applied not to their own but to the Turkish empire. World War I already bore a quasi-ideological character, as evidenced by the "Prussian militarism" against which the Entente Powers were allegedly fighting, the espousal by the Central Powers of a variant of national self-determination in their abortive moves on the Polish question, and finally the Wilsonian rhetoric. Paradoxically, the legalistic and conservative order established by the Congress of Vienna enabled liberal and eventually democratic institutions to take root in a number of countries. The result of World War I, fought in the name of lofty principles, was to make the world very unsafe indeed for democracy.

The Soviet Union adapted skillfully to the drastically changed nature of international relations. After 1933 its position appeared to be the acme of paradox. Here was the state that proclaimed itself opposed to every other existing form of government and yet claimed to be a firm supporter of the international order threatened by fascism. The League of Nations had been branded by Lenin a "league of imperialist brigands"; yet in 1934 the USSR entered the League. Hitler's dramatic successes in the 1930s should not obscure the fact that he failed in his first and most basic diplomatic objective: to isolate the USSR and to be acknowledged a defender of the

European order against Communism. His anti-Communist posturings gained adherents among some groups and politicians in the West and contributed, though not nearly so much as is commonly believed, to the French and British toleration of his early treaty violations and aggressions. But the British and French governments did not repair to Hitler to help save them from international Communism. Once their hopes of appeasing Hitler had been exposed as illusory, they went to Stalin to help save them from war and, if that were impossible, to help them in a war against resurgent Germany. The official myth sedulously propagated by the Soviet propaganda and still believed by many in the West—that the USSR was patiently trying to collaborate with the democracies and only when repulsed by them turned regretfully to a treaty with Germany— cannot obscure the brilliant achievement of Soviet diplomacy. Alone of the great powers in 1939 the Soviet Union achieved its aim: to gain territorial aggrandizement while remaining at peace. Both the Franco-British hopes of drawing Russia into an alliance and thus preserving peace, and Hitler's hope of so dazzling the French and British by the Soviet-German Pact as to let him have his will with Poland, turned to ashes. To be sure, Stalin's brilliant gambit was within two years to bring him close to irretrievable disaster, but then, who in 1939, including the German General Staff, could have realized the full extent of the French army's weakness?

It was not merely Stalin's diplomatic skill and unscrupulousness that enabled him first to pose as a defender of democracy and then in the name of the interests of the fatherland of socialism to make an alliance with Hitler. There was ample warrant in the ideology for both courses of action. It was Hitler who compromised what little ideological content his hideous doctrine contained by signing with Stalin. Stalin could revert to the traditional Communist tenet in international relations: differences between capitalist states were ones of degree rather than substance. A major and prolonged war between the main capitalist powers would create a favorable climate for the spread of revolution. Thus, quite apart from personal and nationalist reasons, Stalin could claim that the course he took in 1939 was in full accord with the Communist doctrine. It was not his fault that some people in Britain and France thought that since 1934 or 1935 the character of the Soviet state had changed drastically, that the Popular Front period represented more than just a phase in the foreign policy of his country, and that he would obligingly pull Britain's and France's "chestnuts out of the fire," risking in the process the destruction of his own regime, if not indeed of the whole Communist experiment.

The Grand Alliance of the USSR with the United States and Britain demonstrated once again the incongruous character of the Soviet state and of its position in the community of nations. The Western allies could not accept the simple fact that the USSR had become their partner in the war because and only because she was attacked by Hitler. If for the Germans the Japanese became "honorary Aryans," then for the British and Americans, especially the latter, Stalin for the duration of the war became an "honorary democrat." Pretense notoriously leads to self-deception. Even if the most humane type of Communist rather than Stalin had disposed of Russia's policies during the war, he still could not have fulfilled the hopes that public opinion in the West as well as official American (if not British) circles had entertained about the Soviet Union's postwar behavior in international relations. Unfounded illusions during the war; unfounded disillusionment following it— here in a nutshell was the main source of America's unhappy experience with the USSR and the world. The tragedy was compounded by the fact that while the basic ideological incompatibility between the two super-powers could not have been wished away, some of its disastrous consequences could have been avoided by greater realism on the part of the West. Stalin could not have been transformed into a Jeffersonian democrat recognizing the sanctity of popular will elections. But he did entertain the possibility of the Soviet Union becoming an imperial power in the traditional sense of the word. In the very beginning of the Grand Alliance he formulated his proposals in a crass way. The Anglo-Soviet treaty of alliance of 1942 was to be supplemented by a secret protocol that would provide for the Soviet Union to retain its 1941 frontiers (its territorial gains from the period of the Soviet-Nazi collaboration) in return for the British right to have bases in France, the Low

Countries, Norway, and Denmark. Apart from the crudity of such proposals, they testify to Stalin's readiness to consider the postwar world in terms of spheres of influence.[8] Any and all such attempts broke down because of American refusals even to consider the sinful idea of spheres of influence. Russia was, in Washington's view, to be integrated into the world system, and peace was to be guaranteed through the United Nations. The result was then predictable: the Soviet Union did get its sphere of influence, but the Western Allies did not. Eastern Europe was by 1946 unchallengeably in the Soviet grip, while much of American policy during the next two decades consisted of devising stratagems and policies to protect Western Europe from the Soviet or Communist danger. Furthermore, there is much to suggest that hard, businesslike bargaining could have enabled Poland or Czechoslovakia to preserve their internal autonomy while remaining within the Soviet sphere, that is, to acquire the status of today's Finland rather than undergoing the brutal process of Communist *Gleichschaltung*. Not only the United States but the alleged objects of her solicitude were thus to pay a high price for American virtue and repugnance for power politics.

This is not to suggest that with a different attitude by the West the Soviet Union would at the end of the war have washed its hands of the international Communist movement. But there is a great deal of evidence that for a considerable period of time the USSR might have deemphasized the use of foreign Communists as an auxiliary arm of its foreign policy. The Comintern was dissolved in 1943. With more than just a hint from Moscow, the great Communist parties of the West, the Italian and French, were pursuing moderate policies within the context of parliamentary government. The Sino-Soviet Treaty of August 1945 showed that the USSR expected Chiang's regime to remain the main political force on the Chinese mainland for a long time. All such maneuvers suggest that Stalin was leaving himself an option of observing certain rules of the international game, provided that those rules were spelled out clearly by his Western partners. But they were not. Washington, which after 1945 held the direction of Western policies, no longer sought to bargain with the Soviet Union. It had expected the USSR to behave in a manner consonant with the Charter of the United Nations and, since it did not, American policy makers concluded that the usual tools of diplomacy were unavailing when dealing with this mysterious power. To absurd expectations succeeded grotesque apprehensions. If the Soviet Union violated its wartime pledges and the Charter, this meant it might at any point launch its armies in a drive to the English Channel. In April 1946 the ambassador of the country that had the monopoly of the atom bomb and which then produced half of the industrial output of the world asked of the leader of the state whose economy still lay shattered by the war and which had lost more than 20 million men, "What does Russia want and how far is Russia going to go?" Stalin not very reassuringly answered, "We are not going much farther."[9]

America's naiveté (much though this term has been used, there is no ready substitute) could not be reassuring to Stalin; quite the opposite. If the United States at the height of her power failed to realize her strength and her bargaining assets, this meant that the Soviet Union should cash in on its opportunities before the Americans woke up and tried to mount a basic challenge to the new Soviet position both in Europe and elsewhere. It was thus easy for Stalin to see the Marshall Plan not merely as the means to put Western Europe on its feet but also as a sinister scheme to use the rearmed West as America's cat's-paw to reverse Russia's postwar expansion and deny her the fruits of the victory. If so, the East European countries had to be more firmly bound to the USSR, their governments and societies receiving the Communist mold. There was likewise no reason for Moscow to press the Chinese Communists to moderate their ambitions and to content themselves with Manchuria alone. A Communist China, or even China torn by a civil war, was bound to distract American attention and resources from Europe. There is yet another paradox, and the most startling one: the weakness of America's original reaction to the Soviet usurpations was what fed Stalin's fears and apprehensions for the future and set the stage for the cold war. The West's confused and contradictory policies led the Soviets to fear an eventual war; Russia's ominous and self-imposed isolation move, like the 1948-1949 Berlin blockade and the 1948 Communist coup in Czechoslovakia, made the West fear imminent Soviet aggression. Here then was a tragedy of errors, or rather of mutual misperceptions, which largely shaped the postwar world.

The Cominform, born in 1947, was a ponderous Soviet response to what was perceived as the long-range American threat. This Communist Information Bureau of nine parties might well have been called the Anti-Marshall Plan Bureau, since its original function was to fight the economic recovery of Western Europe. Its secondary function was to exercise control over those Communist parties that now ruled as the Kremlin's deputies in their own countries. The whole effort was transparently clumsy: the Soviet Union did not need the Cominform to keep the French or Bulgarian Communists in line. But it was obviously hoped that this would be a more decorous way of synchronizing policies of foreign Communists and of making sure that they would combat the nefarious designs in the West. Once this body failed in its first test, when the Yugoslav Communists refused to submit their dispute with Moscow to the "impartial" arbitration of the Cominform, it obviously became a fifth wheel, and its dissolution in 1955 was hardly noticed.

Stalin's obsession with the Marshall Plan and his misconception of its military implications, his personal pique at a Balkan upstart whom he also falsely suspected of harboring ambitions to become completely independent from the USSR, were to have fateful and irreversible historical consequences. The period of the Berlin blockade, which began in early summer of 1948 and ended in May 1949, coincided with the time when the Chinese Communists scored their greatest and most decisive successes in the civil war. Facing crisis with the United States, with real war not inconceivable (even though Stalin did not believe that the risk was great), the USSR did not wish to put a brake on the Chinese Communists' progress and their welcome diversion of Washington's attention from its European schemes. This was not the time to negotiate with the Americans about what had been the original Soviet aim in China: to establish a Communist state but one confined to Northeast China and Manchuria, which would have given the Soviet Union a Chinese satellite rather than a rival Communist power. And after the

Berlin confrontation had ended in the summer of 1949, even Stalin could not have stopped Mao's forces, in view of their dazzling victories and the complete collapse of Chiang's regime.

The rise of Communist China transformed many of the basic perspectives of Soviet foreign policy. Between roughly 1933 and 1950 the Soviet Union had been accepted as a normal member of the community of nations, at the same time that the Soviet state was claiming and receiving the loyalty of a worldwide movement on account of its ideological character. The Soviet Union was the sole "exporter" of revolution, the sole arbiter of tactics of Communist movements everywhere. Although after World War II the USSR had become one of the two super-powers, it still basked, just like the weak and backward Russia of the twenties, in the protective feeling and affection of millions of supporters and sympathizers throughout the world. Now this enviable situation was gone forever. No longer would the USSR be able to enjoy complete freedom of maneuver, confident that no matter how drastic or unexpected its policies—such as the Nazi-Soviet Pact—they would be met with a chorus of approval from every Communist party in the world.

How did Stalin propose to deal with the new problem? The scraps of information about his dealings with the Chinese leadership throw fascinating light on the Sino-Soviet relations during this phase. It is clear that he counted first of all on his unmatched prestige to secure at least outward deference and obedience from Peking. But even the megalomaniac despot realized that China could not be treated in the same way he dealt, say, with Bulgaria. The Sino-Soviet Treaty of 1950 envisaged the Chinese as repossessing Port Arthur and the Manchurian Railway. Stalin now hastened to offer Soviet military help for Mao's consolidation of his power over the mainland. According to a recent Soviet source, "Soviet aviation units took part in the concluding phase of the [civil] war, having been sent there in accord with the Sino-Soviet Treaty of February 14, 1950."[10]

But Stalin did not confine himself to soothing Mao's pride and to providing him with belated help. The Manchurian port of the Chinese Communist empire enjoyed at first an autonomous position, being ruled by people with special ties to Moscow, headed by Kao Kang. It was only following Stalin's death in December 1953 that Mao moved "to remove or to push aside those leaders of the party, who were known as partisans of increased proletarian influence in the party and of friendships with the Soviet Union."[11] In 1955 Kao Kang died in jail.

The story of the Korean War suggests strongly that it was exploited by the USSR for preserving Soviet leverage over Peking, if not indeed instigated for that purpose. After China's involvement in the war, Soviet air units moved into Manchuria, ostensibly to protect her from American air raids.[12] But it is at least reasonable to conjecture that this was the means of establishing a Soviet presence in that rich province should Chiang's forces, with American support, descend on other parts of China and rekindle the civil war.

Stalin's death was bound to put an end, at least for some time to such games. His successors were conscious of how the awe and imperturbability exuded by the late despot had marked various internal and external weaknesses of the Soviet Union. They could not and would not conduct foreign policy in the same way. Above all, they realized that their position might be weakened, perhaps fatally, by any realization, whether in the West or even in their own country, of the precarious nature of Sino-Soviet relations. It is revealing that the announcement of George Malenkov's assumption of leadership was accompanied by a picture showing him with Stalin and Mao, as if in addition to the late dictator's blessing he also had the approval of the head of what for the next seven years would be officially referred to as the Great People's Republic of China.[13] For both internal and external reasons the Kremlin needed the "unshakable friendship of the Soviet and Chinese people," and it had to pay a price for that friendship. For some twenty years the relationship between the Soviet Union and foreign Communists had been fairly one-sided: to the USSR accrued most of the advantages of this relationship, to foreign comrades most of the dangers and costs. Now the Soviet leaders hastened to appease Peking. Economic and technological help was extended to China on a much more generous scale than originally planned in Stalin's time. The special position of the USSR in Manchuria and Sinkiang was liquidated with no demur from Moscow. In 1954 Khrushchev headed a delegation to China, where it fell to him to negotiate the final stage of the liquidation of the Soviet presence on Chinese soil: Port Arthur and the East Chinese Railway were turned over to Peking; the joint companies—Stalin's favorite method of exploiting fellow Communist states—were liquidated and their total assets given over to the Chinese. For Mao this was evidently but a beginning: Mongolia too should be returned to Chinese suzerainty, he told his visitors.

Developments in the international field during the next five years left the Kremlin no option but to continue what was in fact a policy of appeasement of Peking. The period 1956-1957 was a time of crisis in the Soviet Union's relations with the satellites, at the same time that the leadership of the Russian Communist Party was shaken by serious internal dissensions. It was imperative for the Kremlin to receive public support from China, and that support did not come free. In October 1957 the Soviets took a step that would have been unimaginable in Stalin's time: they promised to help China develop its nuclear technology, and as the Chinese were later to reveal, the agreement included a promise that the USSR would deliver its ally a sample atom bomb.[14]

Both sides were under no illusion as to the nature and reasons for their collaboration. Peking was aware that time was growing short for its exploitation of the Soviet predicament. A détente with the United States would enable the Kremlin to face a public rupture with China with greater equanimity. Understandably Mao had every reason to press the Soviet Union toward a more militant posture vis-à-vis America and to constrain Moscow to support anti-Western revolutionary movements all over the world. The Soviets chafed under these constraints. Then August-September 1958, "in an attempt to intensify the 'Big Leap' by means of creating a center of tension close to China, Mao and his partisans embarked, without any consultation with the USSR . . . upon provocative artillery shelling of islands in the Taiwan Straits . . . As became known later, the Maoists had counted on the possibility of starting a 'local war' with the United States there and eventually of involving the USSR in it."[15]

History had thus caught up with the USSR. What had been the

source of additional strength, of her privileged position vis-à-vis other states, had now become also a burden, a source of entanglements and danger. Communist China's declaration of independence vis-à-vis the Soviet Union was to affect much more than just Sino-Soviet relations; it was bound to change the Soviet position within the whole Communist movement. No longer would the USSR enjoy a completely free hand in foreign affairs, be able to perform the most breathtaking maneuvers and shifts in its policies, confident that no matter how much they might hurt the interests of foreign Communists, the latter would obediently follow Moscow's wishes. Some foreign parties, notably Albania's, went over completely to Peking's camp. Others, such as North Vietnam's, saw the conflict between the Communist giants as an opportunity for maneuvering between the two and for asserting a degree of independence of both. The Sino-Soviet break, which became public knowledge in 1960, meant that any conflict between the interests of a given Communist party and those of the USSR could no longer be resolved by Moscow, automatically and without fear of repercussions in favor of the other party. Peking became a fervent advocate of what might be called the underprivileged members of the Communist family, those parties whose revolutionary strivings were either ignored or restrained by Russia out of her concern to avoid a dangerous confrontation with the United States. Much as the Soviet leaders saw through the Chinese game and in fact by the early 1960s had come to believe that Mao wanted nothing less than to force them into a war with America, they were still vulnerable to such pressures. The loyalty of foreign Communists could no longer be taken for granted; it had to be fought for in competition with China. Thus, the Soviet regime was forced to offer repeated proofs of its "internationalism" and of its solicitude for anti-Western revolutionary movements throughout the world, even though by doing so, it was frustrating or at least delaying that thoroughgoing détente with the United States and that definitive settlement of the German problem which had been cardinal objectives of Soviet policy since the middle fifties.

   An outside observer, when first confronted with the evidence of the Sino-Soviet split, might well have concluded that its logical outcome would be a basic change in the Soviet Union's foreign outlook and policy. The USSR would become explicitly what she was already in fact, a status quo power. The umbilical cord linking the Soviet state to the international Communist movement, if not severed, would become attenuated. It obviously made no sense to export revolution if—and here China offered a constant and irrefutable proof—each new state entering the "camp of socialism" brought with it new headaches for the USSR: entanglements, expense, danger. Even within its special preserve, Eastern Europe, the USSR had to put up with a semi-independent posture by Rumania. Other loyal East European Communist regimes still had to be watched carefully: in 1968, for example, Brezhnev might well have borrowed the dominoes simile of the American policy makers about Southeast Asia to justify the Kremlin's intervention in Czechoslovakia. A few more months of the Czechoslovak liberalization and the Warsaw and East German regimes would have had to follow suit or collapse in the face of popular pressures. The maintenance of Communist regimes in Eastern Europe could no longer be assumed to bring economic profits to their protector. The pattern of Soviet exploitation that prevailed in Stalin's time could not be maintained following his death. In the sixties the satellite empire occasionally became an economic burden. Following the 1968 invasion Soviet economic help had to be extended to Czechoslovakia to keep that country's economy from crumbling. And in the winter of 1970-1971, to prevent Gomulka's fall from endangering the Warsaw Communist regime, food shipments had to be rushed to Poland.

As against the costs and danger of ideological imperialism, the Kremlin leadership could ruefully contemplate the case of Finland. This small country, since 1945 as firmly within the Soviet sphere as any of the Communist satellites, had nevertheless been allowed for a variety of reasons to preserve her internal autonomy and democratic institutions. Hence, Finland's internal crises and dilemmas were of no concern to Moscow, no drain on Soviet resources. The Finnish government did not have to be watched anxiously for any sign of flirtation with Peking; the freedom of the press in Helsinki was unlikely to lead to untoward impressions and strivings in Warsaw, Sofia, or Kiev.

But neither the Sino-Soviet conflict nor the recent troubles in

Eastern Europe appear to have persuaded the Kremlin to alter drastically the pattern of its relations with the world Communist movement or to abstain from ideological imperialism. In fact, the dispute with China has, at least until recently, sharpened the ideological thrust of Soviet foreign policy. During the Khrushchev era the Soviet Union sought to outbid Peking in the appeal to revolutionary movements, especially in the Third World. Moscow decided not only to try to remain the directing center of World Communism but also to become the chief sponsor of non-Communist revolutionary movements and regimes, throwing its support behind practically every organized force combatting the waning Western influence in the Third World. In fact, fissures within the Communist bloc have apparently served to strengthen the Soviets' determination to stake a claim to yet another area of ideological influence and appeal in world politics. Amidst official guests at recent congresses of the Communist Party of the Soviet Union, there have been not only delegations of fraternal parties from all over the world, but also delegations of the ruling parties of Algeria, Egypt, and Mali, and of the Socialist Party of Chile. To be sure, their presence could only partly offset the absence of representatives of the largest Communist-ruled nation in the world, but the mere fact of admitting non-Communists to what had traditionally been a closed family gathering has a significance that goes beyond the symbolic. The Soviet Union now proclaims itself to be the fatherland not only of socialism but also of anti-imperialism. For a traditionalist thinking in terms of pre-1914 international law and diplomacy, this must have been an even more shocking and ominous development than the Soviet-Communist link. The latter might just be rationalized in terms of a worldwide ideological fraternity, masked by the polite fiction that when Michael Suslov and Boris Ponomarev talk with their British, French, or Argentinian comrades, they do so as fellow Communists rather than as members of the highest ruling body of the USSR. But this new intimate link between the Soviet Union and a variety of movements and regimes whose only common denominator is hostility to the West has an eloquence of its own.

How can one explain the persistence of this anti-Western syndrome and activity even at times, as at present, when the Soviet Union's "other" official policy seeks, and to a degree has achieved, a far-reaching détente with the United States and other Western powers? There are several explanations, including the very momentum, so to speak, of the Soviet Union's ideological past; the competition with China; and especially, the character of the Soviet regime as predicated on its international role. Every denial of internal freedom, each restriction on the Soviet citizen's liberties, is rationalized eventually by the image of a world divided into two hostile camps, in which the forces of light—Communism—are forever contending with those of darkness—capitalism and imperialism—in a struggle that never abates even when relations between the Soviet and Western governments are of the friendliest. Furthermore, and equally important, the Soviet regime feels that by now it has gained a prescriptive right to have what are, in fact, two foreign policies. It reacts strongly when the West shows the slightest sign of imitating the Soviet practice of having a bifurcated foreign policy: an ideological as well as a state one. One example was Khrushchev's probably unfeigned indignation because the United States "celebrated" the Captive Nations Week. The Soviet example has nevertheless influenced the American approach to foreign policy. The United States has even grown so used to Soviet unorthodox practices that they hardly arouse any surprise, not to mention diplomatic protest. It is no longer news when a secretary of the Central Committee and an American Communist leader sit down to a "cordial exchange of views." Yet the reaction in the USSR and America would be stunned were a presidential assistant to hold a similar publicly announced exchange with the head of an anti-Soviet Ukrainian or Russian émigré organization.[16]

The situation illuminates two melancholy facts, one a platitude: the emergence of the Soviet state and then its achievement of superpower status has, perhaps irretrievably, changed the nature of international relations and corroded that rudimentary international order which existed prior to 1914. The mainstays of that order were national sovereignty and the principle of noninterference by foreign powers in the affairs of sovereign states. To be sure, these were often honored in the breach, but still they were recognized as desirable aspirations and as necessary prerequisites of any real world order that would banish war. The Soviet Union was the first state in modern history which explicitly rejected national sovereignty as the basis of political legitimacy. In view of its ideological premises, the Soviet state has to consider every non-Communist government as de facto rather than de jure. That by itself would not have led to a heightening anarchy of international relations. After all, one tenet of the popular American philosophy of international relations has been that nondemocratic governments are both immoral and, in the long run, doomed by the forces of history. But in addition, the Soviet Union has assumed and exercised leadership over a worldwide movement whose stated, even though long-run, aim has been to replace every other form of government by the dictatorship of the proletariat.

Another almost inevitable result of the Soviets changing the rules of the international game was a transformation in the character of the foreign policy of Western powers, principally the United States. Once committed to an active world role, the United States— not only the government but also public opinion—found it impossible to get a handle on the Soviet phenomenon. The United States could and did deal in a forthright manner with palpable aggression. But following the war this country became an occasional partner as well as an almost constant competitor not only of another state but also of a worldwide system. Who, then, was the United States dealing with, the guardians of Russia's national interest or the high priests of an international ideological movement? In fighting to curb Soviet expansion, was America dealing with an imperial power, a worldwide conspiracy, or was she really fighting the forces of history? Could the Soviet threat, Communism, be contained by the virtuousness of American policies, exacting similarly virtuous policies from her allies, or should the United States, to be "realistic," descend into the grubby game of worldwide subversion? Could the Russians be scared off their evil designs by a crushing superiority of power on the other side, or were they to be dissuaded from their real fears by continuous examples of American high-mindedness and solicitude for freedom and democracy throughout the world? At one time or another American foreign policies during the last twenty-five years reflected each of these variants.

Almost inveitably, therefore, the ideological component of American policies was enhanced by competition with the Soviet Union and by what America's rulers and public opinion conceived of as the exigencies of the cold war. Though not altogether undesirable, this aspect of the American response to what was thought to be the Soviet-Communist challenge was to have disruptive consequences both for international politics and for the inner workings of the American democracy. In announcing the doctrine that bears his name, President Harry S. Truman proclaimed the basic conflict to be between two ways of life: the Communist one, spreading "in the evil soil of poverty and strife," and the democratic one, "based upon the will of the majority . . . free elections . . . guarantees of individual liberty . . . freedom of speech."[17] This rhetoric, necessary as it may have been to convince the American taxpayers to assume additional and unaccustomed burdens, still appeared to suggest that the United States was engaged in an ideological crusade rather than a sober endeavor to restore a degree of stability to international relations. America's power was enlisted once more in a drive to make the world safe for democracy rather than from war, and for the right of individual states to be free from direct or indirect aggression. Many of the contested areas—Iran, Turkey, certainly Kuomintang China—could not be described as free in the sense that the term is employed in the lexicon of American politics. The time would come when public opinion would demand evidence of irreproachable democratic virtues from each of the allies and protegés of the United States, and when they were found wanting, many Americans would conclude that this country had no business protecting their independence. Thus, the ideological veneer of the policy of containment was to contribute to the paradoxical situation of recent years when, to many critics at home and abroad, the United States stands revealed not as a defender of international security and order, but as an enemy of social and political change throughout the world. Yet what most critics and moralists overlook is the lesson of one of the most justifiable and rewarding acts of postwar United States foreign policy: the decision to extend American help to a regime which by no stretch of the imagination could be characterized as democratic, but which in no sense could be described as opposed to social and economic change: Tito's Yugoslavia. Here was a government which, though utterly lacking in democratic or capitalist virtues, showed its determination to retrieve its national independence as well as its capacity to do so by barring an invasion by an overwhelming force. American aid to Communist Yugoslavia could be seen as an act of sheer power politics. Yet in extending a helping hand to a Communist dictatorship, the United States stumbled into an acknowledgment of what must be the basic principle of international morality: the right of any state, no matter what its ideological complexion, to be free from foreign domination. Livelihood must come before virtue, proclaimed an ancient philosopher. And international security must come before democracy or social progress as the foundation of a viable international order.

The Soviet state, or rather the privileged position that this state has assumed in its foreign relations, has thus deflected even its rivals from perceiving what must be the guiding principle of an effective endeavor for peace. The ideological virus that has infected the world body politic could not be conjured away by contrivances like the United Nations. When beginning in 1947 the United States in her exasperation over this predicament sought a formula for an ideological counteroffensive against what it perceived as the Soviet drive for world domination, this served only to deepen the crisis that the world had reentered immediately following the war. Both super-powers have rationalized their ideological imperialism in terms of higher principles allegedly transcending national sovereignty. What made matters worse from the Western point of view was the fact that America's posture as leader of the "Free World" was bound to be ineffective: unlike the Soviet Union, the United States is not bolstered by the loyalty of a disciplined world movement that will unquestionably follow her commands. Furthermore, a democratic society is badly equipped to sustain a prolonged ideological crusade. It is expected by its own people as well as by its allies to adhere rigorously to its professed ideals in international relations and not to dilute them in the slightest through realpolitik or national interests. The Soviet state does not, or has not until recently, suffered from similar disadvantages. The Monroe Doctrine has, in effect, collapsed; the Brezhnev doctrine (which should really be called the Stalin doctrine) has been doing quite well, at least insofar as Eastern Europe is concerned.

The problem here is not primarily United States-Soviet relations but rather how the Soviet Union has affected the general character of international relations and politics. Until 1914 there had existed what might be called a rudimentary international order. It was far from providing for the equality of its member states, still less for a peaceful resolution of international disputes. Yet in theory, this system expressed certain basic aspirations and stipulated the necessary conditions for a world order, the cardinal condition being national or, to be more precise, state sovereignty. The rise of the Soviet state and of the international Communist movement could not but pose a basic challenge to the effort to reconstitute this international order after the catastrophe of World War I. Soviet membership, first in the League of Nations and then in the United Nations, could not in itself counteract the disruptive effect of the Soviet Union on the normal functioning of international politics in its pre-1914 sense. Whatever the obligations that the USSR assumed by virtue of its membership in the world organizations, and whatever one thinks of the Soviet record in abiding by them, it is clear that the Russian leaders never even pretended that, in assuming those obligations, they were abdicating their role as guides of a worldwide supranational movement whose legitimacy derived from an ideology and not from any international covenant.

The challenge to the Russian leadership of the Communist movement, the virtual certainty that the monolithic unity of this movement can never again be restored, has not resulted in what might be called the secularization of the Soviet state. In fact, while Soviet policies toward their acknowledged ideological protagonists have become more conciliatory, Soviet ideological pretensions have over the last twenty years grown more all-embracing. Moscow has emerged as the sponsor of a revolutionary ecumenism, but one which, unlike Rome's does not imply a liberalization of the practices of the true church itself.[18] Influence and power outside their own country are seen by the Soviet leaders as a necessary condition for the preservation of their regime in its full autocratic rigor. Stalin could easily afford the collapse of the Greek Communist

17 | THE CONVOLUTIONS OF TERROR

It is not too early to say that Alexander Solzhenitsyn's *Gulag Archipelago, 1918-1956: An Experiment in Literary Investigation* is a literary masterpiece and a historic event. Dismiss for the moment what might be called the politico-sensational aspects of its appearance: the Western publishers' battles and the race to translate it, its relation to détente and to Soviet-American trade. These are important problems, but they are irrelevant to the artistic and historical resonance of this work, to its greatness as well as its shortcomings—for a personality cult of artists and martyrs should be avoided as much as that of political leaders; one leads to the other. *Gulag* is an unusual type of literary production: personal recollections are blended with a historical chronicle and historico-philosophical reflections. As a personal account, it has striking honesty and an integrity of self-analysis. As a chronicle of human injustice and suffering, it impresses by its massiveness and vividness.

By now there is a considerable literature about terror and suffering in Stalin's Russia, some of the most shattering accounts having appeared openly in the Soviet Union between 1960 and 1965. It is fair to say that no single tale recounted by Solzhenitsyn can surpass in horror and in its grip on one's capacity for compassion and indignation some of the stories already told. Osip Mandelstam's very physical ailment—which his wife described as asthma, a gasping for air—epitomizes what happened to him in prison as a man and an artist. Deserving of compassion is even the one-time ally and accomplice of Stalin, Aaron Soltz, who for a trivial gesture of protest was incarcerated in an asylum, became crazed, and when released, spent his time filling up paper with meaningless rows of numbers—some private code of his demented mind—which he kept sending to his former friend and destroyer. But Solzhenitsyn's book reveals the deeper meaning and scope of terror—not in number of victims, for there the writer is as baffled as anyone else not privy to the archives of the KGB, but in the psychological dimension of the horror.

The book is written, one might say, in two languages. When recounting individuals' stories, their hopes, fears, and villainies, the author uses language that is sparse and unemotional. But when it comes to the villain-hero of the book—terror—the idiom is filled with metaphors, touched with mystery, somewhat obscure. Here are Solzhenitsyn's descriptions of the "torrents" of terror and suffering that periodically sweep through the vast land: "a torrent is something elemental, something stronger than even the Organs" of the state security; once you are seized by a torrent, "no one can save you from being drawn into the maelstrom." Terror and suffering on that scale, the author seems to say, require a special language to convey the mystique of the ordeal, which allows no usual explanation. The secret police itself was being purged: "These torrents sprang up from some mysterious law ordaining a renovation of the organs; [a law] which required periodical sacrifices so that those who survived would appear purified." The book has sudden transitions from one idiom into the other, which shock the reader into an awareness of the surrealist landscape of Stalin's Russia.

One day in 1945 Alexander Solzhenitsyn suddenly ceased to be an artillery captain and Soviet citizen; he became part of the human flotsam to be carried by a mighty torrent to one of the islands of the Archipelago. The very minute his officer's straps were torn off, it became inevitable that he should be cast into a whirlpool of investigation, solitary cells, convoys, and camps. It was almost equally inevitable that he should lose not only his physical freedom but part of his quality as a human being. More fortunate than most, he would be restored eleven years later to his full status as a man. Then he would wonder how he could ever have signed the deposition thrust at him by the investigator. But luckily, too, he was never physically tortured nor constrained to denounce a friend or relative.

The book makes clear that the uniqueness of Stalin's terror did not lie in its cruelty. On this count Hitler may well contend for a palm of primacy. But Soviet terror went deeper; it had philosophical, indeed a metaphysical meaning. Why, for instance, go through the fuss and bother of investigations, depositions, false confessions? Why go through the effort and expense of transports, camp installations, for hundreds of thousands, if not millions, who would die in a few weeks or months, their labor not compensating the state even for their miserable food and the other expenses incurred on their behalf? If terror alone had been the aim, why not a neat "final solution" for a hundred thousand or so who might conceivably become troublesome for the Leader? Even official Soviet accounts now imply that not as much as one-thousandth of those repressed were guilty of a real crime, even such a crime as Solzhenitsyn's: a few unflattering remarks about Stalin contained in a private letter. Then why?

Solzhenitsyn's own story may provide a clue, as well as testimony to the superiority of Solzhenitsyn as artist than as analytical historian. In 1945 he was arrested and seized by security officers in the presence of his brigade commander, Colonel Travkin. The colonel, to the fury of the agents and the fearful amazement of his staff, stood up, shook Solzhenitsyn's hand, managed to hint for what reason he was being arrested, and said to the ex-officer, now a state criminal: "I wish you luck, captain." Solzhenitsyn's comment: "Wonder of wonders, one *can* remain a man." Colonel Travkin did not suffer for his humane and foolhardy gesture. Here a historian must be more precise and pedantic, explaining that in 1945 a front-line officer *could* take this risk—though Travkin still must have been an unusually honest and brave man. In 1937-1938, however, such behavior would have been inconceivable, or Travkin would soon have shared the fate of his subordinate. Thus, the reader is made to realize the "higher" reasons for Stalinist terror. The ordeal of the defeat, then the patriotic elation of the war, have managed to rub off from Soviet society much of the fear and hysteria that had solidified the grip of the regime in the late thirties. Travkin was not arrested; with the war still going on, it was impractical, perhaps even dangerous, to arrest too many front-line officers. But Stalin could not allow an esprit de corps to crystallize within the Red Army; with the war's end and new torrents of terror, it was unlikely that in a year's time an officer would dare to shake the hand of an unmasked criminal.

Sometimes Solzhenitsyn the artist provides answers to the questions he himself asks as an analyst-historian. Thus, he wonders why at some crucial moments—say, when thousands of Leningraders were being dragged off, arrested, and deported following Kirov's assassination in 1934—the people did not fight back. What could the security services have done against hundreds of thousands fighting with axes, clubs, even fists? But elsewhere he avows that he, who as an adolescent and young man had lived through terror, nevertheless went to prison and then remained for at least one year afterward a convinced Marxist-Leninist. Terror so vast not only made people obey the regime, it also made them believe the phantasmagoric tales of treason and "wrecking" spread by the regime before 1941.

As for the maker of this surrealist world, Solzhenitsyn begrudges him greatness, even as a force for evil. Stalin was "a blind and (personally) unimportant instrument" of forces created by the system. Yet this is hardly convincing. The author sketches masterfully how the system made Stalin possible. Terror began to be practiced on the morrow of the Revolution as a weapon of class war. Then insensibly it turned into an administrative technique: political prophylaxis. But it remained for Stalin to create a veritable civilization based on terror. Solzhenitsyn in fact pays a perverse homage to the evil wrought by this one man in the very frequency of his references to the "Great Teacher," "the Father of the People." When applying another epithet to the dictator's accomplices, he puts it in lower case; for Stalin it is capitalized: he is The Murderer. No, the system did not make Stalin inevitable; it is conceivable to envisage the Russia of the thirties and forties ruled by a Khrushchev or an oligarchy like the present one, with terror running in rivulets rather than in torrents.

Personal courage is almost an irrelevant consideration in evaluating the behavior of victims of the terror, certainly in those horror-laden years of the thirties. Some brave men can resist physical torture and refuse to break down, to sign a lying confession, to implicate others. Fewer are capable of standing up under psychological torture. The Soviet secret police worked for a purpose and not just with the impatient sadism of the Gestapo. And if by a miracle one could withstand beatings, then sleeplessness and refined psychological chicanery, who could remain insensitive to blackmail: the threat of destruction of one's wife, children, parents? Solzhenitsyn shows no sympathy toward the Communist leaders, like Zinoviev and Bukharin, who broke down and pleaded falsely to the greater glory of the oppressor-in-chief; and perhaps they deserve no sympathy. But certainly they deserve compassion and, from a historian, despite all their past transgressions, understanding. Solzhenitsyn's hatred of the system that robbed him of eleven years of his life and Russia of millions of her best people is so great that he cannot grant the makers of this system, even as revolutionaries, any virtues. Under tsarism, he maintains, the Bolsheviks were not particularly persecuted as compared with other revolutionaries, such as the People's Will of the seventies and eighties, or the Socialist Revolutionaries. But this is an oversimplification and, for a historian, a harmful one. Although as a whole the Bolsheviks (and for that matter the Social Democrats in general) were not treated or punished so severely as other revolutionaries, some of them had to endure long imprisonment and exile; not a few lost their sanity or were driven to suicide. Perhaps even the cruel exile of Stalin may partly account for his future inhumanity and relish in sadism. When it comes to the Communist victims of terror and their false confessions, one must distinguish degrees of guilt, as between Zinoviev, a most unattractive figure (though not as monstrous as Stalin), and Bukharin, in many ways an engaging man, but flawed because of the ideology into moral insensitivity. After all, the author shows compassion toward General Vlasov, though he does not (as Soviet propaganda outrageously and clumsily tries to present) minimize his guilt.

If there is an individual hero in the book, it is another Vlasov. An unsophisticated provincial official, Vasily Vlasov, refuses to humor the local prosecutor and the secret police chief by condoning minor frauds. Arrested as a people's enemy, he defies in court his persecutors and false witnesses. In his death cell, awaiting the news as to whether his sentence will be commuted, he spits in the face of an investigator who addresses him too unceremoniously. A miracle: he gets only twenty years, lives to become free and tell his tale. A happy ending? Not quite. On her father's arrest his eight-year-old daughter Zoe became ill and then died with the words, "Give me back my papa." Solzhenitsyn is not a sentimentalist; he does not grow lyrical about Vasily nor lachrymose over Zoe Vlasov: theirs are merely two such cases among millions. But the reader is not only moved but comforted. Not even at the worst of times could Stalinist reality completely displace the human one. Vasily Vlasov helps explain why the Russian people have managed to survive their oppressors, how they have produced Solzhenitsyns, why there is some hope for the future. Why, asks the author in another place, could not some of the falsely accused, instead of confessing, shout to their investigators-oppressors: "No, if you are, then we do not want to be revolutionaries; if you claim to be Russians, then we do not want to be Russians; if you represent Communism, then we are not Communists"? Vasily Vlasov, in effect, did that, and so now does Solzhenitsyn.

His nation's and his own ordeal makes Solzhenitsyn skeptical about political ideologies in general. Did not Marxism-Leninism help bring suffering to millions and make even more people acquiesce in it because, instead of seeing Stalinism for what it was, they viewed it through an ideological prism? And were not the socialist rivals of the Bolsheviks rendered ineffectual and impotent through their own ideology, because instead of seeing oppression and suffering in their true light, they saw them as misguided and cruel, but still revolution? Thus, every political ideology—and here Solzhenitsyn would include, to the anguish of some of his Western admirers, liberalism and the new left—is harmful insofar as it obscures the reality of human aspirations and sufferings. What *is* real is human individuality and the life of a nation, and if a political system respects human freedom and the tradition of a nation, then what form it takes, whether authoritarian or democratic, is relatively unimportant. Such views as expressed in his "letter" to the Politburo are already implied in *Gulag*. One may, perhaps from the Western perspective, must question them, but if they are examined

316   *Internationalism and Foreign Affairs*

against the experience of the Russian people during the last three hundred years, they certainly are neither simplistic nor a product of political naiveté.

Not that Solzhenitsyn abhors all ideologies. It is the Communist Vlasov who finds the hardihood to withstand his ordeal as much because of his beliefs as because of his inherent honesty. But absolute power joined to an ideology—there, in Solzhenitsyn's view, is the root cause of the evil of our times. Any state is tolerable, indeed to be respected and obeyed, if it is willing to let its citizens render to God that which is God's, or to translate into secular terms, if it respects man's internal autonomy and freedom, and abides by real laws rather than the mockery of "socialist legality." Quite apart from his present beliefs, Solzhenitsyn's Christian orientation is a product of his reflections on his nation's and on his own calvary: internal as well as national anarchy must lead to despotism. The real tragedy of Communism in its Stalinist version—and here again the artist speaks through his work rather than directly— was that over and beyond its physical oppression, it conquered men's minds. To the author the most significant element in the early and, by comparison with the thirties, "mild" period of terror and illegality lay in the persecution of the clergy and of the faithful in general. To be sure, the ex-Mensheviks or Socialist Revolutionaries then being tried and sentenced were in a vast majority of cases as innocent as the Orthodox bishops and priests. But the latter had never had the presumption to try to impose a political system on their people; they sought only to remain faithful to the precepts of their faith. For the most part, they were willing to abide by the laws of the Soviet state as long as they did not clash with those of God. Here Solzhenitsyn castigates the fallacy of the Western liberal critique of the Soviet system insofar as it concentrates on the Soviet suppression of *political* dissent. The source and prime cause of political repression lies in the excessive and unnatural politicization of the life of a nation: once we overlook or minimize the sufferings of a human being because he happens to be a reactionary priest or a rich peasant, we prepare the way for the persecution of "political deviationists," then of the "people's enemies," then of the people as a whole. Not a highly original point, but how vividly this lesson speaks from the pages of the *Gulag*!

Solzhenitsyn emerges as a fervent Russian nationalist. Not in the political sense, for many even among the current dissenters would strongly disagree with his indifference, indeed at times his negative attitude, toward Russian Soviet imperial expansion, and with his avowal of the historical wrongs done by Russia to Poland and to small Baltic nationalities. But Solzhenitsyn's critique in no sense smacks of national masochism and breast-beating; it simply comes out of the realization (quite apart from a humane acknowledgment of other nations' rights) of how often the Russian state's victories have meant slavery and new burdens for the Russian people. In developing this theme, unfortunately, Solzhenitsyn becomes a bit fatuous. Defeats, he writes, are often beneficial for the nations that suffer them, just as personal travails and suffering enrich and ennoble individuals. It was unfortunate for Russia that Peter the Great should have beaten the Swedes at Poltava: victorious Russia went on to become a great power of no benefit to her people, while the fortunate Swedes, now taught to eschew war, became prosperous and the freest nation in Europe, this blessed state continuing until today when, "if one believes what one reads," excessive affluence had brought forth certain moral degeneracy. Russia's own defeats have often brought her people increased freedom; and revolution, pursues our writer, unmindful that the revolution which he deplores would have been inconceivable had the Provisional Government in 1917 been able to score military successes rather than continue to suffer defeats. As to the ennobling force of individual suffering, the Russian example is again instructive of how often an erstwhile political martyr will, with power in his hands, become an oppressor.

But Solzhenitsyn is far from endorsing any mystique of individual or national suffering as the path to salvation. Against the imperial role, he sets up what might be called biological and cultural criteria for a nation's greatness. The Russian nation grew vast and strong because of its impulse to grow and to colonize the wilderness; it has become great because of its culture. No one who reads Solzhenitsyn can retain the slightest doubt that he is fiercely proud to be a Russian or can overlook the utter inconceivability of the writer "choosing the West" in any sense, except as a temporary and involuntary place of exile.

What of the more prosaic aspect of *Gulag*; what does it actually add to our knowledge? Certainly there are no "revelations." A Soviet writer who in many cases has no access to the books and periodicals that have found their way abroad but which are no longer easily available at home is often at a disadvantage vis-à-vis a Western student. Thus, though miniscule, factual errors exist, such as his description of the trial of the Socialist Revolutionaries and his confused account of what was happening in the ministry of the State Security in 1952. To be sure, he benefits from that priceless oral history which he has collected so assiduously and which he analyzes so scrupulously. Again, to be pedantic, there is the problem of a historian's emotional detachment. Solzhenitsyn, in trying to account for what is so difficult to understand, Stalin's personality, raises the question of whether the tyrant in his youth was not in fact an agent of the *Okhrana*. It is a tempting hypothesis, but along with Roy Medvedev, whose feelings toward the leader in question are no more tender than Solzhenitsyn's, we must reject it: the weight of evidence against it is too overwhelming.

But if Solzhenitsyn teaches few new facts, how much more clearly he illuminates the old ones: the factory director who, after about ten minutes of clapping at mention of Stalin's name, first broke off and sat down, and who in consequence was sentenced to "sit" for ten years; the man who during the news broadcasts would turn off his radio at the start of the endless series of "We pledge to you Joseph Vissarionovich" homages or messages, and who, denounced by his solicitous neighbor, was also sent to a camp. All such incidents reveal not only how evil but also how shamefully preposterous was the reality of Stalin's Russia and why it is so difficult for the present leaders, all of them at one time Stalin's servitors, to allow for a full accounting of the past. One can rehabilitate some victims, reveal some cruel episodes, denounce piously the "cult of personality." But how can one rationalize an inane and obscene joke played on a whole nation? Solzhenitsyn and, almost as amply as he, Nadyezhda Mandelstam make certain that future generations will not only stand in awe of this unparalleled period in a nation's life; they will also know that this was not a grandiose human sacrifice on the altar of progress and socialism, no cruelty in the style of "Gods are athirst." This was also, and primarily, a massive idiocy and hysteria superimposed upon inhumanity. And if one can discount the picture of boundless suffering that comes from the pages of *Gulag*, then what remains is the impression of colossal waste and sheer stupidity. It is the latter conclusion that is most damaging to Stalin's successors. They have done away with terror on the surrealistic scale as practiced by their erstwhile teacher and leader. But what they have retained is not only absolute power but the political and verbal apparatus that made this terror possible and which was used as its rationalization. And so, because of writing about horrors that they themselves have largely admitted and condemned, a Soviet writer is now adjudged not a "people's enemy"—too reminiscent—but a traitor; and is no longer sent to a camp—again too reminiscent and, in view of his fame, too embarrassing—but into forced exile. The result is chicanery instead of terror, though the latter is kept in reserve and is occasionally used against those whose incarceration will not create too much fuss, such as Yakir and Krasin, two dissidents who broke down and confessed. This chicanery is undoubtedly more humane, and yet even by the premises on which the current Soviet system is based, it is no more rational and less ridiculous than the terror of yore.

Though it sounds paradoxical and perhaps indelicate, Alexander Solzhenitsyn is as much a product of the Soviet system as, say, Brezhnev. Had the system not decided that it was a high crime to say a few disrespectful things about Stalin in a private letter, perhaps he would have remained a loyal Marxist-Leninist, combining some literary activity with teaching mathematics. Possibly had he been allowed to publish in his own country, he would have remained a critic of the regime rather than been forced to become its enemy, as they see him. At one time he almost became, if not a member of the Soviet establishment, then the closest thing the USSR would have had to a representative of the loyal literary opposition. He recounts in *Gulag* how at an official invitation, presumably Khrushchev's, he held a session with and lectured to the justices of the Soviet Supreme Court. It is not Solzhenitsyn who has changed his position since those days; it is the regime, which thus made it inevitable that Russia's greatest living writer should become a dissenter, then an exile, and then, above all, something he did not aspire to in the early sixties, a political force.

As to the political impact of *Gulag*, one must suspect that in the short run the regime's calculations may well prove to have been justified. Many—and not only those from among the ruling apparatus—must lean toward the conclusion that, in the midst of a more affluent and, all things considered, freer present, one should not dwell incessantly on the horrors of the now almost dim past. Through a mixture of expulsions and judicious chicanery, the regime has coped efficaciously with dissent. Perhaps, except among the intelligentsia, Solzhenitsyn's historical evocation finds little political resonance. But in another dimension the current official policy must be judged not only vile but also near-sighted. In the early sixties—for it was only at the Twenty-second Congress in 1961 rather than in 1956 that Khrushchev entered upon a really consistent critique of Stalin—there appeared to be just a chance that Stalinism could be separated from the living body of Communism and be convincingly presented as an excrescence upon it. By being too faint-hearted to keep on telling the truth, the successors of Khrushchev offered convincing proof that this past still shapes the present, that one cannot pull out the roots of Stalinism without shaking up the whole system. Russia's rulers obviously hope that through expulsions and arrests they can change the past, just as through terror Stalin almost succeeded in imposing his own version of reality on an entire nation. But one cannot exile history, and *Gulag* will be one of the main reasons why this past will remain alive, meaningful, and a challenge to succeeding generations of the people of Russia.

NOTES

INDEX

NOTES

Introduction

1. Quoted in Bernard E. Brown, *Protest in Paris: Anatomy of a Revolt* (New York, 1974), p. 2.
2. *Landmarks: Collection of Essays about the Russian Intelligentsia* (Moscow, 1909), p. 43.
3. John Maynard Keynes, *The General Theory of Employment Interest and Money* (New York, 1936), p. 383.

1 Bakunin, Herzen, and Chernyshevsky

1. Franco Venturi, *The Roots of Populism* (New York, 1960), p. 57.
2. Y. M. Steklov, *Fighters for Socialism* (Moscow, 1923), I, 227.
3. Steklov, p. 288.
4. The study of national character can produce almost any conclusion. It was fashionable among certain English historians of the nineteenth century to attribute constitutionalism to the "Germanic spirit" and to contrast with it the instinctive penchant toward despotism found among the Latin nations and the Slavs.
5. Discussed at length in Martin Malia, *Alexander Herzen and the Birth of Russian Socialism* (Cambridge, 1960).
6. Quoted in Malia, p. 408.
7. Most of the serfs were landholders, unlike the Negro slaves in the South; that is, apart from their duties on the landlord's lands (sometimes commuted by money payment), they had their "own" collectively held land. Unfree tenants rather than "serfs" would be a more technical description of their status. The peasants' folklore emphasized the contrast of personal unfreedom with the conviction that the land—all the land, their master's as well as the commune's—was legitimately theirs.
8. The burst of enthusiasm for Alexander, explicable by the contrast with his hateful father, was not unusual at the time, even among the radicals. Prince Kropotkin, the famous revolutionary and anarchist, recounts

in his memoirs how enraptured he was as a young man by his first encounter with the Tsar-Liberator.

9. E. H. Carr, *Romantic Exiles* (London, 1949). Carr's account, colored by irony but also by compassion, was received rather huffily by such socialist scholars as the late G. D. H. Cole. Cole implied unfairly that Carr with a kind of Anglo-Saxon condescension represents the great revolutionary and his circle as a bunch of mixed-up foreigners, thus provoking in a casual reader doubts as to what kind of people become socialists. Even if so, the casual reader can be reassured by the stories of the Marx and Lenin households, with their connubial bliss and bourgeois orderliness.

10. Steklov, p. 159.

11. There is a strong temptation to fall into the current sociological slang and to use the magic word "alienation." But the history of the Russian revolutionary movement shows exactly the limitations of this term. Were the Decembrists alienated from their society? But they represented the ideas and emotions, certainly not of the numerical majority, but of a considerable proportion of members of their class. The later intelligentsia radicals exhibit the same phenomenon. They were often the more active, more drastic exponents of ideas that were endemic in their society. Perhaps it was the staunch reactionaries and the defenders of the status quo in tsarist Russia who were alienated and "rebels against their own class."

12. Y. M. Steklov, *N. G. Chernyshevsky* (Moscow, 1928), I, 8.

13. One may feel that this was a clever courting technique, but it was more than that.

14. T. A. Bogdanovich, *Loves of the People of the Sixties* (Leningrad, 1929), p. 24.

15. An unkind relative in her sketch of Olga Chernyshevsky suggests that her husband's sardonic words about having been happy in Siberia were not unconnected with his wife's absence there.

16. The authorship of the letter has been in dispute, most of the authorities crediting it to Chernyshevsky, others to Dobrolyubov. Nobody questions that it expresses faithfully Chernyshevsky's ideas.

17. To an ultra-Bolshevik historian, Pokrovsky, the "moderation" and the counsel for patience of the proclamation to the peasants compared unfavorably with the proclamation signed "Young Russia" by a group of student hotheads who advocated wholesale carnage of the imperial party, abolition of the family and the republic. This Bolshevik worthy, whose historical views after his death in 1932 were branded by Stalin as a vulgarization of Marxism, saw in Chernyshevsky's advice a prototype of Menshevism. Steklov, *Chernyshevsky*, 294.

18. G. V. Plekhanov, *Works* (Moscow, 1924), V. 115.

19. Quotations from *What Is To Be Done?* are mostly from the Vintage Books edition (New York, 1961), trans. Benjamin R. Tucker, rev. and abr. Ludmilla B. Turkevich. The abridgment omits some of the politically most important passages.

20. For the tracing of the characters of *What Is To Be Done?* see Bogdanovich.

2   Socialism and Utopia

1. Sir William Beveridge, *Full Employment in a Free Society* (New York, 1945), p. 254.
2. Frederick Engels, *The Conditions of the Working Class in England in 1844,* in *Karl Marx and Frederick Engels on Britain* (Moscow, 1953), p. 52.
3. William Morris, *News From Nowhere* (London, 1912), pp. 84-85.
4. Francis Place, quoted in Graham Wallas, *The Life of Francis Place,* 3rd ed. (New York, 1919), pp. 383-384.
5. This argument is developed at greater length in Adam Ulam, *The Unfinished Revolution* (New York, 1960).
6. *A Handbook of Marxism* (New York, 1935) p. 57.
7. Karl Marx, *Capital* (New York, 1932), I, 648.
8. B. Kozmin, *P. N. Tkachev and the Revolutionary Movement of the 1860's* (Moscow, 1922), p. 19.
9. *Landmarks: Collection of Essays about the Russian Intelligentsia* (Moscow, 1909), p. 43.

3   The Marxist Pattern

1. Quoted in Bertram Wolfe, *Khrushchev and Stalin's Chost* (New York, 1957, p. 88.
2. P. Tkachev, *Collected Works* (Moscow, 1933), II, 22.
3. Maxim Gorky, *The Russian Peasant* (Berlin, 1922), p. 45.
4. Samuel H. Baron, *Plekhanov* (Stanford, 1963), p. 324.
5. Israel Getzler, *Martov* (Cambridge, 1967), p. 139.
6. Julius Martov, *Notes of a Social Democrat* (Berlin, 1922), p. 268.
7. *Martov and His Circle* (New York, 1959), p. 58.
8. V. I. Lenin, *Sochinenya,* 4th ed. (Moscow, 1954), XXIII, 438.
9. Baron, p. 352.
10. Adam Ulam, *The Bolsheviks* (New York, 1965), pp. 382-386.
11. One cannot help wondering how Tolstoy could have been so sure; after all, *he* was never in jail.
12. For these personal characteristics, see Ulam, pp. 208-216.

4   Lenin's Last Phase

1. V. I. Lenin, *Works,* 4th ed. (Moscow, 1964), XLV, 381, 377, 362, 346, 358.
2. *Lenin's Miscellany* (Moscow, 1970), XXXVII, 35, 362.

3. *Lenin's Miscellany,* XXXVII, p. 364.
4. Quoted in Lenin, XLV, 380.
5. Lenin, XLV, 380.
6. Record Book of the Secretaries attending V. I. Lenin, *Problems of the History of the Communist Party of the Soviet Union,* 1963, no. 2, p. 84.
7. One of the minor mysteries of the period, on which light may sometime be thrown, is why Rykov and Trotsky, two full members of the Politburo, were not mentioned by Lenin in this connection, while Pyatakov, considerably junior in status, was.
8. See Adam Ulam, *The Bolsheviks* (New York, 1965), p. 569.
9. Lenin, XLV, 343 (my italics).
10. Lenin, XLV, 347.
11. Lenin, XLV, 387.
12. Here it is significant to quote a couple of utterances at the Twelfth Party Congress. Vladimir Kosior: "Comrade Zinoviev spoke about collective judgment of the Party. But comrades . . . collective judgment ought not to be formulated by [a few] individuals . . . We have no clubs, no other groups where Party members might exchange opinions." Lutovinov: "It would appear that the Politburo has become the infallible pope; everything I do, I do correctly, don't you dare to criticize, no one has the right to criticize." *Twelfth Congress of the Russian Communist Party (b)* (Moscow, 1970), pp. 109, 116.
13. Lenin, XLV, 405.

6   Lenin, Stalin, and Trotsky

1. Record Book of the Secretaries attending V. I. Lenin, *Problems of the History of the Communist Party of the Soviet Union,* 1963, no. 2, p. 85.
2. First revealed in Khrushchev's 1956 speech. Bertram D. Wolfe, *Krushchev and Stalin's Ghost* (New York, 1957), pp. 98-99.
3. For Trotsky's version, written when he was in exile in 1929, see Trotsky, *My Life* (New York, 1931), pp. 482-488, repeated with some but not all and not completely reproduced documents of the case in Trotsky, *Stalin* (New York, 1946), pp. 362-364.
4. The *Trotsky Archive* T 792, Mar. 28, 1923.
5. One wonders how Fotyera managed to survive the Stalin era.
6. *The Trotsky Archive* T 793.
7. Quoted in Wolfe, p. 278.
8. *The Trotsky Archive* T 794, 795.
9. *The Trotsky Archive,* T 796.
10. A careful reading of Trotsky's account in *My Life* (pp. 483-486) shows that he intentionally confuses the dates when the various letters were

dispatched by Lenin and completely omits the fact that on March 5 he was asked point-blank over the phone whether he was going to undertake the defense of the Georgian case.

11. *The Eleventh Congress,* p. 430.

12. *The Twelfth Party Congress,* Apr. 17-23, 1923, *Stenographic Report* (Moscow, 1923), p. 1.

13. *The Twelfth Party Congress,* p. 105.

14. *The Twelfth Party Congress,* p. 172.

15. *The Twelfth Party Congress,* p. 113.

16. *The Twelfth Party Congress,* p. 564. Lenin had washed Bukharin's head for precisely the same reason at the Eighth Party Congress.

17. N. Semashko and others, *What Was the Disease from Which Lenin Died?* (Leningrad, 1924), p. 35.

7   Stalin

1. Stalin, *Collected Works* (Moscow, 1946-1952), XIII, 119.

2. Quoted in J. J. Marie, *Stalin* (Paris, 1967), p. 8.

3. Jane Degras, *The Communist International,* 1919-1943: *Documents,* vol. II: 1923-1928 (London, 1960), p. 525.

4. Jane Degras, ed., *Soviet Documents on Foreign Policy,* vol. III: 1933-1941 (New York, 1953), p. 49.

5. Seemingly, because Ehrenburg's ruminations brought him a severe dressing-down by Khrushchev.

6. Nicholas Virta, *The Great Days,* produced on the Soviet stage in 1948.

7. *The Correspondence of the Chairman of the Council of Ministers of the U.S.S.R. with the Presidents of the United States and Prime Ministers of Great Britain* (Moscow, 1957), I, 339.

8. Stalin must have smiled on receiving this plaintive message from Churchill: "The trend of developments in Yugoslavia is such that I do not think that the ratio 50:50 as between our interests is being observed. Marshal Tito . . . himself admits he is warmly devoted to the Soviet Union." *Correspondence,* p. 349.

9. It was at San Franciso that Molotov shocked Edward R. Stettinius and Anthony Eden by announcing that the sixteen Polish underground leaders who had disappeared were being held prisoners on charges of sabotage against the Red Army. Asked what was going to happen to them, he gave the famous answer, "The guilty ones will be tried."

8   The Uses of Revolution

1. V. I. Lenin, *Works,* 4th ed.(Moscow, 1954), XXXIII, 438.

2. Lenin, XXXIII, 439.

3. J. V. Stalin, *Economic Problems of Socialism in the USSR,* quoted in *Current Soviet Policies,* ed. Leo Gruliow (New York, 1953), p. 3 (italics mine).

4. Maxim Gorky, *The Russian Peasant* (Berlin, 1922), p. 21. Gorky adds that the speaker was "in his way" a humane person who treated his soldiers well and enjoyed popularity among them.

5. Lenin, XXXI, 233.

6. *15th Conference of the Old-Union Communist Party (b)* (Moscow, 1927), p. 721.

7. Gorky, p. 43.

8. The argument also shows how unequal are the terms of the dialogue between the East and the West. Would a Soviet historian or philosopher reciprocate his liberal Western colleague's stance and grant that whatever its past crimes and present dificiencies, capitalism in the last twenty years has shown an amazing power of adjustment and vitality? Or that it is likely to reform itself still further and cease entirely to be an oppressive and hostile force?

9. Lenin said on one occasion, "We often take with one hand what we give with the other." At the victory banquet in the Kremlin for the Soviet commanders at the end of World War II Stalin matched this frankness: the Communist regime had made many mistakes, he said, in an obvious reference to its collaboration with Hitler in 1939-1941, and any other nation might well have chased out its rulers when the war broke out. But not the Russians!

9   Titoism

1. The Russo-German Pact of 1939, although it disillusioned many people sympathetic to Communism and some especially sensitive individual party members, led to no major defections.

2. See Adam Ulam, *Titoism and the Cominform* (Cambridge, 1952), pp. 29-38.

3. *The Fifth Congress of the CPY* (Belgrade, 1948), p. 105.

4. George W. Hoffman and Fred W. Neal, *Yugoslavia and the New Communism* (New York, 1962), p. 114.

5. One of the earliest relevant references to the term "cult of personality" is in a little-known article on Lenin by his old friend Mikhail Stepanovich Olminsky, written in 1920.

6. The difficulty of trying to combine decentralization and Leninism was most recently borne out at the Eighth Congress of the Communist Party of Yugoslavia, in December 1964.

7. In foreign policy we are often victims of our own successes. Who would have dreamed that the splendid achievements of the Marshall Plan would result in de Gaulle, or that a Greece freed from the Communist threat would complicate our lives by her position on Cyprus? These bitter fruits of our successes correspond to those of Russia in helping to communize China.

10   Marxist Doctrine

1. The relationship between Marx's primary and secondary views on international politics is analogous to the student of the international situation who both hopes and believes that in the long run the United Nations must become the decisive factor in the world, yet whose comments about actual conditions indicate he is well aware that nationalism, national sovereignty, and the inability of the United Nations to resolve the most basic and dangerous conflict are facts of life of the present day.

2. A meeting in favor of Polish independence was in fact the occasion of the creation of the First International in 1864.

3. The Bolsheviks and Communists were not, however, identitical. There were perhaps 10,000-15,000 Bolsheviks on the eve of the March Revolution in 1917 and about 300,000 by the November Revolution. Even among the leaders of the Communist Party there were people, notably Trotsky, who had not been Bolsheviks prior to 1917.

4. The concept of a relatively brief war was inherent in the military planning of all the major powers. Thus, the famous Schlieffen Plan of the German general staff envisaged a lightning blow against the French army which then would allow the Germans to concentrate against the more slowly mobilizing armies of Russia. Implicit in the plan was the conviction that peace could be reached with France after the crushing of her armies, and presumably that, as compared to the standards of 1918 and 1945, it would be a lenient peace.

5. Quoted in James Joll. *The Second International, 1889-1914* (New York, 1956), p. 139.

6. Fourteen of the ninety-one socialist deputies voting were actually against the credits, but by party rule they were bound to vote with the majority.

7. *Lenin's Miscellany* (Moscow, 1924), I, 208.

8. To be sure, this Chinese application of Communism went beyond Lenin's original injunction. According to Lenin, although the peasant was a desirable ally and enlisting the peasant on one's side or at least securing his neutralization was a necessary task for the socialist revolutionary, the active force in the revolution was still to be the city proletarian.

11   Communist Doctrine and Soviet Diplomacy

1. No more fundamental mistake could be made than that of certain British Labour circles in 1945, who believed that a socialist government was bound to have an easier time with the Russians than a nonsocialist one; that because it inspired greater sympathy and trust in the Communists, it was bound to enjoy certain advantages in dealing with Moscow.

12   The Perils of Khrushchev

1. Some time later the Chinese Communists, never at a loss for the last

word, answered that Khrushchev did not mention all the remnants of colonialism tolerated for the time being by the Chinese: how about the territories wrested from China by Russia from the seventeenth to the nineteenth century?

2. On December 19 Khrushchev wrote to Kennedy: "The time has now come to put an end once and for all to nuclear tests." Arthur M. Schlesinger, Jr., *Thousand Days* (New York, 1965), p. 895.

3. The Sino-Soviet talks took place July 5-20; the United States-USSR-British ones, July 15-25.

4. The theatricalities of hostility included the Russians' expulsion of some Chinese diplomats and students who had circulated the Chinese letter of June 14, 1963, in Russia, and Chou En-lai's personal welcome of these men on their return to Peking.

5. Schlesinger, p. 908.

6. An ingenious procedure enabled the United States, USSR, and Britain to eschew the ticklish problem of recognition: other countries could signify their adhesion to the treaty by signing with any one of the three main signatories—East Germany signing in Moscow, Bonn in Washington.

7. Some of the administration's opponents, however, considered the treaty a devilish ruse invented by the Russians to outwit the United States.

8. Chinese statement of Sept. 1, 1963, quoted in William E. Griffith, *The Sino-Soviet Rift* (Cambridge, 1964), p. 371.

9. Chinese statistics, not entirely above suspicion, in 1967 moved this figure up to 700 million.

10. Griffith, p. 320.

11. Griffith, p. 410.

12. Griffith, p. 423.

13. *Plenum of the Central Committee of the CPSU, June 18-21, 1963* (Moscow, 1964), p. 267.

14. *Plenum,* p. 266.

15. *Plenum of the Central Committee of the CPSU, March 24-26, 1965* (Moscow, 1965), p. 36.

16. *Plenum of the Central Committee of the CPSU, June 18-21, 1963* (Moscow, 1963), pp. 23, 263. Ilichev was a close collaborator of Krushchev's and one of the few top officials to fall with him.

17. Such a delay often reflects official uncertaintly as to how much of the proceedings should be published. It is thus entirely possible that some of the most interesting passages have been censored.

18. The phenomenon of the new left, impatient of the old organizational forms and doctrines, clearly reflects the deep split in international Communism. The slogan "better red than dead," which could perhaps have a rational justification in the days when Communism was a monolithic movement, has also lost most of its appeal for the same reason.

19. The presence of numerous officials was purportedly connected with

the first part of the Central Committee's session, devoted to agricultural problems, but the fact that they stayed on for the "Chinese" part could not be accidental. The Chinese later alleged that the final session was attended by 6,000 people.

20. *Plenum of the Central Committee of the CPSU, February 10-25, 1964* (Moscow, 1964), p. 546.

21. *Plenum,* pp. 572, 578, 551.

22. *Plenum,* pp. 470, 471, 495 (my italics).

16 The Soviet Union and the International Game

1. Maxim Gorky, *The Russian Peasant* (Berlin, 1922), p. 22.

2. Stanislaw Pestkovsky, "The October Days in Petrograd," *The Proletarian Revolution,* October 1922, no. 10, p. 99.

3. From Lenin's speech on May 14, 1918, in Jane Degras, ed., *Soviet Documents on Foreign Policy,* vol. I: *1917-1924* (New York, 1951), p. 78.

4. *Lenin's Miscellany* (Moscow 1959), XXXVI, 338.

5. Jane Degras, ed., *Soviet Documents on Foreign Policy,* vol. III: *1933-1941* (New York, 1953), p. 36.

6. Quoted in Degras, III, 132.

7. *Papers Relating to the Foreign Relations of the United States: Russia 1933-39* (Washington, 1941), pp. 221-222.

8. See Adam Ulam, *Expansion and Coexistence: History of Soviet Foreign Policy, 1917-1967* (New York, 1968), pp. 331-332.

9. Walter Bedell Smith, *My Three Years in Moscow* (New York, 1950), p. 50.

10. V. I. Glunin, A. M. Grigorev, K. V. Kukuskin, and V. N. Nikiforov, *Recent History of China* (Moscow, 1972), p. 246.

11. Glunin et al, p. 266.

12. Glunin et al, p. 259.

13. The picture in *Pravda,* Mar. 10, 1953, was a composograph of a photograph taken at the signing of the Sino-Soviet alliance on Feb. 14, 1950, when in addition to the three gentlemen in question, a score of other officials were gathered for the occasion.

14. Ulam, p. 599.

15. Glunin et al, p. 319.

16. We may console ourselves with the reflection that for the time being at least, Communist China is willing to tolerate a similarly abnormal pattern of relations between Washington and Peking. We have de facto diplomatic relations with the People's Rupublic at the same time that we have a de jure link with and are pledged to defend another Chinese regime viewed by Peking as a rebel one. To be sure, this is viewed by the Chinese Communists as but a temporary accommodation and realistically as an efficacious way of eroding the United States protection of Taiwan.

17. Harry Truman, *Memoirs* (New York, 1958), II, 106.

18. Perhaps emblematic of the whole current state of relations is the issue of a dialogue between Catholicism and Marxism as advocated by certain circles within the church. The Communists are quite willing to carry out such a dialogue, provided it takes place in the West. At home they insist on a monologue.

INDEX